Common Core
for the
Not-So-Common
Learner

GRADES **K–5**

We dedicate this book to our respective families who are our greatest source of support for all of our endeavors, Tim, Dave, Jason, Christine, Sara, Meadow Rose, and Gavin Joseph; Howie, Benjamin, Jacob, and Noah. We also dedicate this book to all educators who are committed to the success of the Not-So-Common Learner.

Common Core
for the
Not-So-Common
Learner

English
Language Arts
Strategies
GRADES
K–5

MARIA G. DOVE
ANDREA HONIGSFELD

CORWIN
A SAGE Company

CORWIN
A SAGE Company

FOR INFORMATION:

Corwin
A SAGE Company
2455 Teller Road
Thousand Oaks, California 91320
(800) 233-9936
www.corwin.com

SAGE Publications Ltd.
1 Oliver's Yard
55 City Road
London EC1Y 1SP
United Kingdom

SAGE Publications India Pvt. Ltd.
B 1/I 1 Mohan Cooperative Industrial Area
Mathura Road, New Delhi 110 044
India

SAGE Publications Asia-Pacific Pte. Ltd.
3 Church Street
#10-04 Samsung Hub
Singapore 049483

Copyright © 2013 by Corwin

Printed in the United States of America

ISBN 978-1-4522-5782-2

MIX
Paper from
responsible sources
FSC
www.fsc.org
FSC® C014174

This book is printed on acid-free paper

Acquisitions Editor: Dan Alpert
Associate Editor: Megan Bedell
Editorial Assistant: Heidi Arndt
Production Editor: Amy Schroller
Copy Editor: Diane DiMura
Typesetter: C&M Digitals (P) Ltd.
Proofreader: Susan Schon
Cover Designer: Rose Storey

15 16 17 10 9 8 7 6 5

Contents

Preface

One of the ways that teachers improve is by learning from other teachers . . . Isolation is the enemy of all improvement.

—Andy Hargreaves

Foreword, *Finnish Lessons*

The intention of this book along with its companion volume, *Common Core for the Not-So-Common Learner, Grades 6–12: English Language Arts Strategies,* is to provide a carefully selected sample of instructional strategies that address each anchor standard to help teachers meet the Common Core State Standards (CCSS) with diverse students. It is not a step-by-step prescriptive manual for successful implementation of the CCSS, nor does it attempt to provide a comprehensive guide to meet the academic, linguistic, social, and emotional needs of diverse learners. This book identifies the CCSS anchor standards for English Language Arts, how to interpret those standards for K–5 diverse learners in terms of academic performance, and suggests possible strategies to achieve them. Teachers are encouraged to examine the strategies contained herein, experiment with them in their own classes, investigate as well as interpret their effectiveness, modify them to support their own instructional goals, and work collaboratively with fellow teachers to create methods, techniques, and activities that are most suitable for their own population of diverse learners.

It is our hope that some of the instructional and implementation strategies addressed in these pages will spark new ideas and begin conversations about teaching practices for diverse learners that are shared by many. In this way, this book should not be perceived as the definitive account of necessary strategies to use with diverse learners but as the impetus that compels all educators to better understand research-based best practices for diverse learners, to further search for answers to critical questions regarding the CCSS implementation with this student population, and to collaboratively share their findings with colleagues.

It is no surprise that the CCSS will present many challenges for teachers who instruct diverse students. Educators will read and try to interpret each individual standard for their grade level and no doubt be faced with numerous questions such as the following:

- What does each standard actually require students to know and be able to do?
- How do I help struggling students meet the standards?
- Must I change what I normally do in my daily instructional practices in light of the CCSS?
- Where am I going to find the resources to create lessons that address individual standards?

These questions are answered in detail in this book. We address the CCSS by first explaining what each anchor standard requires students to know and do in broad terms. We identify what we call an *anchor performance* for each of the 32 anchor standards, which represent a critical skill students should be able to develop in light of the CCSS. We further suggest both broad and specific strategies for helping diverse and struggling learners succeed with each of these standards and share our ideas for changing instructional practices. Furthermore, we offer a range of additional resources at the end of each chapter for readers to explore instructional ideas that are too numerous to contain within these pages.

In light of the complexity of implementing the CCSS, teachers can no longer work in isolation to overcome the various obstacles in order to initiate effective instructional practices. There are no quick fixes, and although it may be a starting point, adding a few instructional strategies to one's teaching repertoire will not bring about the systemic change that is vital for diverse learners to succeed. As *Washington Post* blogger Valerie Strauss (2010) also noted, "No set of standards has much meaning without equitable resources to ensure that teachers are trained well enough to reach kids who live in widely different circumstances" (para. 11). We hope that this book and its companion version for Grades 6 to 12 will be added as a ready-to-use, practical resource to the professional libraries of schools across the country.

Further, we would like to invite our readers to reflect on their own teaching effectiveness, to engage colleagues in collaborative efforts to do so as well, to investigate new models of instruction, to review and revise curricula, and to go beyond the scope of this book to begin and sustain the essential collaborative conversations and interventions that are vital to school reform.

HOW THIS BOOK IS ORGANIZED

Chapter 1 establishes the framework for the rest of the book and discusses who the not-so-common learners are and what the Common Core State Standards mean for them and their teachers. Chapters 2 through 7 follow the same internal organization. Each chapter focuses on one strand of the Common Core State Standards in the following order: Language (Chapter 2), Reading Literature (Chapter 3), Reading Informational Text (Chapter 4), Foundational Reading Skills (Chapter 5), Writing (Chapter 6), and Speaking and Listening (Chapter 7). The order of the chapters follows the order in which the CCSS are presented (see www.corestandards.org), with one exception. Since academic language development is so critical for linguistically, culturally, and academically diverse students, we emphasized the importance of paying attention to language skills by intentionally disrupting the CCSS order and placing that chapter ahead of all others.

Within each chapter, we offer the rationale for explicit, strategy-based instruction related to the target CC anchor standards. Following the presentation of our recommended set of core strategies that are aligned to the CCSS and anchor performances, we discuss anticipated outcomes and instructional challenges readers may encounter. We close each of these six chapters by offering an authentic classroom vignette documenting promising practices from K–5 schools with diverse student populations. A list of key resources related to the chapter is also added to encourage further exploration of the topic.

Chapter 8 stands apart from the previous seven. As a continuation of our earlier work, *Collaboration and Coteaching: Strategies for English Learners* (Honigsfeld & Dove, 2010), here we outline the types of instructional and noninstructional collaborative practices that teachers may wish to engage in to support the successful implementation of the CCSS for all learners.

It is our hope the CCSS will represent a new window of opportunities for consistency in grade-appropriate expectations, ensuring equitable education for and meaningful engagement of all learners, and enhanced teacher collaboration in curriculum development and instructional delivery. We wish you an *uncommonly* productive time exploring this book!

Acknowledgments

We would like to express our sincere appreciation for all of those who made a contribution—either directly or indirectly—to this volume: Benjamin Honigsfeld, Jackie Nenchin, Virginia Rojas, Maria Segura, Ellen Tournour, teachers and administrators at the Park Avenue School, Westbury, NY, and the Patchogue-Medford first-grade teachers.

Our gratitude goes to our graduate assistants Katherine "Kat" Lapelosa and Taylor Volpe for their technical assistance with the research for and organization of this text.

We would also like to thank our reviewers whose detailed and honest feedback enhanced the writing of this volume.

We cannot say enough about the unyielding support and the overwhelming confidence bestowed on us by our editor, Dan Alpert. For this and so much more, we sincerely thank you. We would also like to express our appreciation for the entire Corwin team, and especially to Heidi Arndt and Amy Schroller, for their work on the manuscript preparation and production process.

A special thank you to Joanne Lufrano, whose insistence on the development of an inservice course on the Common Core State Standards for the Valley Stream Teacher Center not only led to the development of this project, but also inspired the name of the two volumes—*Common Core for the Not-So-Common Learner.*

We would like to thank our friends and colleagues at Molloy College, Rockville Centre, New York, who continually support and encourage our scholarship efforts, and a special thanks to Jackie Nenchin and Vicky Giouroukakis, who read and commented on earlier drafts of this manuscript.

Last but not least, to our families and friends who frequently cheer us on; your love and support for our work is paramount for us.

PUBLISHER'S ACKNOWLEDGMENTS

Corwin gratefully acknowledges the contributions of the following reviewers:

Denise Carlson, Mathematics Consultant
Heartland Area Education Agency, Johnston, IA

Elizabeth Gennosa, English/AIS Teacher
Sagamore Middle School, Holtsville, NY

Dolores Hennessy, Reading Specialist
Hill and Plain School, New Milford, CT

Connie Molony, K–12 ELA Specialist
South East Education Cooperative (SEEC), Fargo, ND

Kristina Moody, SPED Teacher
West Elementary, Gulfport, MS

Joyce Smithok, Teacher
Shaw Avenue School, Valley Stream, NY

Catherine Alaimo Stickney, Director of Curriculum,
    Instruction, and Assessment
Ashland Public Schools, MA

Barbara L. Townsend, K–5 Reading Specialist
West Side Elementary School, Elkhorn, WI

About the Authors

Maria G. Dove, EdD is Assistant Professor and Coordinator of the MS TESOL Program in the Division of Education at Molloy College, Rockville Centre, New York, where she teaches courses to preservice and inservice teachers on the research and best practices for developing effective programs and school policies for English learners. Before entering the field of higher education, she worked over thirty years as an English-as-a-second-language teacher in public school settings (Grades K–12) and in adult English language programs in Nassau County, New York.

In 2010, she received the Outstanding ESL Educator Award from New York State Teachers of English to Speakers of Other Languages (NYS TESOL). She frequently provides professional development throughout the United States for educators on the teaching of diverse students. She also serves as a mentor for new ESL teachers as well as an instructional coach for general education teachers and literacy specialists. She has published several articles and book chapters on collaborative teaching practices, instructional leadership, and collaborative coaching. Her coedited book, *Coteaching and Other Collaborative Practices in the EFL/ESL Classroom: Rationale, Research, Reflections, and Recommendations (2012)* is published by Information Age Publishing while her best-selling coauthored book, *Collaboration and Co-Teaching Strategies for English Learners* (2010) is published by Corwin.

Photo by Scott Levy

Andrea Honigsfeld is a professor in the Division of Education at Molloy College, Rockville Centre, New York. She teaches graduate education courses related to cultural and linguistic diversity, linguistics, ESL methodology, and action research. Before entering the field of teacher education, she was an English-as-a-foreign-language teacher in Hungary (Grades 5–8 and adult), an English-as-a-second-language teacher in New York City (Grades K–3 and adult), and taught Hungarian at New York University.

She was the recipient of a doctoral fellowship at St. John's University, New York, where she conducted research on individualized instruction and learning styles. She has published extensively on working with English language learners and providing individualized instruction based on learning style preferences. She received a Fulbright Award to lecture in Iceland in the fall of 2002. In the past ten years, she has been presenting at conferences across the United States, Great Britain, Denmark, Sweden, the Philippines, and the United Arab Emirates. She frequently offers staff development primarily focusing on effective differentiated strategies and collaborative practices for English-as-a-second-language and general education teachers. She coauthored *Differentiated Instruction for At-Risk Students* (2009) and coedited the five-volume *Breaking the Mold of Education* series (2010–2013), published by Rowman and Littlefield. With Maria Dove, she coedited *Coteaching and Other Collaborative Practices in the EFL/ESL Classroom: Rational , Research, Reflections, and Recommendations* (2012), and coauthored *Collaboration and Co-Teaching: Strategies for English Learners* (2010)—a Corwin bestseller.

1 Introduction

It is time for parents to teach young people early on that in diversity there is beauty and there is strength.

—Maya Angelou

Over the past decade, linguistic diversity has increased dramatically across the United States, a concern for many school districts that struggle to develop policies, curricula, program models, and instruction for pupils who speak languages other than English. Not only is there great language diversity in large urban areas such as New York City and Los Angeles, but also pockets of both immigrant and first-generation, US–born students are arriving in classrooms in Des Moines, Iowa; Knoxville, Tennessee; St. Louis, Missouri; and Cheyenne, Wyoming. In addition, our heterogeneous classrooms are filled with students ranging from students with disabilities, struggling learners, average achievers, and gifted and talented pupils. Furthermore, some of our English learners (ELs) may have a combination of language and learning issues; some may be highly educated and literate in their native language, while others come from areas of the world where they have not had the opportunity for consistent, formal schooling.

Never before have school districts across the nation been so challenged by an increase in educational initiatives coupled with the lack of financial resources. Schools are being asked to do so much more with so much less. Enter into the mix the implementation of the Common Core State Standards (CCSS), a substantial challenge for preparing schools to meet these rigorous benchmarks with their students, and an even greater one for those schools who have large populations of academically and linguistically diverse students.

The challenges of instruction for academically and linguistically diverse pupils are multifaceted and, therefore, require multistep solutions that involve all stakeholders—administrators, teachers, parents, students, and community members—in their development. In our view, efforts to achieve successful solutions require the following:

1. A shared vision and mission for all students reached through consensus along with the determination of measurable, achievable goals with an understanding of how to accomplish them

2. Curriculum mapping and alignment to ensure that instructional content and practices for academically and linguistically diverse pupils are consistent with the Standards and the learning outcomes for all students

3. Collaborative planning, instruction, and assessment among teams of teachers—content-area, ESL, special education, and literacy specialists, among others—to foster the use of teaching and learning strategies to make academic material comprehensible for all learners

4. Strategies to integrate language and content instruction to foster literacy and language development while acquiring content information

5. A direct focus on teaching academic language needed to access rigorous content and opportunities for students to apply newly learned language through various methods of discourse

6. The explicit teaching of literacy and language-learning strategies to develop students' understanding of their own thinking and learning processes

All too often, only partial efforts are initiated to spearhead change, and the results are neither rewarding nor permanent. Fullan (2007) identified *clarity* as one of the variables of successful change; in short, "the more complex the reform the greater the problem of clarity" (p. 89). Teachers, left to their own devices, often are not clear about which strategies are appropriate for diverse student populations or how to implement them. Teacher interpretation or beliefs in the use of particular teaching and learning strategies play a significant role in effective change (Fullan, 2007). However, powerful instructional practices do not alone fall on the shoulders of teachers. Both school and district leaders need to take an active role in reform efforts to effect school improvement (Fullan, 2011) and the teaching and learning of academically and linguistically diverse youngsters.

Complex change requires that school administrators do their part to foster a shared understanding of the needs of diverse learners, to develop an inclusive curriculum, and to provide the time and necessary resources for collaborative teacher practices. In turn, to respond to the essential changes in instructional practices due to the CCSS, teachers are challenged to develop proactive methods and strategies to deal with the various levels of student need in their classes.

WHO ARE OUR NOT-SO-COMMON LEARNERS?

Walk inside most public school classrooms today and you will find students from different cultural, linguistic, and socioeconomic backgrounds with different assessed levels of cognitive and academic ability. Diversity is a part of our society at large; yet schools often segregate various populations of students with the best intentions—to offer more tailored educational instruction to those who have been deemed not ready or able to learn all or part of the grade-level curriculum within a mainstream classroom. More often than not, the individual needs of these youngsters are overlooked and diverse learners are placed in available programs such as reading remediation, ESL, and Special Education Resource Rooms. Although these programs may meet state and local mandated requirements of remediation and instruction, they often serve to fragment students' schedules and contribute to the discontinuity of curricular instruction (Scanlan, Frattura, Schneider, & Capper, 2012) further impeding an already academically disadvantaged population. Furthermore, when diverse students are labeled and segregated from the mainstream classroom, their abilities, language, and culture are subject to "subtle forms of unintentional rejection" (Cummins, 2001, p. 2) often coupled with teachers' low expectations for them.

Our intention in identifying the *Not-So-Common Learner* is not to fuel the marginalization and segregation of these youngsters. In our portrayal of these students, we hope that teachers and administrators will embrace the education of these pupils in every classroom and provide the appropriate resources to support the use of meaningful strategies and techniques, many of which are outlined in this volume, to assist their learning.

Common characteristics and labels associated with *Not-So-Common Learner* include the following:

- English Learners (ELs). These are students who are either foreign-born immigrants or US–born citizens of immigrant parents, speak a language other than English, and have yet to develop proficient skills (listening, speaking, reading, or writing) in English.

- Students with Interrupted or Limited Formal Education (SIFE). A subgroup of English learners, these school-age youngsters often have significant gaps in their education and, on the average, two years or less schooling than their same age peers.
- Students with Disabilities. Pupils with special learning needs due to physical and/or mental impairments who require special assistance to meet with academic success.
- Nonstandard-English-Speaking Children. Often racially or ethnically diverse, these US–born students speak a dialect of English in their communities and have yet to acquire standard American English skills.
- Children of Poverty. Youngsters under the age of eighteen whose families have incomes below the US poverty threshold; approximately sixteen million of America's poor are children who are often malnourished, live in substandard housing, and have unequal access to education opportunities.
- Struggling Learners. Students who are not performing at grade level in the core subject matters.

THE STANDARDS MOVEMENT

A Nation at Risk (National Commission on Excellence in Education, 1983) is frequently cited as the beginning of the educational standards movement in the United States. Yet here we are 30 years later, with a reaffirmation and commitment to a common set of academic standards that have been adopted to date by 45 states, and there still remains some debate about the value and effectiveness of learning standards. Inasmuch as multiple variables account for student success, it can be easily concluded that standards alone will not reform public education. However, a set of learning standards, grounded in research and aligned to essential criteria for college and career success, might be a powerful anchor to initiate school reform. According to Reeves (2000),

> Although standards alone are clearly an insufficient instrument for the improvement of student achievement, the essence of standards—the clear articulation of what students should know and be able to do—forms the basis for the essential transformations necessary for school success. (p. 5)

However, standards cannot be viewed as a panacea to cure all educational ills or the silver bullet that will dispel the monster crisis facing US schools.

More than a decade has passed since higher academic standards, additional test accountability, and Adequate Yearly Progress (AYP) requirements have been in place due to *No Child Left Behind* (NCLB) legislation. As AYP specifications have increased, the number of failing schools has increased as well. In 2007, 28 percent of schools failed to make AYP, and by 2011, that number had risen to 38 percent (McNeil, 2011).

Some educators suggest that policies and schools practices that rely on standards and accountability are not sufficient to increase academic success (Rowan, Correnti, Miller, & Camburn, 2009), and that despite administrative, faculty, and community commitment to planned change, reluctance to establish reforms is often fueled by cultural, traditional, political, and economic obstacles, as well as the means to efficiently support and promote educational improvements (Thomas, 2002).

Many researchers agree there is no straightforward way to institute reforms, or the Common Core Standards for that matter, without directly connecting educational policies with classroom practices (Fullan, 2007; Supovitz, 2006)—examining and changing school policies and classroom practices as well as fostering a culture of inclusion where all children feel they belong can improve student learning. In order to create inclusive schools, policymakers, administrators, and teachers need to become aware of how to make educational reforms a reality, which is most often due to the investment of training (Elmore, 2008) and capacity building through collaborative practices (Honigsfeld & Dove, 2010) regarding essential skills for teachers and school-level administrators to understand and meet the academic challenges of diverse learners.

COMMON CORE ADVANCES

The Common Core State Standards for English Language Arts & Literacy in History/Social Studies, Science, and Technical Subjects—*the Standards*—offer a number of advances or shifts in instruction for the teaching of English language arts. First and foremost, they were developed to ensure that all students are college and career ready by the end of twelfth grade. With this in mind, they contain sets of anchor standards in reading, writing, speaking and listening, and language that are consistent across all grade levels and promote an integrated model of literacy.

The Standards identify students' literacy development as a shared responsibility. All teachers will be expected to foster students' reading and writing skills across the disciplines. Another advancement incorporated into the Standards is the promotion of student research and communication skills. To be college and career ready, students must be able to gather, critically examine, and report information as well as analyze and synthesize a range of available text and nontext materials through the integrated use of media and technology.

In Grades K–5, the CCSS prescribe an increased emphasis on the reading of nonfiction text. The Standards call for a 50–50 balance between the reading of literary and informational texts. Reading expository texts is viewed as an essential skill to be college and career ready in as much as the required reading in post-high school training and college programs depends upon students being able to comprehend informational texts proficiently.

The Standards require students to read grade-appropriate texts to increase their exposure to what is often called "the staircase of complexity" (www.engageNY.org), text that becomes increasingly more challenging throughout each grade. To develop these reading skills, teachers must shift their practices from delivering information through direct instruction to helping students obtain information through thoughtful reading, learning how to gather information from ever-increasing, complex text, and participating in meaningful interactions and sustained collaborations. In order to meet this challenge, teachers will need to engage students in close, careful reading of text and scaffold instruction to support learning for those who are reading below grade level.

To fully focus on students being able to obtain information from and staying connected to text, a paradigm shift will have to take place. Classroom conversations and discussions will now focus on text-based information, questions, and answers. Students' ideas, opinions, arguments, and conclusions will be supported with evidence from text. Teachers will advance their instruction to facilitate text-dependent conversations so students read more closely and deeply. These evidenced-based conversations will be routinely established in addition to discussions that activate students' prior knowledge, build background information from students' personal experiences, or motivate students through their personal connections with the topic, which are not text dependent.

Another shift in instruction is the development of students writing from sources. Students will be expected to produce their own writing by gathering data from various media, spending an increased amount of time writing nonfiction pieces and less time engaged in writing personal narratives. Using evidence from various data sources, students will be able to compose their own arguments, offer their opinions, and draw their own conclusions. Teachers must facilitate opportunities for students to write about a single topic with information from multiple sources.

The Standards also emphasize student acquisition of academic vocabulary. Teachers must identify vocabulary that most frequently appears in text across disciplines and grade levels; incorporate before, during, and after reading strategies to explicitly teach critical vocabulary in context; and associate new words with previously known or learned vocabulary. Shared reading and read-alouds are perfect opportunities for teachers to emphasize not only key academic vocabulary but sentence- or text-level academic features as well.

The advancements set forth by the CCSS will create a new set of challenges for teachers and administrators. Support must be provided so that all teachers enhance their skills to develop student literacy across the disciplines. Curricula must be examined so that teachers are given the time to conduct close, careful reading with grade-level text. Teaching strategies need to be enhanced to scaffold instruction for academically and linguistically diverse learners. Moreover, professional development must be an ongoing initiative for teachers and administrators to better understand how overall instruction should change for all students to meet the Standards.

WHAT IS NOT COVERED IN THE COMMON CORE DOCUMENT

It is critical that all those implementing the CCSS read the beginning pages of the *Common Core State Standards for English Language Arts & Literacy in History/Social Studies, Science and Technical Subjects,* even if your main focus is teaching mathematics. These pages contain essential information on the development of the Standards, the key design considerations in creating them, the focus of instruction and assessment as it pertains to individual grade-level standards, the characteristics of students meeting the CCSS as well as what the Standards are and are not. To this end, we would like to focus on the design limitations of the CCSS. Our main goal for emphasizing these limitations is to dispel any misconceptions about the purpose of the Standards with the following information:

How do we develop this?

- The CCSS were created to ensure that students are college and career ready. By design, they identify what students should know and be able to do. However, the Standards do not specify any particular curriculum to be taught or the techniques and strategies teachers must use to teach students.
- The Standards only describe the essential skills that must be taught; it is beyond the scope of the CCSS to identify "all that can and

Can you just apply Standards for a higher or lower grade?

should be taught" (Common Core, p. 6). Therefore, a curriculum that only addresses the Standards, in our estimation, is not a complete curriculum.

- The methods, materials, and instructional interventions necessary to foster academic growth with students who are not yet working at grade level or the nature of assignments for students working above grade-level expectations are not specified by the Standards.
- The instructional supports necessary for English learners or students with disabilities to succeed are not specified by the Standards. In our opinion, teachers must continue to apply research-based strategies, best practices, and appropriate accommodations for working with these student populations.
- The Standards do not address the necessary social, emotional, physical, and cultural growth of students to be college and career ready.

These limitations, which are directly stated in the Common Core State Standards document, are specifically outlined to ensure that teachers maintain a strong sense of autonomy when making instructional decisions for their students, and district members involved in curriculum development have the flexibility to create a program of study best suited to their specific student populations.

APPLICATION OF THE COMMON CORE TO ADDRESS INDIVIDUAL DIFFERENCES

The CCSS can be viewed as an opportunity for teachers to identify essential grade-level skills and help individual learners to gain those skills. Not all learners acquire academic proficiency in the same way (Dunn & Dunn, 1992), and students from diverse backgrounds bring with them different sets of experiences, cultural knowledge, linguistic ability, and understanding of the learning process (Tomlinson & Imbeau, 2010). The Standards are an opportunity for diverse learners to have access to rigorous curriculum and high quality instruction.

Although not an easy task, educators will need to maintain high expectations for all students and to provide differentiated and scaffolded instruction to move students working below grade level toward making academic progress. Tomlinson and Imbeau (2010) identified key elements of differentiated instruction; among them are the following:

- Teachers have a responsibility to ensure that all of their students master important content.
- Teachers have to make specific and continually evolving plans to connect each learner with key content.
- Teachers are required to understand the nature of each of their students, in addition to the nature of the content they teach.
- A flexible approach to teaching "makes room" for student variance.
- Teachers should continually ask, "What does this student need at this moment in order to be able to progress with this key content, and what do I need to do to make it happen?" (p. 15)

In order to address students' individual differences, many teachers not only examine their instructional practices regularly, but also in some cases consider their overall attitudes and beliefs about the abilities, strengths, and value of diverse learners in their classes. If these youngsters are continually perceived as limited, their progress most likely will remain at a deficit; however, if teachers believe diverse learners are an asset to their school community, their different cultural perspectives, personal experiences, multilingual abilities, street smarts, and so forth, can be capitalized upon to meet with school success.

The CCSS are an opportunity for teaching specialists of diverse learners (ESL, SPED, AIS, Literacy, etc.) to examine their curricula and to challenge students in ways that they may never have before. Teachers must aim higher by infusing grade-appropriate texts and content into instruction so that students not yet working at grade level remain connected to the general education class content while receiving the support they need to succeed.

STUDENT DIVERSITY AND TEACHER CHALLENGES

There are a number of challenges teachers perceive in implementing the Standards with diverse learners. Generally speaking, teachers recognize the considerable task of identifying, planning, and executing effective instruction to meet the Standards with these youngsters. Teachers have other concerns as well, and depending upon the administrative style of the building principal or central office administration coupled with the general collaborative nature of the school or district culture, they may or may not have influence over how their concerns are addressed. Nonetheless, much teacher anxiety is due to possible changes to curricula, service delivery, program models, instructional practices, adopted program materials, and state as well as local assessments, much of which they have no control over.

Classroom practices can no longer remain status quo due to the advancements or instructional shifts brought about by the CCSS. Teachers question how to go about introducing struggling readers or those who have yet gained grade-level academic proficiency in English to more complex texts. In addition, they are concerned with providing these students with the necessary tools to write their own nonfiction texts while gathering evidence from multiple sources and teaching these youngsters academic vocabulary when some students have yet to develop basic vocabulary and concepts.

Some educators are apprehensive regarding the implementation of the CCSS. They fear a lack of support at the school or district level in terms of not having the necessary resources or training to make the implementation of the Standards effective. Additionally, all teachers require pertinent solutions to the following dilemmas:

- Identifying how to meet the grade-level Standards with diverse students
- Interpreting what the CCSS mean for severely learning-disabled youngsters
- Understanding how to execute the CCSS with emergent bilingual students
- Applying the CCSS to Students with Interrupted Formal Education (SIFE)
- Creating CCSS aligned units of learning for students working below grade level

Student diversity certainly will create multiple challenges for teachers implementing the CCSS, and teachers no longer will be able to arrive at adequate solutions working in isolation. For this reason, it is our belief that teacher collaboration is a vital way to bring about a resolution to these issues. We discuss collaborative practices in greater detail in Chapter 8.

FOCUS ON RESEARCH-BASED STRATEGIES TO ADDRESS LEARNING NEEDS

There is much information being generated about how teachers can work to meet the Standards. Unfortunately, some of it is misguided and not based on research or best practices for working with diverse learners. In spite of documented differences about how students learn (Dunn & Dunn, 1992), some are touting uniformity of practices to present instruction to all learners based on the CCSS. We would like to take the opportunity to identify some general guidelines and techniques for working with diverse learners as follows:

- Convey information in the form of photographs, drawings, and other graphic representations;
- Bring to class real objects (realia) and artifacts for students to examine, discuss, and explore;
- Offer information in ways that meet students' perceptual preferences for learning: auditory, visual, tactual, and kinesthetic;
- Use nonverbal cues to relate information: gestures, facial expressions, and body language;
- Provide information through alternative formats: audio, video, and multimedia presentations;
- Scaffold speech so that complex sentences and difficult vocabulary are supported through the repetition of information using less complex sentences;
- Frontload vocabulary to make text more accessible;
- Increase wait time for students to process information;
- Increase student engagement by having students turn and talk to a partner or work in cooperative learning groups;
- Maintain a low-anxiety learning environment; and
- Model and demonstrate procedures. (Walker & Walter, 1996)

In addition to the general strategies listed above, Fisher and Frey (2008) offer a unique perspective on how to deliver instruction and incrementally increase student independence. Their four-step process of structured teaching, based in part on the gradual release of responsibility model (Pearson & Gallagher, 1983), is as follows:

 1. Focus lesson: Teachers begin by setting a purpose for the lesson and modeling a skill, strategy, or learning task.

2. Guided instruction: Students have the opportunity to practice alongside the teacher; instruction during this phase of the lesson can be differentiated.

3. Student collaboration: Students work in cooperative learning groups to engage in meaningful activities and problem solve to gain a clearer understanding of the purpose of the lesson.

4. Independent practice: Students are released to work on their own to apply what they have learned.

Lessons structured in this manner give diverse students multiple opportunities to listen, observe, and practice before having the responsibility of performing transferred to them.

CONCLUDING THOUGHTS

The increase in linguistic diversity in the United States is showing no sign of abating, and students across the nation will continue to be academically challenged with the onset of the CCSS. Educators will continue to have many concerns for teaching diverse learners in the years ahead, and yet to foster success with this population of youngsters, the CCSS must be viewed as an opportunity to carefully examine curricula, resources, materials, and classroom practices to reach all learners. The following chapters offer sets of essential strategies that address each individual anchor standard in order to provide teachers with different tools to work with and meet the Standards with a diverse student population.

Paper work
Work sheet

2 Strategies for Academic Language Development

The mastery of content is dependent on language that students can understand.

—Sherry Vermette
Special education teacher in
Hampton Bays, NY

OVERVIEW

It has been well established both by researchers and practitioners that academic language is critical for student success in the content areas (see key resources on this topic at the end of the chapter). Judith Lessow-Hurley (2003) cautioned that "simplistic notions of language and language development are all too often at the heart of both the politics and programs for students who don't speak English" (p. 15). Academic language is commonly defined as the language competence required for students to gain access to and master content taught in English. Connecting it to the Common Core State Standards (CCSS), academic language is the type of abstract and cognitively demanding language students need in order to be college and career ready. Along with new concepts and complex information presented in the content areas, students must recognize, internalize, and apply the unique ways language is used in English language arts, math, science, social studies, and all other subject matters. As such, special attention must be paid to

- discipline-specific vocabulary;
- phrases and idiomatic expressions associated with the target content;
- typical sentence structures used in the lessons;
- grammatical constructs used in academic text; and
- text-level features of standard American English.

In sum, for our purposes, academic language is possibly best defined by WIDA (World-Class Instructional Design and Assessment, 2011) as "the language required to succeed in school that includes deep understandings of content and communication of that language in the classroom environment. These understandings revolve around specific criteria related to discourse, sentence, and word/phrase levels of language" (p. 1).

WHY DIVERSE LEARNERS NEED EXPLICIT INSTRUCTION IN ACADEMIC LANGUAGE

Diverse learners may have dissimilar issues which amount to the same difficulties with developing academic language. Some students are unfamiliar with standard American English either due to their families speaking a dialect other than Standard English, or they come from homes where little or no English is spoken. Poverty also places certain children in tenuous situations. Children coming from low-income families with parents who have little or no education often lack the background knowledge that is a stepping-stone for acquiring academic language. In addition, some students with disabilities are speech and language impaired and struggle with expressing their ideas, which impedes their learning.

There is a growing population of language-minority youngsters that often appear to be fluent in English but are not. This pseudo fluency is apparent in the distinction between BICS (Basic Interpersonal Communication Skills) and CALP (Cognitive Academic Language Proficiency), which may be traced back to Cummins's (1984) most frequently cited contributions to the field of English to speakers of other languages (ESOL). BICS refers to the ability to use language in social contexts, whereas CALP identifies the type of language necessary to develop conceptual understanding of cognitively and academically challenging content matter. More recently, however, Cummins and Man (2007) further refined the original dichotomy and distinguished among three types of language skills:

1. *Conversational fluency*, which refers to a learner's ability to engage in everyday conversations that often take place in familiar, face-to-face situations

2. *Discrete language skills*, which refer to the learning of rule-governed aspects of language

3. *Academic language proficiency*, which indicate the learner's command of the type of oral and written academic forms of English necessary for successful participation in school

Cummins and Man (2007) also noted that there is limited transfer between the development of the first two language skills (conversational competence and distinct language skills) and of academic language proficiency. They also suggested that all three types of language skills should be developed using appropriate methodologies. The most important implication of this distinction is that these three language skills often have three distinctive developmental trajectories both for first- and second-language learners.

Among many others, Collier and Thomas's (1999) research suggests that it takes most ELLs five to seven years to develop native-like academic language proficiency and literacy. However, they documented that students with interrupted formal education (SIFE) or those whose native-language literacy was below grade level took seven to ten years to develop grade-level proficiency and literacy skills in English. Hakuta, Butler, and Witt (2000) concurred that ELLs need a minimum of three to five years to develop oral proficiency (communicative skills), whereas academic English proficiency can take even longer, at least four to seven years.

Goldenberg and Coleman (2010) noted that learning content area matter will require students to acquire and use the specific register associated with that subject, going beyond the vocabulary unique to the content taught. Coleman and Goldenberg (2010) emphasized that "students may know the meanings of individual content-specific words, yet still not be able to understand the larger meaning when reading them in a sentence or be able to combine them to write a sentence" (p. 62) or produce even longer, more complex oral or written responses to content-based prompts.

An additional challenge in the acquisition of academic language is that students need not only develop their receptive language skills (having opportunities to comprehend academic English by listening to or reading challenging language input) but also to build their productive language skills by creating sentences, paragraphs, and longer academic texts both orally and written. In sum, students need both explicit instruction in academic language and sustained, meaningful opportunities to continue to acquire and develop the necessary language skills.

CORE LANGUAGE AND VOCABULARY STRATEGIES

The strategies contained in this chapter follow the expectations of the six College and Career Readiness Anchor Standards (CCRAS) for Language. They are framed by the CCRAS strand-specific sets of *Conventions of Standard English, Knowledge and Application of Language,* and *Vocabulary Acquisition and Use.* Although language standards are placed at the very end of the CCSS document following reading and writing standards, for the sake of working with diverse learners, we positioned them to be the first chapter addressing CC strategies. Not only do we place special emphasis on language standards by putting them in a prominent place (Chapter 2), we will also present specific strategies to support the six language standards that address the needs of English learners as well as those who may come from bilingual or bidialectal homes or may not use Standard American English consistently.

Box 2.1 College and Career Readiness Anchor Standards for Language

Conventions of Standard English

1. Demonstrate command of the conventions of standard English grammar and usage when writing or speaking.

2. Demonstrate command of the conventions of standard English capitalization, punctuation, and spelling when writing.

Knowledge of Language (Begins in Grade 2)

3. Apply knowledge of language to understand how language functions in different contexts, to make effective choices for meaning or style, and to comprehend more fully when reading or listening.

Vocabulary Acquisition and Use

4. Determine or clarify the meaning of unknown and multiple-meaning words and phrases by using context clues, analyzing meaningful word parts, and consulting general and specialized reference materials, as appropriate.

5. Demonstrate understanding of word relationships and nuances in word meanings.

6. Acquire and use accurately a range of general academic and domain-specific words and phrases sufficient for reading, writing, speaking, and listening at the college and career readiness level; demonstrate independence in gathering vocabulary knowledge when encountering an unknown term important to comprehension or expression.

From each of the six CCRAS for Language, we derived and aligned a series of related *Anchor Performances*—skill sets that all students need to develop—and suggest strategies to help diverse students build these skills in order to meet the standards. Some strategies may be more appropriate than others depending upon the grade levels or language proficiency levels of the students. To that end, we also include suggestions on how to adapt strategies to meet the needs of diverse individual learners.

Conventions of Standard English

Anchor Performance 1: Apply the Conventions of Grammar and Usage in Writing and Speaking

What Goldenberg and Coleman (2010) stated in reference to English learners is likely to be beneficial for all students with diverse academic, linguistic, and cultural backgrounds:

> Effective second-language instruction provides a combination of (a) explicit teaching that helps students directly and efficiently learn features of the second language such as syntax, vocabulary, pronunciation, and norms of social usage and (b) ample opportunities to use the second language in meaningful and motivating situations. (p. 68)

Overall, we concur with Anderson (2005) that grammar instruction must be deliberate and well planned; to facilitate that process, we created a helpful tool presented in Table 2.1, which teachers may use for lesson planning or reflection.

Table 2.1 Grammar Lesson Planning Checklist

Will my lesson provide:	✓
1. A simple explanation of the grammar point at issue?	❏
2. Students' immersion in correct models of grammar?	❏
3. A demonstration of the particular pattern in a piece of writing (model texts)?	❏
4. Multiple meaningful activities for better understanding grammar point?	❏
5. Examples posted in the classroom?	❏
6. Ample student practice to apply new grammar knowledge?	❏
7. Time for students to edit their own writing?	❏

Essential Strategy to Support Anchor Performance 1: Grammar Connections

Long gone are the days when sentences were diagrammed and grammar was taught as a stand-alone academic subject in the elementary classroom. Instead, grammar is embedded or organically linked to literacy and content-based instruction so as to demonstrate its connectedness to how language is used at the word, sentence, and text levels. The purpose of the next section is to present research-based strategies that connect grammar to subject-matter texts, to literature and mentor texts, and to students' authentic experiences with varied linguistic input.

Sentence Dissection. Though sentences are no longer diagrammed, sentence-level language analysis can be helpful for diverse learners. Jeff Anderson (2005) publicly identified himself as a *sentence stalker*—using a phrase he borrowed from Vicki Spandel (2005)—and noted that he is "always on the lookout for great mentor texts, sentences, paragraphs, essays, articles, advertisements, and novels" (p. 17). During a structured instructional conversation session of no longer than 15 to 20 minutes, offer students exposure to and guided exploration of a carefully selected, sufficiently complex sentence (or two). It is best if the excerpt comes from a text you are using for literacy or content-based instruction and is loaded with information as well as opportunities for discussing grammar and usage. See two examples—one from fiction and one from nonfiction—below: The first sentence dissected in Table 2.2 is excerpted from *Stellaluna* by Janell Cannon (1993), and the second one is from *National Geographic Kids* (http://kids.nationalgeographic.com/kids/animals/creaturefeature/vampire-bat/) analyzed in Table 2.3.

Table 2.2 A Dissected Sentence From *Stellaluna*

Sentence: Each night, Mother Bat would carry Stellaluna clutched to her breast as she flew out to search for food.		
Sentence Chunk	**Possible Discussion Points**	**Linguistic Features**
Each night	How does the author say *every night*? Which is more expressive: *each* or *every*?	Time marker at sentence opening position
Mother Bat would carry Stellaluna	How does the author express that Mother Bat did something regularly?	Habitual past expressed with the auxiliary *would*
clutched to her breast	Why does the author choose *clutch* and not *hold onto*? Who clutched to whom?	The rich meaning of *clutch*; Past participle form of the verb

as she flew out	Who flew out? Who does the author mean by *she*? Why does the author say *flew out*? Out of what? Why didn't the author say *flew away*?	Temporal clause; Reference use of the personal pronoun *she* to refer to Mother bat The adverb *out* indicating direction
to search for food.	Why did Mother Bat fly out? What are some synonyms for *search for*?	The infinitive used to express purpose Phrasal verb: *search for*

Table 2.3 A Dissected Sentence From *National Geographic*

Sentence: Rather than sucking blood, vampire bats make a small cut with their teeth and lap up the flowing blood with their tongues.		
Sentence Chunk	**Possible Discussion Points**	**Linguistic Features**
Rather than sucking blood,	What does *rather than* mean in this sentence? Who is this part of the sentence talking about?	Comparative adverbial clause with a present participle
vampire bats make a small cut	What kind of bats? What kind of a cut?	Noun phrases
with their teeth	How do bats make a small cut? What instrument do they use? In other words, with what do they make a cut?	Prepositional phrase
and then lap up the flowing blood	What do vampire bats do first to get to the blood? What do they do next? What does *lap up* look like, sound like?	Compound sentence; Present participle used as an adjective
with their tongues.	How do bats drink the blood? What instrument do they use? In other words, with what do they lap up the flowing blood?	Prepositional phrase

Some successful ways to conduct this activity are using sentence strips, a chart paper, or the interactive whiteboard and color-coding the language chunks. Sentence dissection can be performed on all text types at all grade levels. It is especially important to apply this strategy to content-based, academic text so students could gradually become independent readers of textbooks and other informational texts. Introducing ELLs to one "juicy sentence" a day based on a shared text is a similar strategy promoted by Lilly Wong Fillmore (2009).

Patterned Writing, Patterned Speech. Among others, Oczkus (2007) also recognized the importance of borrowing from authors: "When students study the textual patterns in fiction and nonfiction, first analyzing and then borrowing another author's organizational pattern or word choice, their writing improves" (p. xiv). Not only does using patterned writing and speech help students improve their writing, but it also allows diverse students to become familiar with the way words are strung together to make meaning, the way verb tenses are used appropriately, the way parts of speech fit together, and the way simple, compound, and complex sentences are formed.

In Norma Simon's (1954/1997) classic *Wet World*, a recurring sentence pattern—*A _____ waited when I _____.*—can be found on every page; then a variation on this sentence pattern is introduced at the end of the book. Using this pattern, invite students to create their own compound sentences while learning about using (a) the simple past tense, (b) time adverbial clauses, and (c) prepositional phrases appropriately and authentically. Offer a sentence frame, model your use of the sentence pattern, and encourage your more confident language users to share their examples first. See student examples in Box 2.2.

Box 2.2 Patterned Sentences Based on Norma Simon's (1997) *Wet World*

A wet world waited when I looked out of my window this morning.

A warm breakfast waited when I went into the dining room.

A warm lunch waited when we went to the cafeteria after Math.

As Butt, Fahey, Feez, Spinks, and Yallop (2003) also pointed out, "the challenge to language educators is to develop ways of incorporating 'reflection, enquiry, and analysis' into teaching about the structural patterns of texts" (p. 250), or in other words, to invite students to carefully examine how the words are put together to form a patterned sentence or longer units of discourse and not merely echo samples provided by the teacher.

Real Grammar, Real Life. The elementary school is a place for exciting events that support learning in their own unique ways: going on field trips, browsing books at book fairs, taking care of class pets, or celebrating crazy hat (or crazy hair) day are some of our favorites. As a much better alternative to *drill and kill* practice books, why not take these authentic experiences and turn them into meaningful opportunities to teach about and practice grammar as it applies to real situations? Our colleague, Jackie Nenchin, shared with us her *Crazy Hat Activity*, which is a way to make learning relative clauses fun. For a successful activity, the teacher should have a collection of fun hats and other head coverings, such as scarves and shawls. Alternatively, the teacher can ask students to create their own hats with construction paper, ribbons, felt, glue, and other materials. It is important for each hat to have a distinct look. With their hats on, students should sit in a circle and observe all of their classmates' hats. The students should be provided with a sentence starter that includes one or more relative pronouns (*who, which, whose, whom, that*) as follows:

- *I spy someone **who** is wearing a (adjective) hat.*
- *I spy someone **who** is wearing a (adjective) hat **that** has/is (more information about the hat).*

For example:

- *I spy someone who is wearing a striped hat that has orange and purple fuzzy balls attached to it.*

To begin the activity, the first player describes one of the students' hats, and the student to raise his hand first and guess correctly *who* is wearing it becomes the next one to describe a hat. When everyone has had a turn, the game is over; if more practice is needed, the guessing can continue with other items of clothing. To extend this activity into a content area or for upper grades, change the purpose of the guessing game to identify historical figures, scientific discoveries, and important events. For example, in a unit on inventions, have students write complex statements in the following fashion:

- *I am thinking of a person who invented a tool that helped automate the production of cotton.*
- *I am thinking of a scientist who invented a communication device that helped people talk to each other across the country.*

Anchor Performance 2: Apply the Conventions of Capitalization, Punctuation, and Spelling When Writing

As students move from kindergarten through fifth grade, the expectations for knowing how to spell words and how to use capitalization and punctuation conventions of English become incrementally more challenging. Spelling instruction and spelling tests are still commonly practiced even though decades of research indicate that spelling is best learned through meaningful, active engagement with the target words through reading, writing, and other contextualized activities (Weaver, 1998). The following strategies support such meaningful activities for acquiring and practicing the conventions of writing.

Essential Strategy to Support Anchor Performance 2: Hands-on Work With Words Using Reference Materials, Authentic Literary and Informational Texts, and Manipulatives

Rather than rote memorization or drill and kill exercises, students must participate in meaningful, age-appropriate, engaging activities of increasing complexity. Authentic materials, reference books and online resources, as well as teacher and student-created hands-on materials will contribute to such learning opportunities.

Resourcing. In order to assist students with their spelling, provide them with explicit instruction to access and use available print resources; create regular opportunities to develop their skills to be efficient and successful with reference materials, such as monolingual and bilingual print and online dictionaries, glossaries, and other reference books. Some suggestions for becoming familiar with dictionary use include (a) examining the letter distribution in a dictionary, (b) locating guide words (the first and the last words on the page), (c) practicing scanning a dictionary page through game-like activities such as scavenger hunts, and (d) exploring long entries and multiple meanings given for a word. *Guide Word Wonders* is one activity that gives students practice with reference materials. Using print dictionaries and teams of three or four students, the teacher displays a set of guide words for one of the pages in the dictionary. Students must use their dictionaries to find the page on which the guide words are located and identify the page number. First team to find the guide word page wins the round. Play continues in like manner until students have had ample practice finding dictionary guide words.

Personal Dictionaries or Word-Study Books. Turn a blank marble notebook into either an alphabetized personal dictionary or a subject-matter word study book by inserting appropriate tabs. Have students collect their own words and develop ownership of the spelling and meaning of the words by writing the words, putting them into personally meaningful sentences, and illustrating them.

Authentic Literature and Mentor Texts. Authentic literature and mentor texts may be aligned to a range of core standards and anchor performances (also see Chapter 6 on writing). When students are asked to examine a mentor text for use of writing mechanics such as punctuation, they see an authentic example of how and where the author chose to insert a colon as opposed to a semicolon, or a period versus an exclamation point. When grammar and mechanics are taught in the context of authentic reading and writing, students learn how authors use language effectively to achieve their goals, and they, too, aspire to do so. An engaging way to use authentic literature is to select one of the books in Box 2.3 that more explicitly lends itself to examining capitalization, punctuation, and spelling as well as offer teaching opportunities about a range of grammar points and conventions of English.

Box 2.3 Teaching Punctuation, Spelling, and Other Grammatical Conventions

Author	Books
Brian P. Cleary	Words Are CATegorical® series, including
	• *Dearly, Nearly, Insincerely: What is an Adverb?*
	• *Hairy, Scary, Ordinary: What is an Adjective?*
	• *I and You and Don't Forget Who: What is a Pronoun?*
Ruth Heller	A World of Language series, including
	• *A Cache of Jewels and Other Collective Nouns*
	• *Up, Up and Away: A Book of Adverbs*
	• *Mine, All Mine: A Book about Pronouns*
	• *Many Luscious Lollipops: A Book about Adjectives*
Robin Pulver	• *Nouns and Verbs Have a Field Day*
	• *Punctuation Takes a Vacation*
	• *Silent Letters Loud and Clear*
	• *Happy Endings: A Story About Suffixes*
Marcie Aboff (and others)	Word Fun series, including
	• *If You Were a Prefix*
	• *If You Were a Suffix*
Rick Walton	Language Adventures series, including
	• *Around the House, the Fox Chased the Mouse: Adventures in Prepositions*
	• *Bullfrog Pops: Adventures in Verbs and Objects*
	• *Herd of Cows, Flock of Sheep: Adventures in Collective Nouns*
	• *Just Me and 6,000 Rats: Adventures in Conjunctions*
	• *Once There Was a Bull . . . (Frog): Adventures in Compound Words*

Interactive Word Walls. One method of teaching the spelling of high-frequency or sight words is through building a Word Wall, a strategy promoted by Patricia Cunningham, Dorothy Hall, and Cheryl Sigmon (1999). High-frequency words—ones that beginning readers and writers need to know "by heart," and that do not always have predictable spelling patterns—account for about half of the words we read and write; thus, building a word wall with these words would be highly beneficial for struggling learners. You can add frequently misspelled words and make sure the major spelling patterns are represented on the Word Wall. Each week, select four or five words and add them to the designated bulletin board or wall in the room. Have sections for each letter of the alphabet and check to see that the words are visible and accessible to all students. Include at least one daily activity when students read, write, chant, clap, find, or play interactive games with the Word Wall words.

Knowledge and Application of Language

The grade-specific standard for knowledge and application of language does not begin until second grade, indicating that the metacognitive or metalinguistic awareness that is necessary to think abstractly about the language is developmentally more appropriate for students in Grade 2 and up.

Anchor Performance 3: Understand How Language is Used in Different Contexts

Students need exposure to language used in a variety of ways and in a variety of contexts—formally and informally, in written and spoken formats, and in varied genres and situations. If students internalize the knowledge they have about how language functions in different contexts, they are likely to comprehend more fully when reading and listening or make more effective choices when speaking and writing.

Essential Strategy to Support Anchor Performance 3: Integrate all Four Language Skills (Listening, Speaking, Reading, and Writing) Meaningfully, Purposefully (and Playfully Whenever Possible)

Students' knowledge and understanding of how language is used in various contexts will begin by listening to and reading texts in a variety of styles; at the same time, such understanding must be transferred to actual opportunities for students to produce language by making not only the grammatically correct word-, sentence-, and text-level choices but also the most appropriate and powerful choices for words and sentence structures when speaking and writing.

Skits and Role-plays. To have students understand the difference between formal and informal language use, explore a range of scenarios in which language is used to various degrees of formality. Start with simple one- or two-line role-plays and move on to longer skits. Some possible scenarios include speaking to a teacher, a police officer, an elder, or the principal versus speaking to a younger sibling, an older brother, a cousin, a friend from the neighborhood, or a classmate. Have students read short skits representing formal versus informal language use, and compare language choice and sentence complexity. When the students are ready to apply what they have learned about language variety, invite them to generate and perform their own skits.

Read It and Speak It (and Write It, too). Students need to understand that how we use language in writing and language in speech will differ. To practice identifying the differences between written and spoken English, direct students' attention to grade-appropriate language patterns frequently found in written texts, but rarely in everyday, spoken language. Create a T-chart comparing two versions of the same sentence: See how the same idea is expressed in two different ways and how the sentence published in a *Kids Discover* issue titled "Great Wall of China" (DuBose, 2008) compares to the sentence that is more likely to be used in spoken English (Figure 2.1).

Figure 2.1   Read It and Speak It Comparison Chart

Written in a Book (Great Wall of China)	Spoken in Everyday Situations
1. One of the most magnificent structures on earth arose in the East Asia nation of China many centuries ago. (p. 2)	1. They built a very famous and beautiful wall in China a long time ago.
2. Like earlier walls that were built in China, the purpose of the Great Wall was to keep out invaders who wandered the arid grasslands north of China's borders. (p. 2)	2. They built the Great Wall to keep out strangers who lived in the north. They built other walls before the Great Wall of China.

One extension that this strategy lends itself to is using the sample sentences as mentor text and encouraging students to write original sentences that parallel their sentence structure. This activity reinforces for students that careful examination of what they read can help improve their writing. Another extension of this activity is exposing students to longer texts and spoken discourse about the same topic. Students can compare a news report on TV with a news article online, or a newspaper or magazine article with a podcast about the same current event.

Theme Reading, Theme Listening Across Genres. Supporting several other Common Core Standards, this strategy shows students how writing style changes when they read or listen to a range of literary resources about an essential grade-appropriate topic represented by various genres. To address this Common Core language standard, the goal is to compare how authors chose to write about a shared theme and used words and sentences as well as text-level organization while operating within the framework of their chosen genres. In Box 2.4, see a collection of our favorites on the topic of community for the second-grade classroom.

Box 2.4 Theme Reading/Listening Collection on Neighborhood Communities

Title	Author
Poems:	
"Tempest Avenue"	Ian McMillan
Wake Up, House: Rooms Full of Poems!	Dee Lillegard
My House is Singing	Betsy Rosenthal
"Childhood Tracks"	James Berry
Nonfiction	
Homes in Many Cultures	Heather Adamson
Wonderful Houses Around the World	Yoshio Komatsu
Homes Around the World	Max Moore
At My House: A Lift-the-Flap Shadow Book	Roger Priddy
The ABC Book of American Homes	Michael Shoulders
Houses and Homes	Ann Morris
Fiction	
In These Walls and Floors (What's Lurking in This House?)	Nancy Harris
The Little House	Virginia Lee Burton
The Biggest House in the World	Leo Lionni
Ira Sleeps Over	Bernard Wab

Songs, Rhymes, Fairy Tales, Riddles

"This is the House that Jack Built"

"Home on the Range"

The Three Little Pigs

Goldilocks and the Three Bears

Anthologies with Various Genres

Home: A Collaboration of Thirty Authors & Illustrators   Michael J. Rosen, Editor

Bilingual Books

The House is Made of Mud   Ken Buchanan

My House/Mi Casa   Gladys Rosa-Mendoza

My Very Own Room/Mi Propio Cuartito   Amada Irma Perez

Jeopardy Game for Style Shifting. Style shifts in authentic situations often occur automatically: confident and experienced speakers of the language naturally change the level of formality they use based on the situation, the context, the audience, or the topic. To practice identifying the difference between formal and informal English, consider playing an adapted version of the game "Jeopardy," the goal of which is for students to switch from the informal or slang version of a phrase or sentence to the formal one. Featured on *Do you Speak American?* (http://www.pbs.org/speak/), Daniel Russell, an elementary school teacher used "Jeopardy" to validate his students' knowledge of their dialect—also known as African American Vernacular English (AAVE)—when he asked them to provide the standard English equivalents of various common phrases in AAVE. For example, students can easily recognize and relate to the sentence "I didn't do nothing." The task is to be able to produce the same sentence in standard American English. The Jeopardy board will contain a selection of commonly used, similar, nonstandard English expressions and the challenge for the students is to come up with the standard phrase. One possible way to make this an effective activity is to include authentic student-generated linguistics examples so learners could recognize their own informal speech patterns. To get started, see a jeopardy template on one of these websites: http://www.superteachertools.com/jeopardy/ or http://www.techteachers.com/jeopardytemplates.htm.

Vocabulary Acquisition and Use

Anchor Performance 4: Determine or Clarify the Meaning of Unknown and Multiple-Meaning Words and Phrases

Successful vocabulary learning and accurate vocabulary use in all content areas are two strong predictors of academic success. Determining or clarifying the meaning of unknown words, deciphering multiple word meaning, using context clues, analyzing meaningful word parts, and consulting general and specialized reference materials are some of the most challenging tasks that ELLs and at-risk students face on a daily basis. For over a decade, Isabel Beck, Margaret McKeown, and Linda Kucan's (2002) work has been frequently cited to provide a rationale for and to create a manageable framework for robust vocabulary instruction. Some of the strategies presented below build upon their suggestions, whereas others represent additional researchers' and practitioners' recommendations.

Learning new words and figuring out word meaning often present an added challenge for struggling learners. If they are less-than-fluent speakers or competent readers in English, context clues and contextual understanding may not be as effective as they are for more proficient speakers and readers. Thus, scaffolding vocabulary acquisition and creating multiple meaningful opportunities to encounter and to actively use robust vocabulary should be a primary goal.

Essential Strategy to Support Anchor Performance 4: Offer Visual and Contextual Support

Pictures ranging from ad hoc line drawings to magnificent photographs, from quick sketches to intricate illustrations found in picture books may all offer an appropriate context and much needed visual support for new and difficult words. Showing brief video clips and bringing in realia (the real object you are teaching about) may further enhance students' understanding of complex word meanings. Additionally, providing a variety of authentic contexts in which the target words are used will lead to the type of rich instruction that gives students numerous meaningful experiences with the words.

Picture It. Robert Marzano and Debra Pickering (2005) suggested that "when you ask students to construct a picture, symbol, or graphic representation of a term, they are forced to think of the term in a totally different way" (p. 21). When students are learning about various land features (plateau, peninsula, mountain range, delta), have them generate their own illustrations, where the expectation is that the drawings will look similar. At the same time, when exploring big concepts such as respect, natural disasters, freedom, each student's conceptualization may vary considerably.

These drawings will also spark rich conversations and lend themselves to opportunities to use academic language in discourse. Student-created illustrations (with appropriate guidance and scaffolding) will contribute to internalizing word meaning while engaging learners in a multimodal task.

Student-Friendly Definitions and Concept Maps. The definition of *outrageous* as "exceeding the limits of what is usual" or "not conventional or matter-of-fact" as found in an online dictionary is *outrageously* difficult for struggling learners. Why? These dictionary definitions use sentence fragments and synonyms that would need to be defined and explained so they are just as difficult as the target word. Stahl and Nagy (2006) claimed that "having children restate definitions may be the only way a teacher can find out whether the children actually understand them" (p. 65). A precursor to that recommendation should be presenting definitions to students written in an accessible, student-friendly way; then, letting students use their own words to define new concepts is expected to lead to greater access and greater retention. So what would be a child-friendly definition of *outrageous*? Let's try this:

> *When something is outrageous, it shocks you. You can hardly believe it has happened. For example, if someone had broken into the school and vandalized the main office, that would be outrageous.*

When child-friendly definitions are augmented with visual or graphic support such as a concept map, students also understand the connections and associations that go with the target word.

Look Inside and Outside of the Word. We are inspired by Nancy Frey and Douglas Fisher's (2009) framework for learning words "inside and out." To look *inside* a word, students are directed to identify root words, prefixes, suffixes, or word parts of compound words they recognize. Invite them to also look *outside* the word and try to figure out the meaning from the sentence or paragraph where they came across the word or look for any illustrations or other visuals that could help. Another take on the inside-outside strategy is to examine how the word is used inside the context of the subject matter or literacy task as opposed to outside in the students' own experiences if applicable.

Anchor Performance 5: Recognize Word Relationships, Figurative Language, and Nuances in Word Meanings

Knowledge of vocabulary and application thereof gets increasingly complicated when complex word relationships are introduced, figurative language is used, or nuances in word meanings need to be recognized or defined.

Essential Strategy to Support Anchor Performance 5: Active Engagement With Challenging Language Segments Presented in Context

Although ELLs and at-risk students need support and scaffolding, and although they highly benefit when difficult academic content is made accessible, teachers should not shy away from exposing them to the complexity of the English language. Diverse learners cannot afford to be exposed to less-than-robust language learning opportunities. Instead, they need engaging explorations of meaningful language segments as well as exposure to the complexity of carefully chosen whole text selections

Word Sorts. Depending on the objective of the lesson, frequently engage students in sorting activities, in which they need to match single words or phrases to preestablished categories. Similar to a word sort, Doug Fisher, Nancy Frey, and Carol Rothenberg (2008) suggested expanding task to concept sorting and have students sort larger language chunks or even sentences into categories that relate to the concept they are studying. Using interactive whiteboard technology gives a hi-tech twist to tactile learning, although sorting words that are written on index cards or placed in a T-chart will also do. Older students may contribute to a shared wiki page to document the outcomes of their word or concept sorts. Since word relationships may range from synonyms and antonyms to whole and part, from parts of speech to idioms, these relationships may lend themselves to sorting activities across the curriculum.

Act It Out: Language nuances are hard for diverse learners to understand unless they are made tangible and visible for ELLs and other at-risk students. Demonstrating word meanings by acting out subtle differences, playing charades, pantomiming, and participating in other kinesthetic activities will make the shades of meaning more explicit and memorable for students. Box 2.5 illustrates a range of synonyms for three verbs with more or less subtle differences in meaning.

Box 2.5 Shades of Meaning for *Walk, Cry,* and *Eat*

Walk, strut, stroll, wander, march, roam, swagger, tiptoe

Cry, weep, wail, sob, whimper

Eat, devour, wolf down, nibble, chew, gobble up, munch, pig out, dine

Create a pantomime activity for students by preparing cards with *Shades of Meaning* words. Have teams of students take turns selecting a word card, discussing what it means, and having one team member act it out. Have the other teams try to guess the word being pantomimed.

Idioms From Around the World. In multilingual classrooms, an exciting and highly motivating activity is to compare how students' native languages work in contrast to English. Choose age- and grade-appropriate common idioms and proverbs and invite students (with parental input) to provide versions of the same idiom or proverb in their home languages. Such an exercise in comparative linguistics in the elementary classroom not only enhances students' understanding of figurative language in English, but it will also help develop cross-cultural understanding as the class discusses what information is revealed about different cultures and people through these idioms and proverbs. Box 2.6 has some of our favorites.

Box 2.6 Proverbs Compared Across Languages

Example 1:

English: *Two heads are better than one.*

Chinese: 一人計短,二人計長. ("One person's plans are short, but those made by two people are long.")

Hungarian: Több szem többet lát. ("More eyes see more.")

Japanese: 三人寄れば文珠の知恵 ("Three people together have the wisdom of a Buddha.")

Spanish: Cuatro ojos ven más que dos ("Four eyes see more than two eyes.")

Example 2:

English: *Out of the frying pan and into the fire.*

Hungarian: Csöbörből vödörbe. ("Out of the cup into the pail.")

Russian: От волка бежáл, да на медвéдя попáл. ("He ran from the wolf, but ran into a bear.")

Spanish: Saliste de Guatemala y te metiste en Guatapeor ("You left Guate-bad and you ended up in Guate-worse." A play on the words Guatemala, mala and peor.)

Turkish: Yağmurdan kaçarken doluya tutulmak. ("Out of the rain into the hail.")

Story Connections to Teach Figurative Language. Exposing students to authentic literature in which figurative language is used in a meaningful context remains to be a much favored strategy. In Box 2.7, there is a collection of our favorite K–5 children's books to use when teaching figurative language. An important challenge to keep in mind is that many linguistically and academically diverse learners tend to interpret figurative language literally or are puzzled by it. One best way to approach it is to dissect the target expression, discuss the literal and connotative meaning, and engage students in rich conversations about the language chunk you are analyzing.

Box 2.7 Children's Literature for Teaching Figurative Language

Title	Author
Similes	
My Dog is as Smelly as Dirty Socks: And Other Funny Family Portraits	Hanoch Piven
My Best Friend Is As Sharp As a Pencil: And Other Funny Classroom Portraits	Hanoch Piven
Crazy Like a Fox: A Simile Story	Loreen Leedy
Stubborn as a Mule and Other Silly Similes	Nancy Jean Loewen
Metaphors	
Skin Like Milk, Hair of Silk: What Are Similes and Metaphors?	Brian P. Cleary
Tulip Sees America	Cynthia Rylant
Idioms	
In a Pickle: And Other Funny Idioms	Marvin Terban
Figurative versus Literal Meaning	
Parts	Tedd Arnold
More Parts	Tedd Arnold
Even More Parts	Tedd Arnold
Owl Moon	Jane Yolen

Anchor Performance 6: Acquire and Use Accurately a Range of General Academic and Domain-Specific Words and Phrases

To be on the path to college and career readiness, students in all grades need to build and accurately use a range of general academic and content-based words and phrases.

Essential Strategy to Support Anchor Performance 6: Deconstructing and Reconstructing Academic Language

In-depth understanding is needed of not only word-level but also sentence- and text-level complexities that characterize general academic language use as well as content-specific language use. Diverse students need explicit guidance in examining language as it works in the various content areas, taking language apart to see how the micro- and macro-level pieces fit together, and then also have the opportunity to use the language in appropriate contexts.

Vocabulary Self-Assessment. Start by raising awareness about word knowledge, which is a complex task but can be made accessible to all learners. You can start by sharing and regularly using the Vocabulary Self-Assessment Tool in Figure 2.2, which is a simplified version of a classic by Isabel Beck and colleagues (2008).

Figure 2.2 Vocabulary Self-Assessment Tool

Vocabulary	My Knowledge of Key Words			
	I have never heard of it	I have heard of it, I think I know what it means	I know it very well	I can tell or write a sentence with it

Tiered Vocabulary Instruction. Since Isabel Beck and colleagues' (2002, 2008) work, a fairly well-known conceptualization of vocabulary is the following three-tier model:

Tier 1: Basic words that are often recognized and used with ease by most native speakers of English (e.g., book, girl, happy, he). ELLs face a special challenge and need vocabulary instruction also targeting these words.

Tier 2: General academic words that tend to be more complex and polysemous (having multiple meanings). Some of these words travel across content areas (e.g., origin, system, table) and have different meanings; whereas others perform similar textual or discourse level functions regardless of the content (e.g., therefore, for instance, nevertheless).

Tier 3: Domain-specific words and less commonly used words that are critical for understanding the subject matter of the instruction (e.g., photosynthesis, circumference, expedition). New content can only be acquired if these Tier 3 words are clearly understood and internalized by the students.

The ultimate purpose of this type of categorization goes beyond merely identifying the level of complexity or challenge certain words will pose. Instead, teachers can make important instructional decisions based on this categorization and commit to building students' Tier 2 vocabulary across the content areas to offer the most access to critical words that afford students to comprehend a wide range of texts.

Simon Says, Science Says. A simple yet effective game to play is a modified version of Simon Says, renamed as Simon Says, Science Says by Virginia Rojas (personal communication, July 10, 2012). The purpose of the game is to showcase and practice how conversational vocabulary and everyday language use differ from the precision of academic, domain-specific words. For example: Simon says, "The water dries up"; Science says, "The water evaporates." Or, Simon says, "It is getting cold"; Science says, "The temperature is decreasing." It can be played in a teacher-led, whole class setting or in small groups or pairs.

Chunk It! Teaching and practicing language chunks rather than isolated words help students see how collocations are formed in English (i.e., how certain words go together to create a larger unit of meaning). When teaching the word *according*, it makes much more sense for diverse learners to see language chunks such as "according to the author," "according to the first paragraph," "according to the title," for example. Phrasal verbs (e.g., get in, get over, get back, get ahead) pose a challenge for linguistically diverse students, so special attention to contextualizing and offering a sentence chunk where and how these words are used can be especially helpful. Consider keeping a *Chunk It!* chart displayed in class that keeps a record of language chunks discussed in class and is available for students to add language chunks that they find in their reading.

Songs, Chants, and Other Mnemonic Devices. When words are set to music, when rhythm accompanies them as in chants, or when hard to learn information is turned into a song, remembering facts, recalling concepts, and following procedures—once a daunting task—may become easier for all students. English language learners face the added challenges of acquiring a new language while also committing new and difficult information to memory. Basic mnemonic devices are among the most frequently used memory-enhancing learning tools that teachers and students alike find beneficial (Honigsfeld & Barnick-Eonidis, 2009). Teachers we work with use all sorts of mnemonic devices to remind their students to edit their work:

> SCOPE: *Spelling, Capitalization, Order of words, Punctuation, Express complete thought*

> GPS: *Grammar Punctuation Spelling*

> GAS CAP: *Grammar And Spelling, Capitalization And Punctuation*

Gray (1997) argued that certain mnemonic devices are highly relevant to English learners. He particularly recommended the use of mnemonic devices that encourage visualization and use of imagery. Brain-based learning proponents emphasize the power of music and rhythm to create an environment that optimally stimulates the brain (See, for example, Ashcraft & Radvansky, 2009; Jensen, 2008; Sousa, 2008; Willis, 2006). In a different approach, Schumaker, Denton, and Deshler (1984) introduced RAP, which is a paraphrasing strategy to remind students with learning disabilities of the three steps they need to take to understand what they have just read:

1. *Read a paragraph.*

2. *Ask yourself, "What were the main idea and details in this paragraph?"*

3. *Put the main idea and details into your own words.*

ANTICIPATED OUTCOMES

When diverse learners are exposed to complex language and are engaged in tasks that expect them to use such language, and when these expectations are well supported with instructional scaffolds, diverse learners are anticipated to have their vocabulary acquisition accelerated. Further, if students are given the tools to manage challenging academic texts as well as provided with ample opportunities to practice these skills, they learn to tolerate ambiguity and will handle more complex texts with less frustration and more success.

We believe that teaching and learning academic vocabulary and language is critical to student success in all content areas. Complex language permeates students' ability to make progress in all four skill areas—reading, writing, speaking, and listening. Without fluency and facility with academic language, students will not be able to meet the CCSS.

INSTRUCTIONAL CHALLENGES

As Halliday (1996) so aptly stated, "Language is powered by grammatical energy" (p. 4). Learners whose language use—whether in writing or speech—lacks the necessary grammatical structures or *grammatical energy* will not be able to go far, with their speech halting or writing faltering. Thus, when teaching the conventions of English grammar and language use, we need to move beyond incidental learning, in which grammar is left for students to pick up on their own. Rather, teachers must offer all students daily opportunities to use standard American English in varied contexts and through a variety of authentic experiences. To be able to do so, we urge all teachers to commit to developing their own knowledge of the grade-appropriate grammar points to be taught. Through collaborative planning sessions, consider discussing the following questions:

- What grammar points should be targeted?
- Why should these points be targeted?
- Do I understand the grammar point?
- Have I based my explanation on reliable sources?
- Do I have grammar resources on hand at home and in the classroom?
- What do I want my students to do with the target form/structure?

Even if there is a strong individual teacher commitment to implementing a variety of successful, research-based strategies for vocabulary instruction that are aligned to the Common Core standards, schools need a schoolwide approach to vocabulary instruction that is comprehensive and integrated. We concur with Camille Blachowitz, Peter Fisher, Donna Ogle, and Susan Watts-Taffe (2006), who stated that vocabulary must be a "core consideration in all grades across the school and in all subject areas across the school day" (pp. 527–528). Additionally, for most effective vocabulary instruction in a school or district it must be based on a common philosophy and shared practices among teachers to ensure greater continuity and instructional intensity. At the same time, we must recognize that students come to school with a vast range of prior knowledge, background experiences, active and passive vocabulary, and language skills, thus differentiated instruction must also be considered.

PROMISING CLASSROOM PRACTICES

Louanne Johnson, a fourth-grade teacher, recognized that vocabulary instruction and academic language development could not be left to chance. It needed to permeate every school day. She organized her vocabulary and language instruction by selecting a word or idiom of the day, words of wisdom (proverbs) on a weekly basis, and other carefully selected phrases or academically challenging expressions that were derived from text that students were reading or had read. She displayed these words and expressions in the classroom, integrated them into instruction, and constantly referred to as well as reviewed them.

After much success with her own class, Louanne proposed the word of the day become a shared school practice; in this way, all students had the opportunity for sustained, focused exposure to Tier 2 words in multiple contexts on a daily basis through both central office morning announcements and prepared activities developed by a committee of interdisciplinary teachers and specialists. For example, if *compare* was selected for a particular day, students, in accordance with their grade-level curriculum, compared measurements or numbers in mathematics, reading selections in English language arts, daily weather patterns during morning circle meetings, and how significant ideas, beliefs, communities, and societies have changed over time. It was found in Louanne's building that this type of systematic, school-wide effort can pave the way for additional collaborative conversations to connect and streamline grade-level curriculum with a focus for building strategies to develop academic language to help all students have multiple opportunities and exposure to critical language learning.

COMMON CORE LANGUAGE STANDARDS— (UN)COMMON REFLECTION QUESTIONS

1. How can all teachers' knowledge-based and skill sets regarding grammar instruction be enhanced?

2. How could English Language Development (ELD) standards be meaningfully connected to the CCSS?

3. How do the Common Core language standards translate into successful instruction for beginner English learners? How about students with language disorders?

4. Which of the ideas presented in this chapter will be the first one(s) you try in your classroom and why? What improvements/growth do you hope to see in your students by engaging in these activities?

KEY RESOURCES

Professional Books

Casagrande, J. (2006). *Grammar snobs are great big meanies: A guide to language for fun and spite.* New York, NY: Penguin Books.

Hale, C. (2001). *Sin and syntax: How to craft wickedly effective prose.* New York, NY: Broadway Books.

Lederer, R., & Shore, J. (2005). *Comma sense: A fundamental guide to punctuation.* New York, NY: St. Martin's Press.

Lukeman, N. (2006). *A dash of style: The art and mastery of punctuation.* New York, NY: Norton.

Noden, H. R. (1999). *Image grammar: Using grammatical structures to teach writing.* Portsmouth, NH: Heinemann.

Truss, L. (2004). *Eats, shoots & leaves: The zero tolerance approach to punctuation.* New York, NY: Gotham Books.

A Specialized Resource to Help Develop the Grammarian in Every Teacher

Anderson, J. (2005). *Mechanically inclined: Building grammar, usage, and style into writer's workshop.* Portland, ME: Stenhouse.

Online Resources

- Office of English Language Acquisition, Language Enhancement, and Academic Achievement for Limited English Proficient Students (OELA)
  http://www.ed.gov/about/offices/list/oela/index.html
- Teaching Diverse Learners
  http://www.alliance.brown.edu/tdl
- US Department of Education's National Clearinghouse for English Language Acquisition
  http://www.ncela.gwu.edu
- Vocabulary and Style
  http://www.vocabulary.com/
  http:/grammar.yourdictionary.com/slang.dictionary
- Vocabulary Development Using Digital Tools
  http://techteachers.com/vocabulary.htm
  http://www.wordsmyth.net/
  http://www.wordsift.com
  http://www.visualthesaurus.com/
- Grammar Practice
  http://grammaropolis.com/games.php
  http://www.roadtogrammar.com/
- Grammar Blast
  http://www.eduplace.com/kids/hme/k_5/quizzes/?x=100&y=19

3 Reading Strategies for Literature

It is better to read a little and ponder a lot than to read a lot and ponder a little.

— Denis Parsons Burkitt

OVERVIEW

Teachers are often at a loss when trying to provide reading instruction in their classrooms that meets the needs of all learners, particularly those who are struggling or are not yet fluent in English. Children acquire new literacy skills differently from each other, thus one challenge teachers face is how to match each learner with just the right reading strategies to bring about success. Other concerns focus on slightly older students who move into the upper elementary grades lacking grade-level reading ability, and as such, they are still *learning to read* instead of being ready for *reading to learn.* How do educators "catch students up" so that the curriculum becomes more accessible to them through the written word?

No one reading method reaches all students, yet elementary teachers are inundated with the latest methodologies touted to bring about results. Districts often adopt new reading trends or anthologies with prepackaged materials and resources before any concentrated, independent review via teacher feedback or piloting programs to determine local results, particularly on their effectiveness with diverse student populations. Classroom teachers are mandated to use new methods or materials after being exposed to them most often in one-day workshops, thus the integrity behind them over time frequently becomes lost (Burns, 1999).

Reading trends should not be a substitute for best practices with individual learners, and reading methods should not dictate instruction in a one-size-fits-all approach. Unfortunately, the problem with adopting new reading philosophies is that too often little has been done to research the method independently, to prepare teachers to implement them effectively, to sustain professional development to support teachers adequately, or to provide the necessary resources and materials for students at all levels of reading. First and foremost, the instruction of each individual child is paramount, and well-informed teachers identify students' instructional needs and combine practices that work best for each one of them.

WHY TEACHING DIVERSE LEARNERS READING STRATEGIES PROMOTES COMPREHENSION OF LITERARY TEXTS

Much research has documented the positive impact of reading strategy instruction on overall understanding of concepts and literacy development (Fang & Wei, 2010; Griffin, Simmons, & Kameenui, 1991; McNamara, 2007). According to McNamara (2009), "strategy instruction is particularly needed and effective for those students who are struggling most, namely those with . . . lower reading skills" (p. 34). In fact, we think most teachers would agree that students who are able to independently apply reading strategies overall have better comprehension of text.

The National Institute of Child Health and Human Development (2000) published report, *Teaching Children to Read,* offered general guidelines for reading instruction. Not only did the report suggest that teachers should teach reading explicitly through strategy instruction but also should model the process of thinking while reading, foster students' curiosity and engagement with the text to ask questions, and provide activities that keep students actively engaged in the reading process.

One important goal is not to be overwhelmed with the task of teaching diverse learners to read. Many strategies that work with average achievers can be scaffolded or modified to work with those students whose reading skills are yet emerging. Furthermore, teaching reading through fiction is a great avenue for diverse learners to discover the joy of reading while being introduced to fundamental strategies for reading improvement.

CORE READING STRATEGIES

This chapter contains strategies that are aligned to the ten College and Career Readiness Anchor Standards (CCRAS) for Reading with detailed application to the strand for literature. They follow the CCRAS that are divided according to *Key Ideas and Details, Craft and Structure, Integration of Knowledge and Ideas, and Range of Reading and Text Complexity.* A series of related *Anchor* Performances are derived for each of the ten standards and accompanied by applicable strategies to help diverse learners. We invite our readers to review each strategy (outlined in Box 3.1) and adapt it according to the grade-level and academic or language abilities of their students.

Box 3.1 College and Career Readiness Anchor Standards for Reading for Literature

Key Ideas and Details

1. Read closely to determine what the text says explicitly and to make logical inferences from it: cite specific contextual evidence when writing or speaking to support conclusions drawn from the text.

2. Determine central ideas or themes of a text and analyze their development; summarize the key supporting details and ideas.

3. Analyze how and why individuals, events, and ideas develop and interact over the course of a text.

Craft and Structure

4. Interpret words and phrases as they are used in a text, including determining technical, connotative, and figurative meanings, and analyze how specific word choices shape meaning or tone.

5. Analyze the structure of texts, including how specific sentences, paragraphs, and larger portions of the text (e.g., a section, chapter, scene, or stanza) relate to each other and the whole.

6. Assess how point of view or purpose shapes the content and style of a text.

Integration of Knowledge and Ideas

7. Integrate and evaluate content presented in diverse media and formats, including visually and quantitatively, as well as in words.

8. Delineate and evaluate the argument and specific claims in the text, including the validity of the reasoning as well as the relevance and sufficiency of the evidence. (*Not applicable to literature; see Chapter 4*)

9. Analyze how two or more texts address similar themes or topics in order to build knowledge or to compare the approaches the authors take.

Range of Reading and Level of Text Complexity

10. Read and comprehend complex literacy and informational texts independently and proficiently.

Key Ideas and Details

Anchor Performance 1: Asking and Answering Questions About the Text

To become skilled readers, students need to know and apply not only a bevy of reading strategies, but they also must understand what habits successful readers engage in to make meaning of text. Good readers repeatedly have and ask questions about what they read, a habit that helps them to remain engaged in the text. By the same token, students also need to know how to derive text-based answers to a variety of questions, whether the answers are *right there* and easily found in the text or different parts of a text need to be examined to develop an accurate answer.

Individual grade-level standards for this anchor performance vary from Grades K–5 requiring students to ask and answer questions with increasing precision and explicitness; expectations change from finding key ideas and details of a text in kindergarten and first grade to referring to examples in the text and drawing inferences in fourth and fifth grade.

Essential Strategy to Support Anchor Performance 1: Sustain the Use of Explicit Reading Strategy Instruction to Enhance Student Text-Based Responses and Support the Development of Student-Generated Questions

Students' comprehension can be fostered through the asking and answering of questions before, during, and after reading. Furthermore, students' abilities to develop their own questions and finding answers

Figure 3.1 Reading Strategies

A Good Way to Read is to . . .

- Think while you read
- Make predictions about what you read
- Make personal connections:
  - Text to self
  - Text to text
  - Text to world
- Jot down words you don't know
- Use context clues to find meaning
- Reread to check your understanding
- Picture the story idea in your mind
- Ask questions about what you read
- Check if you can summarize the story's main idea
- Evaluate and form opinions about what you read

to questions can be best accomplished through teacher modeling. Read-aloud or shared reading is an ideal activity for teachers to showcase their own generation of questions about text. Although read-aloud activities frequently occur in early elementary grades, it is often abandoned by Grades 3–5 due to the increasing demands of the core curriculum and intense attention to standardized test preparation. Modeling one's thinking is essential for diverse learners who often are not aware of what types of strategies to apply to enhance their comprehension of text.

Framework for Strategy Instruction. Reading strategies need to be explicitly taught to students who are emergent readers, particularly to those who have not experienced much reading success or young English learners who have to develop their literacy skills along with their English language acquisition. Students need to be taught one strategy at a time over a length of time, anywhere from a few weeks to a month, depending about the students' age and their readiness to apply each strategy. The selected strategy must be the specific focus of direct instruction, modeled with multiple texts, part of students' guided practice, incorporated into cooperative learning tasks, i.e., literature circles, reader's workshop, buddy reading, guided reading groups, for example, and practiced individually. Figure 3.1 (see opposite) lists common general reading strategies taught in Grades K–5.

Asking Higher-Order Questions (Hill & Flynn, 2008). This strategy—developed in particular for English learners but beneficial for the planned questioning of all students—combines the understanding of the stages of second-language acquisition with the concepts of Bloom's Taxonomy to create a framework for asking higher order thinking questions

Table 3.1 Asking Higher-Order Questions

Story: *A Chair for My Mother* by Vera B. Williams			
Bloom's Taxonomy Concepts	**Sample Stages of Language Proficiency**		
	Preproduction: no English is spoken	**Early Production: one or two word answers**	**Speech Emergence: phrases or short sentences**
Knowledge	Show me the jar where the mother saved money.	What is the girl's name?	In the story, what type of job did the mother have?

(Continued)

(Continued)

Comprehension	Show me why the mother saved money.	Tell me why the mother is saving money.	What happened to the family's furniture?
Application	Show me what would happen if the jar broke.	Tell me what would happen if the jar broke.	How could you save money if you did not use a jar?
Analysis	Show me a chair that is comfortable and a chair that is not comfortable.	Tell me why some chairs are comfortable and some chairs are not.	How are a kitchen chair and a comfortable living room chair the same? How are they different?
Synthesis	Point to the items that belong in a comfortable living room.	Tell me the items that belong in a comfortable living room.	How could you change a bedroom so that it looks like a living room?
Evaluation	Show me things that can start a fire in a house.	What can people do to make their house safe from fire?	What should people do if there is a fire in their house?

to students at different levels of language proficiency. According to Hill and Flynn (2008),

> The beauty of this strategy, which focuses on questions in the classroom, is that it helps teachers specifically address the needs of ELLs while also meeting the needs of every student in the classroom. It allows teachers to integrate learning for ELLs in mainstream classrooms and to help these students achieve academic success at the same levels as their native English-speaking peers. (p. 47)

To ensure rigorous, rich class discussion, it is essential for teachers to carefully develop their questions before a lesson begins instead of thinking up questions *on the spot.* The table below can be used as a planning guide to write not only higher-order questions about a particular story but also in a framework that make questions understandable and answerable for all students. With English learners, picture books often work best with this strategy. Table 3.1 identifies how questions might be developed for emergent bilingual youngsters using the story *A Chair for My Mother*.

On the Line/Off the Line Questions. This strategy is a modified QAR (Question/Answer Relationship) (see chapter 6) which can help diverse learners understand the difference between answers to questions that are easy to find (On the Line) and those answers that require students to piece together information that is in several places (Off the Line). To demonstrate this strategy, examine the excerpt below from the story *A Chair for My Mother* (Williams, 1984) and the questions that follow:

> Sometimes my mama is laughing when she comes home from work. Sometimes she's so tired she falls asleep while I count the money out into piles. Some days she has lots of tips. Some days she has only a little. Then she looks worried. But every evening every single shiny coin goes into the jar.

On the Line Question: *What goes into the jar every single evening?*

Off the Line Question: *How does mama feel when she comes home from work?*

The first question (On the Line) can be answered by repeating the information in the last sentence of the excerpt, *every evening every single shiny coin goes into the jar*. However, the second question (Off the Line) requires information from various parts of the paragraph: *mama is laughing*—happy; *sometimes she's so tired*—sleepy.

Anchor Performance 2: Story Retelling and Summarizing

Students who are able to retell or summarize a story are much better able to comprehend text. However, story retelling and summarizing are skills many students, particularly in the early elementary grades, have difficulty mastering. Young children may not fully understand how to create a summary and have trouble identifying the most pertinent information from the story as well as be able to retell it in chronological order.

All too often, youngsters offer superfluous details, diverting attention away from the main story line. Not only do diverse learners benefit from instruction and practice concerning how to produce oral and written summary accounts, but they can also gain retelling skills through a variety of scaffolded techniques. This anchor performance requires kindergarteners and first graders to retell an often-familiar story including key details, whereas in fourth and fifth grades, students are expected to determine and include a story theme in the retelling or describe how characters respond to challenges.

Essential Strategy to Support Anchor Performance 2: Frameworks for Students to Find the Main Idea as Well as Retell and Summarize Literature

Students often benefit from supportive frameworks and step-by-step strategies to identify essential story meaning and details. These frameworks help students to condense larger pieces of text into summaries by extracting critical information and to distinguish a story's main idea from its superfluous content.

Picture the Main Idea is an activity in which students begin to understand the concept of the main idea versus story details using photographs instead of text. Students are asked to examine and tell what is the most important information being conveyed in a photograph. That information is then identified as the main idea. Then students share some of the details about the picture. The main idea is subsequently contrasted with the photograph's various details and the results are written in a chart. The following is an example of the *Picture the Main Idea* strategy:

Consider a picture of a man, wearing shorts and a t-shirt, riding a bicycle on a boardwalk adjacent to a beach on a sunny day. Student responses might be as presented in Table 3.2.

Table 3.2 *Sample Main Idea—Supporting Detail Chart*

Main Idea	Story Details
A man is riding a bicycle	• It's a sunny day, so he is wearing shorts and a t-shirt • He's riding next to a beach • The weather is warm, he seems to be hot

After modeling this strategy and giving students a chance to try it on their own using various photographs, explain to students that stories have main ideas and details as well. Use guided practice and give students opportunities to now identify story main ideas and details using text. Have students *Picture the Main Idea* as if the text were a photograph by visualizing what the text conveys. To ensure student success, use only short pieces of text with clear main ideas and gradually increase the text difficulty.

5 Wh-Q Sum It All helps students identify the main idea and summarize their reading through the use and guidance of Wh-question words (Who, What, When, Where, and Why). To begin, post the question words on a chart that all students can view. Model the strategy by sharing a short text with students and find the answers to as many listed question words as possible. Not all answers to the question words will be obvious. Consider the following excerpt from *Judy Moody* by Megan McDonald and Peter H. Reynolds (2010):

Judy Moody did not want to give up summer. She did not feel like brushing her hair every day. She did not feel like memorizing spelling words. And she did not want to sit next to Frank Pearl, who ate paste, in class. Judy Moody was in a mood. Not a good mood. A bad mood. A mad-face mood. Even the smell of her new Grouchy pencils could not get her out of bed. (p. 1)

Now let's examine the charted question words and identified answers using evidence from the text in Table 3.3.

Table 3.3 *5 Wh-Q Sum It All Chart*

Question Words	Answers	Text Evidence
Who	Judy Moody	Directly stated
What	Did not want to give summer up. She was in a bad mood.	Directly stated
When	At the end of the summer	Implied; that's when school begins
Where	In her bedroom	"Could not get out of bed"
Why	She did not want to go back to school.	Did not like "memorizing spelling words", or "sitting next to Frank Pearl, who ate paste, in class."

Finally, generate a summary together using the information from the chart.

- *Judy Moody was in a bad mood. At the end of the summer, she did not want to give the summer up and go back to school.*

After demonstrating the strategy and engaging students in guided practice, allow students to read short pieces of text using the strategy in small groups or in pairs before trying it on their own.

Retelling Frames (Moss & Loh, 2010) is a scaffolded approach to summarizing a story. The teacher prepares a framework for students to fill in important information from the text. This strategy is not a simple cloze activity in which certain words are eliminated from the original text and presented to the students. The teacher actually summarizes the story first and then eliminates chunks of text for students to fill in. Students recall information after hearing or reading the story. After several readings, students retell the story either orally or in writing using the retelling framework.

It is important to note that prior to reading, teachers should activate students' prior knowledge about the content of the story. After reading, have students practice in pairs orally retelling the information that was read. Finally, students use the teacher-prepared retelling frame to summarize the story. Review the sample retelling frame in Figure 3.2.

Figure 3.2 Sample Retelling Frame

Ramona Quimby, Age 8 by Beverly Cleary

Ramona Quimby was excited about _____. She now has to take the bus because _____. Her older sister, Beezus, was excited too because _____ although she did not get to take the bus. Beezus had to _____. Mr. Quimby surprised both firls by telling them he was going to _____ also. He was going to study to be a _____.

Anchor Performance 3: Identify Story Elements and Analyze Their Relationship to Story Events

In order to comprehend text, students need to understand the organization of the material they read. When reading literature, that organization includes the knowledge of story elements such as character, plot, setting, point of view, and so on. These elements give students the structure to recall information more readily as well as investigate and interpret the various relationships among the story elements. For this anchor performance, kindergarteners and first graders are asked to identify and describe characters and main story events, whereas fourth and fifth graders are challenged to describe story elements in depth or compare and contrast two or more characters, settings, etc.

Essential Strategy to Support Anchor Performance 3: Use Graphic Organizers to Identify and Examine Story Elements

Graphic organizers can present clear structures for sorting information about story text. They can promote comprehension through the review and analysis of information that is classified into specific categories, namely the elements of fiction. The arrangement of an organizer can spark student interest and encourage students to connect story ideas in different ways. Graphic organizers can also clarify information and assess student understanding of story concepts.

Character Traits are often examined to provide evidence and support conclusions based on what characters say and do. Readers regularly predict story events based on the behavior of certain characters, and the ability to draw these types of conclusions is enhanced by identifying character traits. The author explicitly reveals some character traits while others must be implied. Character traits that are inferred often assist readers in understanding how a character changes during the course of a story and are integral to overall comprehension. There are numerous graphic organizers that identify character traits (see Resources at the end of this chapter). Table 3.4 identifies just one of many possible examples.

Table 3.4 Character Traits: *Harry Potter*

Novel: *Harry Potter and the Sorcerer's Stone* by J. K. Rowling		
Character: Mrs. Dursley/Aunt Petunia		
Trait	**Implied or Stated?**	**Evidence from the text**
Intrusive	Implied	"spent so much of her time craning over garden fences, spying on the neighbors"
Cold-hearted	Implied	"pretended she didn't have a sister"
Busybody	Stated	"Mrs. Dursley gossiped away happily"

Story Mapping is a strategy that helps students identify and organize the elements of a story. This type of graphic organizer can be used as a framework for students to identify story characters, setting, conflicts, and outcomes. Story mapping can guide diverse learners to isolate, extract, and organize pertinent story information. Some story maps can resemble a story sequence or time line in which students identify the beginning, middle, and end of a story while other maps focus primarily on identified story elements. Sequence story maps are often too open-ended for some students in that they do not offer much scaffolded support for generating and organizing story information. With these types of story maps, much teacher and peer guidance is often necessary for their completion. Figure 3.3 illustrates two types of story maps.

Figure 3.3 Story Maps

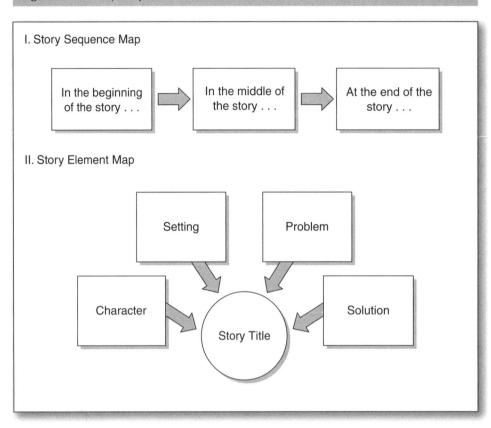

(For additional story maps, review the Resources section at the end of this chapter.)

Foldables (Zike, 1992) are two- or three-dimensional graphic organizers that are constructed by folding 8 × 10 sheets of plain paper and used to identify and organize story information. The creative format of this paper manipulative provides even the most reluctant student with the incentive to write. There are multiple paper configurations that can be constructed using this strategy. One of the four-tab configurations is pictured in Figure 3.4. Each tab can be lifted and information written inside it. (For more information, visit Dinah Zike's website listed in the Resources section of this chapter.)

Craft and Structure

Anchor Performance 4: Determine the Meaning of Words and Phrases Including Figurative Language

Although figurative language can be perplexing for all students, it presents a particular challenge for diverse learners. Figures of speech

Figure 3.4 Sample Foldable

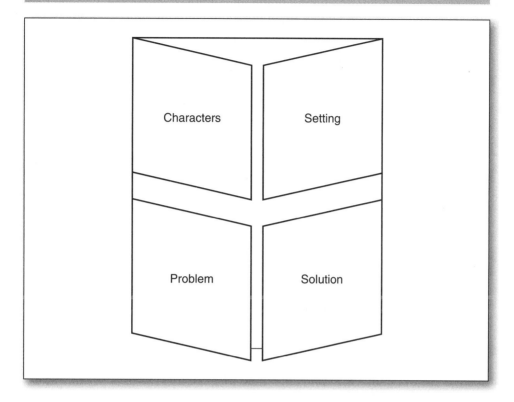

often give prominence to an author's voice, but their lack of obvious connection to the words' literal meaning can play havoc on struggling readers' ability to comprehend a story. Understanding figurative language requires students to be able to infer meaning, and inference requires students to have adequate background knowledge. Additionally, some language expressions are culture bound. This excerpt from *Maniac Magee* (1990) by Jerry Spinelli illustrates the complexity of teaching figurative language:

> [It was] so hot, if you were packing candy, you had soup in your pocket by two o'clock. So hot, the dogs were tripping on their own tongues. And so hot, the fire hydrant at Green and Chestnut was gushing like Niagara Falls. (p. 59)

In order for students to understand this short excerpt, they would need to have experience with candy that melts, grasp that dogs pant when overheated, know fire hydrants are opened on hot summer days in some cities, recognize common names for streets, and identify Niagara Falls. Considering the complexity of this anchor standard, it will most certainly be a particular challenge for teachers to help diverse learners to meet.

Reflecting the difference in the grade-level expectations for this anchor performance, kindergarten and first-grade students are anticipated to ask and answer questions about unknown and sensory words, students in second and third grade describe how certain words supply rhythm and meaning in stories and poems as well as distinguish literal from nonliteral language, and fourth and fifth graders determine the meaning of figurative language such as similes and metaphors.

Essential Strategy to Support Anchor Performance 4: Focus on Context Clues and Students Working in Cooperative-Learning Groups

Using context clues can be a valuable strategy to help readers determine the meaning of unknown words, phrases, and figurative language. Clues may be drawn from information in the same sentence as the unfamiliar words, surrounding paragraphs, and any graphic representations such as pictures or drawings that accompany the text. This strategy can be further enhanced when student teams examine figurative language using context clues. Working in cooperative groups, students have the opportunity to pool their background knowledge and use available clues more effectively.

Guess the Missing Words (Cunningham & Allington, 2011) trains students to make use of the words surrounding unknown words. Begin by writing a sentence or two with a word or phrase either omitted or covered by a sticky note. Model how students might guess the missing word(s). Direct students to read the surrounding words and sentences to look for clues.

Harry walks like a _____. He waddles back and forth.

Model your thinking out loud and write several guesses on the board; then reveal the missing word.

As an alternative, one may choose to reveal part of the word or phrase first in order to elicit other guesses from students or further confirm the possibility of one of the choices already indicated. Conduct a whole-class practice of the strategy and increase the difficulty of the text being used by sharing a direct passage from a story to be read. Continue the use of the strategy by assigning different pieces of text to various student teams. Follow up with independent practice. This activity is appropriate for all elementary grade levels.

Team Trackers (Lorcher, 2011) employs students in teams of three or four to create definitions for unknown or difficult words and phrases in context without the use of dictionaries, glossaries, thesauri, or the Internet. Depending upon grade and reading level, teams are assigned one to five words along with where they may be found in the text (page number, paragraph, etc.) or students may be given handouts of short text in which the words are already highlighted. A graphic organizer such as a semantic web (see Figure 3.5) may be distributed to anchor students in the task. Next, students attend to the following process:

- Read the short text that contains the target word(s) and discuss its meaning. Teacher assists student groups that are having difficulty with the text.
- Write the target word(s) on a piece of paper, whiteboard, or in the center of the semantic web.
- Identify and write synonyms that may mean the same as the target word(s) and that make sense when substituted in the text. If students are unable to write their ideas, they are welcome to compose drawings to convey their meaning.
- Student groups present their answers to the whole class.
- Teacher shares correct definitions in student-friendly terms.

The importance of this strategy is to get students thinking and talking about word meaning. Accuracy is not so much the goal as building student confidence to solve problems and apply strategies in order to figure out new and difficult words in context.

Figure 3.5   Semantic Web

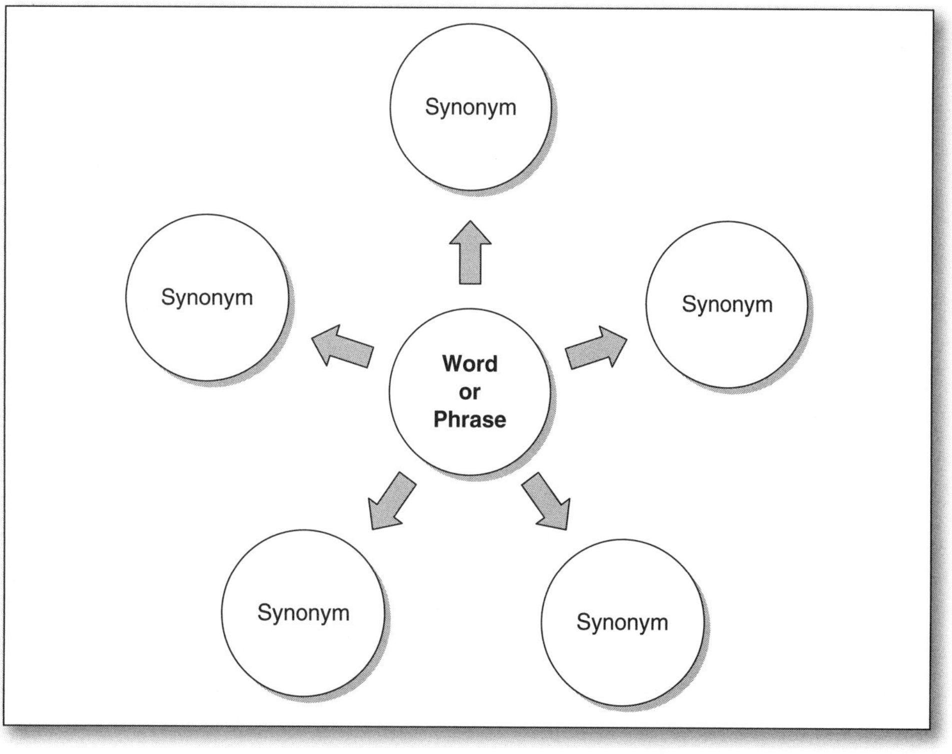

Think Aloud is a strategy that provides students with understanding how to determine the meaning of unfamiliar words by listening to a teacher demonstrate his or her own thinking process for figuring out difficult vocabulary. The following describes the steps for how to share this activity with a group of youngsters:

- Select a short piece of text and project it on a screen using an overhead projector, projection camera, or interactive whiteboard.
- Read part of the text and identify difficult words.
- Model your thinking about the target words. Refer to words in the same sentence and surrounding paragraph that gives clues to the meaning.
- Examine drawings and pictures and talk out loud about possible clues to the meaning.
- Substitute synonyms for the target words and ask students if they make sense in the story.

After modeling the activity for students, engage students in a guided practice using a different, increasingly more complex text. Continue strategy practice by having students work in small groups and *think aloud* with one another. Being explicit about the thinking process and allowing students time to practice provides a framework for students to explore and apply multiple strategies using context clues during their own reading.

Anchor Performance 5: Compare and Contrast Different Types of Texts (Poems, Drama, Using Precise English Language Arts Jargon [Chapter, Scene, Stanza, Etc.])

Students with little reading experience may find it confusing when they attempt to read or listen to a variety of literature. Struggling learners in particular might find a text structure such as a poem is very unlike what they may have been exposed to previously, and they may become frustrated or easily distracted when they cannot make meaning out of what is read. Understanding the structure of different types of text helps students to have better reading comprehension. Knowing text structure also helps students to anticipate important pieces of information and supports them in connecting information to create an overall understanding of the text, as well.

The expectation for this anchor performance varies from grade to grade. Whereas kindergarteners and first graders are expected to distinguish between different types of text, second and third graders describe and refer to different parts of text, and fourth and fifth graders explain differences between and the overall structure of text.

Essential Strategy to Support Anchor Performance 5:
Organizers and Word Sorts to Compare and Contrast Text Types
and Identify Necessary Vocabulary to Discuss Each Text

We cannot say enough about how different text organization strategies can be an ongoing support for all students and in particular diverse learners. Graphic organizers provide vital visual support to analyze, compare, and contrast different text structures. They can frame class discussions as part of an ongoing dialogue with inexperienced and struggling readers who benefit from strategy reinforcement including text organization. Additionally, hands-on activities further enhance student learning about the nature of various text structures.

Figure 3.6 Text Compare and Contrast

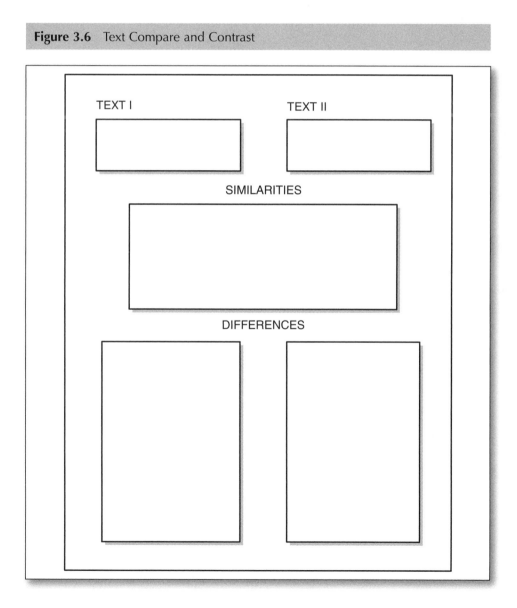

Text Compare and Contrast is an activity that engages students to consider the structure of a text by comparing and contrasting two different types of text. This strategy directs students' attention to the similarities and differences in text organization and supports the discussion of how different types of text convey meaning. Figure 3.6 illustrates one method of comparing and contrasting two types of text.

Other features to add to this type of organization might include an actual checklist of similarities and differences for students such as the following:

- Title
- Author
- Illustrations
- Capital and lower case letters
- Punctuation
- Chapters
- Stanzas
- Subtitles

Text Element Word Sort is an activity in which groups of students sort words that refer to parts of different types of text and categorize them according to the text they represent. To begin, divide the class into groups of four. Select words for students to sort according to text type—for example, sentence, line, paragraph, stanza, rhyme, refrain, fiction, dialogue—and print them on card stock or write them on index cards. Teachers may choose to give students the categories, such as poetry, drama, or prose, for which they must sort the words or just give students the words to sort and have them come up with their own category. Word sort cards may be enhanced with pictures or photographs that illustrate each text concept to assist struggling learners to better participate in the activity. The activity may also be adapted to incorporate interactive whiteboard technology.

Label the Element is a variation of the *Text Element Word Sort*. Instead of students sorting words that refer to different types of text, words that refer to text elements are used to label parts of poems, drama, or stories that are displayed either on posters, chart paper, overheads, or interactive whiteboards.

Theme Reading assists teachers in comparing different types of text written about a particular theme or topic. To prepare this strategy, select an overarching anchor theme (e.g., homes), which is grade appropriate and connected to the curriculum. Organize pieces of literature related to the selected theme. Share each text with younger students through a read-aloud. Older students might work in groups to read and review texts on their own. Have students compare and contrast literature. Scaffold the activity by providing a *Text Compare and Contrast* organizer or a checklist of organizational

Table 3.5 *Sample Scaffolded Text Compare and Contrast Organizer*

Comparative Theme: Homes		
Fiction	**Nonfiction**	**Poetry**
The Little House by Virginia Lee Burton	*How a House is Built* by Gail Gibbons	*This is the House that Jack Built* by Simms Taback

features previously mentioned in this section. Table 3.5 is an example of literature based on the theme of homes appropriate for first grade.

Anchor Performance 6: Distinguish the Point of View of Various Characters as Well as Their Own

Teaching the notion that different story characters have different points of view can be a challenging concept for young learners and diverse students. However, the better able students grasp the concept, the better they can comprehend the text. Authors sometimes choose to tell a story in third person from their own perspective. The excerpts from *Judy Moody* and *Maniac Magee*, highlighted earlier in this chapter, are written in third person, from the author's own point of view. Other children's books, such as *Diary of a Wimpy Kid*, *Junie B. Jones*, *Island of the Blue Dolphins*, and classics such as *Huckleberry Finn* are written from the point of view of the main character of the story. The differences in point of view may be subtle at first for some students to detect; however, providing all learners opportunities to distinguish these differences is vital to improving their overall reading comprehension.

For this anchor performance, students in kindergarten and first grade are expected to answer questions about the author and who is telling the story, second and third graders distinguish differences in the point of view of characters as well as their own point of view from the narrator, and fourth and fifth graders compare and contrast the points of view expressed in different text and describe how the story teller's point of view influences how story events unfold.

Essential Strategy to Support Anchor Performance 6: Games and Activities That Draw Students' Attention to Story Point of View

To promote student understanding of point of view, teachers must consider which clues in the text students might examine to distinguish between first- and third-person storytelling. Generally speaking, first-person narrators participate in the story action; they use pronouns such as *I* and *me* as well as share what they are thinking and feeling with the reader. In contrast, third-person narrators are not a part of the story; they bring into play pronouns such as *she*, *he*, and *they* and are able to share the thoughts and feelings of multiple characters. To support student understanding, the following are a sample of games and activities to further students' attention to clues that reveal story point of view.

Sentence Slam is a game that can promote student understanding of the difference between first-person and third-person point of view. The main objective of the game is for students to categorize randomly selected sentences that have been prepared on paper strips and determine the point of view in which they are written. To play the game, prepare a chart that is divided in half. On one side, write *First Person,* and on the other, *Third Person* (see Figure 3.7). Working in teams, students will select a sentence strip, read it together, and determine its point of view. Finally, one student from the group will approach the chart and "slam" the sentence on the appropriate side shouting first person or third person. Another student from the same group will read the sentence. The whole class will take a few moments to display a thumbs up or down to indicate whether the student has chosen the correct point of view or not. To scaffold the activity, include a list of first- and third-person context clues.

Figure 3.7 Sentence Slam

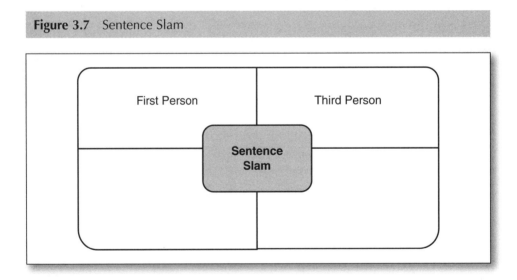

Who Is Telling the Story is a game in which students working in teams must guess the narrator of the story, whether it is the author or the main story character. To prepare for the game, select excerpts either from stories recently shared with students or from texts students have yet to read or discuss. Project text excerpts on screen either with a document camera or prepared overheads or make copies of the text and have them ready to distribute. Have available one hand-held whiteboard per team or other method for teams to write their answers. Create a chart to keep track of each team's score (see Figure 3.8 for a partially completed sample scoreboard).

Figure 3.8 *Who is Telling the Story* Scoreboard

	Story 1	**Story 2**	**Story 3**	**Story 4**	**Story 5**	**Story 6**
Team 1	Author ✓					
Team 2	Main Character x					
Team 3	Author ✓					
Team 4	Author ✓					

To begin play, follow these steps:

1. Distribute small, personal whiteboards to each team.

2. Project the first story excerpt and either read the text aloud or teams may take turns reading text chorally.

3. Give students 30 seconds to confer and write their team answer on the hand-held whiteboards—author or main character.

4. Give a signal for student teams to hold up their answers at the same time.

5. Score their answers on the prepared chart.

6. Have students rotate the whiteboard among team members so everyone has an opportunity to write and hold up team answers.

Point of View Clues is an activity in which students use word clues to draw their own conclusions about point of view. Working in small groups, students receive a list of sentences that they must categorize as having either first-person or third-person word clues. Consider the following list of sentences taken from the popular children's story, *The Little Engine That Could* (1978) by Watty Piper:

- Our engine has broken down.
- Her cars were filled full of good things for boys and girls.
- The toy clown waved his flag and the big strong engine came to a stop.
- I am a very important engine indeed.
- He looks very old and tired, but our train is so little, perhaps he can help us.

Some of these sentences have few clues to determine the speaker and one has both first-person and third-person clues. Considering these challenges in determining the speaker, the main idea of this activity is to foster students' awareness and use of context clues in order to draw conclusions about whether a story character or the author as narrator is speaking. To complete this activity, student groups must identify and sort the sentences according to the type of the word clues (first-person or third-person) each of them contains. With sentences that have both categories of word clues, students must ultimately choose whether a story character or the author is speaking (see Table 3.6).

Table 3.6   *Point of View Clues*

First-Person Word Clues	Third-Person Word Clues
(I, me, my, we, our, mine, ours)	*(he, she, his, her, hers, they, their, theirs)*
Our engine has broken down.	**Her** cars were filled full of good things for boys and girls.
I am a very important engine indeed.	
He looks very old and tired, but **our** train is so little, perhaps *he* can help **us**.	The toy clown waved **his** flag and the big strong engine came to a stop.

Integration of Knowledge and Ideas

Anchor Performance 7: Make Connections About a Story's Events, Characters, Setting, Plot, Specific Descriptions, and Overall Meaning by Comparing the Printed Word With Text Illustrations as Well as Visual, Oral, or Multimedia Representations of the Text

In order to explore a piece of literature's deeper meaning and to create avenues for further discussion, students should be able to synthesize various story elements, events, and circumstances and evaluate different media associated with the text including visual, graphic, oral, or multimedia depictions of the story. Starting from kindergarten and continuing through fifth grade, students should have increasing opportunities to compare grade-appropriate story text with its featured illustrations. Additionally, they should examine variations of the same story as it is represented through drama in combination with visual, oral, and combined media in order to better analyze character, setting, plot, and such. Consequently, students should be better able to interpret why a story unfolds in certain ways rather than just repeating what has occurred. The analysis of combined media should increase students' ability to discover how characters change as a result of story events, what lessons a story may contain, and overall what the author is trying to say.

For this anchor performance, students in kindergarten and first grade are expected to recognize which part of the story an illustration depicts and use illustrations to clarify story elements. In contrast, upper elementary grade students need to discern between different representations of the text and determine how each version reflects certain descriptions and text direction as well as contributes to the overall meaning and tone of the text.

Essential Strategy to Support Anchor Performance 7: Create Opportunities for Students to Work With Visual, Oral, and Multimedia Representations of Literature

For this anchor standard, students will need to combine their knowledge of the story text with different media presented including photographs, audio, and video clips that reveal different aspects of the story. By integrating these elements, students should be better able to construct meaning beyond the written text. Providing students with multiple experiences with multimedia representations of a story is often beneficial for diverse learners to support their overall comprehension.

See It-Hear It-Read It is a strategy that uses literature in recorded form either on audiotape, compact disc (CD), or through other recorded means ranging from downloadable files via the Internet to hand-held listening devices such as MP3 players, iPods, and iPads. It is advisable for students to have the written text in front of them as they listen to the story being read. Most young students take great pleasure in listening to recorded stories, and although it is common to find listening centers in kindergarten through second-grade classrooms, they are rare in third through fifth grade, where students would continue to benefit from listening to selections of high levels of text complexity. Teachers often set up a listening center so that two to four children can listen to the same book at the same time. Developing these types of listening activities in upper elementary grades are often essential for the reading development of struggling readers and in particular for English learners who have yet to establish a fluency and facility with English and hearing the language spoken is beneficial to that end. Students can listen to the same book over and over again connecting what is spoken to the written word, and in turn learn new vocabulary.

Many recorded books have multiple readers narrating various parts of the story making the characters come more alive for listeners; other recordings include sound effects as well as music to enhance the listeners' experience, and those books available on hand-held tablets and devices sometimes include animation, adding a multimedia dimension to the story telling.

Read It-Picture It is an activity in which students listen to a story read by the teacher but are not shown any of the illustrations in the book including its cover. During the reading, the teacher pauses periodically and invites students to draw their own illustrations to match the section of the book that was just read. Students may create a quick sketch of the story idea on paper or whiteboard. To prevent students from creating elaborate drawings during the reading and hinder the progression of the book, teachers can request students divide their paper or whiteboard into four equal boxes to reduce the area for students to sketch their illustrations. In a variation of this activity, invite students to create their own book jackets for the story in question. With all book illustrations, students can participate in a *gallery walk* in which all of their drawings are displayed, and students have an opportunity to walk by and examine each student's drawing and compare the artistic elements that were apparent in the collection.

See It-Say It. Using only drawings, photographs, or other still images to tell a story, wordless books can promote rich conversation, discussion, and the use of Standard American English. Focusing on illustrations gives students the opportunity to gather information from visual representations of a story, a strategy that can bolster reading comprehension. Begin by previewing the wordless book page by page. Refrain from telling the story, but name items in the illustrations and invite students to do so as well. Subsequently, ask students to tell the story from the wordless book, either whole class with students taking turns telling part of the story using one illustration at a time or in small groups that are teacher-led or student-led depending on grade level and student ability. Additionally, use books with text for this activity by covering the words, having students tell the story from the illustrations, and then by reading the story. Wordless books promote student use of varied vocabulary and oral language as well as present ideas for story writing.

Reader's Theatre. A way to engage reluctant readers and English learners to a whole new dimension in storytelling, Reader's Theatre provides students the opportunity to read and write story scripts. Students perform a play in small groups but do not memorize their parts; instead, they read them and enhance their performances with a minimal amount of props and costumes. To introduce Reader's Theatre to your students, here are some suggestions:

- Begin by selecting a story script that is appropriate for your students' age and grade level, duplicate it, and distribute one to each student.
- Read the script to the students aloud and ask them to read the script with you chorally.

- Next, divide the class in half, and have each group read the character parts alternately.
- Further divide students into small groups and assign each one a part. Have students practice their parts.
- Invite students to perform for the class.

When students have the idea, assign a different script to each group. Have students practice reading their scripts in their groups frequently.

This reading format helps students develop their fluency, pronunciation, intonation, and expressiveness. Additionally, scripts may be altered to accommodate various reading levels so that all students can participate. Depending upon their age and ability, students may write their own scripts from stories they enjoy. After much rehearsing, some teachers like to invite other classes and parents to a special performance of the stories. Many Reader's Theatre scripts are available online. Performances of Reader's Theatre scripts may also be viewed on YouTube (www.youtube.com).

> Note: Anchor Standard 8 is not applicable to the Reading for Literature section of the CCSS, thus no Anchor Performance 8 is presented here. See Chapter 4, which addresses this standard in Reading for Informational Texts.

Anchor Performance 9: Compare and Contrast Story, Themes, Settings, Characters, and Plots With Different Versions of the Same or Similar Stories and Topics

Students who make story connections have better comprehension overall. To this end, it is vital to explicitly teach diverse learners how to become active readers—to think closely and carefully about what they are reading, to activate their prior knowledge about the theme or topic, and to be thoroughly engaged in the story. As a result, students will be better able to ask questions, clarify information, and share their understanding of the text.

For this anchor performance, Kindergarten and first-grade students are expected to compare and contrast the undertakings of characters from different stories, those students in second and third grade compare different version of the same story and more specifically their story elements, and fourth- and fifth-grade students compare and contrast themes, topics, and stories in the same genre.

Essential Strategy to Support Anchor Performance 9: Contrast Multidimensional Versions of Familiar Stories

Working with different pieces of literature with related content, such as characters, theme, or other story elements, helps students to comprehend more easily. When students have developed some familiarity and facility with a particular story element, they are better able to activate their prior knowledge and use what they already know to support their understanding of new text.

Stories in a Series. Reading stories that are a part of a book series allows students to become truly familiar with the series' shared characters, settings, general themes, and vocabulary, which helps all readers to have better comprehension because their familiarity with the reoccurring story elements supports their understanding. One idea would be to use the first book in a series for deep reading and discussion to assure students understanding of the text. Subsequently, have students read other books in the series and promote their use of prior knowledge of the previous text. Further support this strategy by having students predict what will happen in the text based on their previous readings. Some of our favorite book series are listed in Figure 3.8.

Figure 3.8 Book Series for K–5 Readers

Kindergarten and First Grade	
Babar	Jean de Brunhoff
Curious George	H. A. Rey
Frog and Toad	Arnold Lobel
Little Bear	Else Minarik
Second and Third Grade	
Horrible Harry	Suzy Kline
Amelia Bedelia	Peggy Parish
A is for Amber	Paula Danziger
Fourth and Fifth Grade	
Judy Moody	Megan McDonald
A Series of Unfortunate Events	Lemony Snicket
The Spiderwick Chronicles	Tony DiTerlizzi and Holly Black

Author Studies. Reading books by the same author allows teachers to create an author study, an activity that promotes examination and discussion of elements that are similar in each of the same author's literature. This activity promotes students to make text-to-text connections, which further supports readers to activate their prior knowledge, visualize the story, and commit their understanding to memory. As part of the study, information about an author's life is shared with the class so they are better able to make further connections about the author and text.

The following suggestions about how to conduct an author study come from Primary Education Oasis (www.primary-education-oasis.com):

- Devote a section of the classroom or bulletin board to the selected author. Display artifacts, photographs, story illustrations, for example, that represent the real life of the author.
- Identify the particular themes, topics, and characters about which the author generally writes.
- Examine story illustrations as an essential part of the author study.
- Discuss in detail the author's style and encourage students to share their thoughts and opinions.

Theme Studies. This type of study allows students to delve more deeply into a particular topic and compare how the same subject is treated by different authors and in different genres. A theme study provides a framework for in-depth learning. It can help students to think more critically about what they read and support efforts to develop their research skills. For example, a theme study might involve the topic of wolves in which students read a selection of fiction and nonfiction as well as examine nontext items and images about these animals. Students would have the opportunity to read and compare tales about wolves with critical cross-curricular information from science, art, music, and social studies. Some texts, music, and art that would lend themselves to this theme include: (fiction) *Fantastic Mr. Fox* by Roald Dahl and Quentin Blake, *The True Story of the Three Little Pigs* by Jon Scieszka and Lane Smith; (nonfiction) *Wolves* by Seymour Simon; (poetry) *Wolf Pack* by Yvette Yvonne; (music) *Peter and the Wolf* by Sergei Prokofiev; and (art) *Midnight-Black Wolf* by Robert Batemen.

Multicultural Fairytales. Common themes of make-believe stories for children are present in many different cultures. Comparing these stories is one way to help students discover similarities and differences between story topics and story development. Using graphic organizers for comparisons is one way to compare these stories (see previous anchor performances in this chapter for graphic organizer ideas). Perhaps, the story of Cinderella is one of the best-known tales, with hundreds of versions of the story told throughout the world. As an example Figure 3.9 identifies only some of the literature available for story comparisons with the Cinderella theme.

Figure 3.9 *Cinderella Stories*

Multicultural Fairytales: Cinderella
Cinderella by Marcia Brown
Mufaro's Beautiful Daughters: An African Tale by Jon Steptoe
The Rough-Face Girl by Rafe Martin (American Indian)
Domitila: A Cinderella Tale from the Mexican Tradition adapted by Jewell Reinhart Coburn
Yeh-Shen: A Cinderella Story from China by Ai-Ling Louie
Tattercoats: An Old English Tale by Flora Annie Steel
The Golden Sandal: A Middle Eastern Cinderella Story by Rebecca Hickox

Range of Reading and Level of Text Complexity

Anchor Performance 10: Read and Comprehend Literature Including Stories and Poetry at Grade Level

At the end of the school year, the expectation is that all students will be reading and comprehending literature on grade level. Of course, this anchor performance is most challenging for diverse learners. Goals and expectations must be high for all students; yet, teachers and administrators must also be realistic about goal setting for youngsters who have learning difficulties, have had inadequate schooling, or are English learners. Goals should be attainable and achievable, and when students are reading well below their grade levels, students must be given adequate time to develop their skills.

Educators should review students overall progress toward meeting targeted goals as specified by the standards. For this reason, a portfolio assessment apart from standardized testing is most helpful in ascertaining the amount of progress diverse learners have met. In the long run, the overarching goal for these youngsters should be direct and sustained progress toward meeting grade-level literacy. To this end, documented evidence that students have increased not only their reading and writing skills but also their speaking and listening abilities can support this overarching goal.

Essential Strategy to Support Anchor Performance 10:
Multiple Opportunities for Exposure, Patience, and Time

Diverse students need multiple opportunities to learn new and difficult information; they should be exposed to the same ideas and skills through multimodalities incorporating auditory, visual, tactual, and kinesthetic activities. At the same time, these students need to be in a learning environment that supports their development of persistence, perseverance, and the belief that they will succeed over time. Learning to read is not an easy process, and for struggling learners, it is even more difficult because these students generally have not met with success readily, and for some not at all. The following general strategies are essential in helping students meet this anchor performance:

- Evaluate, investigate, and offer students accommodations to support their reading; those accommodations may include but are not limited to audio or bilingual versions of texts, extended time to complete assignments, and alternative methods for presenting information.
- Be flexible in assessing student progress and provide multiple ways in which students can be evaluated.
- Provide one-on-one time to work with students whenever possible.
- Investigate second-language acquisition and understand the basic steps in the acquisition of English for those who are not native speakers.
- Create and maintain a low-anxiety classroom environment where all students feel they belong and can thrive.

ANTICIPATED OUTCOMES

The strategies introduced in this chapter will assist diverse learners to have better access to the complex nature of various types of literature. The following are general principles conveyed by these strategies:

- Explicit strategy instruction coupled with guided practice is essential to increase students' reading skills.
- Frameworks and scaffolding for story retelling and summarizing will assist diverse learners' spoken and written discourse.
- Graphic organizers arrange text information in an accessible manner for all students.
- Cooperative learning increases the chances for diverse learners' success.
- Activities requiring multimodalities engage even reluctant students in the text.

Keeping in mind that teachers generally have control over their planning and selection of instructional strategies, what is most crucial is for teachers to recognize the need to alter their classroom practices to meet the CCSS with diverse youngsters.

INSTRUCTIONAL CHALLENGES

One of the key charges of the CCSS for English Language Arts is to expose all students to increasingly more complex texts, a particular challenge for teaching diverse students literature. Compared with informational text, the meaning behind a piece of literature is often not explicit and less obvious to struggling readers. Meaning is frequently revealed on a number of levels involving various story elements. Complex literary text contains exceptional vocabulary, idiomatic expressions, figurative language, and elaborate sentence structures. Furthermore, events in a story may not unfold in a logical or linear fashion. All in all, when the proper amount of scaffolding of instruction is in place from the onset, the more guided practice and grade-level reading skills will be developed ultimately resulting in increased independence to learning on the part of the student.

PROMISING CLASSROOM PRACTICES

Second-grade teacher Jake Escalante developed a unit of study with the objective to compare and contrast different versions of the story, *Three Little Pigs*. His unit consisted of the following texts:

- *The Three Little Pigs* by James Marshall
- *The True Story of the Three Little Pigs* by Jon Scieszka
- *The Three Little Wolves and the Big Bad Pig* by Eugene Trivizas
- *The Three Little Javelinas* by Susan Lowell

For the lesson to introduce the unit, Jake began with the version of the story by James Marshall. Although the *Three Little Pigs* is a popular tale in mainstream American culture, he did not assume that all students knew the story, particularly his diverse learners, and he read the story aloud for their enjoyment. Next, Jake read the story again in order to model the strategy, *Good readers think while they read*. During this shared reading of the text, he conducted a *Think Aloud* for his students, demonstrating his own thought processes for figuring out what the characters might be thinking and feeling, asking the question "I wonder why . . ." (e.g., "I wonder why that pig chose to build a house with sticks?"). Halfway through this reading, he invited his students to practice the strategy. He distributed a prepared handout that had the phrase "I wonder why" repeated on several lines followed by blank space for writing. During this part of the reading, Jake paused periodically and asked his students, "What are you wondering?" Students wrote their responses on the handout. The activity culminated with students sharing some of their written "I wonder" statements. Keeping his class as a whole group, he mapped the story with his students, identifying the characters, setting, problem, and solution.

With subsequent lessons in the unit, the following strategies were incorporated among others:

- The character traits of the wolf and the pigs were compared in the different story versions.
- A four-door *Foldable* identifying characters, setting, problem, and solution was completed by the students in cooperative groups for the *Three Little Wolves and the Big Bad Pig* and compared with the original story map completed by the whole class.
- The class played the game *Who is Telling the Story* to identify each story version's point of view.
- A Reader's Theatre script was devised for each story version, and students read and performed the different versions using simple props.
- The cultural aspects of the *Three Little Javelinas* were explored with the students and its vocabulary was compared to the other versions of the story.

COMMON CORE READING STANDARDS— UN(COMMON) REFLECTION QUESTIONS

1. Which of the ten anchor standards or the grade-appropriate equivalents will present the greatest departure from your previous literacy instructional practices regarding teaching fiction or narratives?

2. Which of the ten anchor standards or the grade-appropriate equivalents will present the greatest challenge to your students?

3. How are you planning to strategically address the difficulties your students will face with select standards?

KEY RESOURCES

Key Professional Books

Alber-Morgan, S. (2010). *Using RTI to teach literacy to diverse learners, K–8: Strategies for the inclusive classroom.* Thousand Oaks, CA: Corwin.

Cloud, N., & Genesee, F. (2009). *Literacy instruction for English language learners.* Portsmouth, NH: Heinemann.

Fisher, D., & Frey, N. (2011*). Teaching students to read like detectives: Comprehending, analyzing, and discussing text.* Bloomington, IN: Solution Tree.

Online Resources

- Practice point-of-view
  http://www.studyzone.org/testprep/ela4/o/pointofviewp.cfm
- Character traits list
  http://www.readwritethink.org/files/resources/lesson_images/lesson175/traits.pdf
- Character trait maps
  http://www.dubois.cps.k12.il.us/PDFs/character_study.pdf
- Story maps
  http://www.enchantedlearning.com/graphicorganizers/storymap
- Foldables
  http//www.dinah.com
- Reading comprehension: Context clues
  http://www.learningtoday.com/player/swf/RC_Context_Clues_L5_V1_T4a.swf
- Inferences and context clues
  http://beyondpenguins.ehe.osu.edu/issue/learning-from-the-polar-past/teacher-resources-for-making-inferences-using-context-clues
- Think aloud
  http://wvde.state.wv.us/strategybank/ThinkAloud.html
- Audiobooks for children (free)
  http://storynory.com
  http://www.booksshouldbefree.com/genre/Children

4 Reading Strategies for Informational Texts

Teaching reading IS rocket science.

— Louisa Moats

OVERVIEW

Teachers have become so accustomed to teaching the content contained in instructional materials directly that they sometimes give little class time for students to read and examine the written texts themselves. Since student understanding of the subject topic has often been the goal of planned lessons, teachers generally have focused much of class time on targeted, concrete explanations, group discussions, and classroom activities designed to insure students have understood the basic concepts and vocabulary prescribed by the content curriculum. With elementary school subjects such as social studies or science in particular, students spend little time reading about assigned topics and more time listening to the teacher, having information read to them, copying notes, and completing worksheets.

One of the several advances in instruction prescribed by the CCSS requires Grades K–5 teachers to incorporate more informational texts into the curriculum for students to read to achieve a balanced approach between exposure to information and literature. Students are also required to engage more with subject-specific, grade-level texts in which they directly and carefully read and answer text-based questions. As a result, students are expected to derive more information from reading and less information from teacher lectures and note-taking in order to meet college- and career-ready anchor standards.

WHY DIVERSE LEARNERS NEED READING STRATEGIES FOCUSING ON INFORMATIONAL TEXTS

Understanding grade-level informational texts is challenging for English learners and others not reading on grade level. Although some frameworks for teaching such as sheltered instruction help diverse students to learn language and content concepts in tandem (Echevarria, Vogt, & Short, 2012), these frameworks often focus on providing comprehensible input to students (Crawford & Krashen, 2007) in specific subject areas and do not emphasize or prescribe direct reading instruction or necessarily expose students to grade-level texts. To boost the ability of students who are reading below grade level or are nonnative English speakers, targeted literacy instruction is essential.

Diverse learners require scaffolded lessons to bridge the gaps in their language and literacy acquisition. They need to read a variety of short, nonfiction texts, to learn from multiple texts on the same topic, and be exposed to academic vocabulary consistently and repeatedly (Feldman & Kinsella, 2005). These students, like their grade-level peers, must tap into their background knowledge to fully analyze and interpret text and to go beyond the printed word to accurately understand the intended meaning and the author's purpose.

Much research has documented the positive impact of reading strategy instruction on overall understanding of concepts and literacy development (Fang & Wei, 2010; Gaskins et al., 1994; Griffin et al., 1991; Romance & Vitale, 1992). The teaching of comprehension strategies helps all readers to analyze, evaluate, interpret, organize, and synthesize information contained in text to strengthen and sustain their understanding. Good readers apply various strategies automatically, but they need to be explicitly taught and modeled for struggling readers to make sense of text. This type of instruction helps students working below grade level to become independent, confident readers and improves their overall understanding of language.

CORE INFORMATIONAL READING STRATEGIES

The strategies contained in this chapter follow the expectations of the ten College and Career Readiness Anchor Standards (CCRAS) for Reading with particular attention to the reading strand for informational texts. They are framed by the CCRAS strand-specific sets of *Key Ideas and Details, Craft and Structure, Integration of Knowledge and Ideas,* and *Range of Reading and Text Complexity.* From each of the ten CCRAS, we derived and aligned a series of related *Anchor Performances*—skill sets that all students need to be able to do—and suggest strategies to help diverse students build these skills in order to meet the Standards. Some strategies may be more appropriate than others depending upon the grade-level or language facility of the students. To that end, we make suggestions on how to adapt strategies to meet the needs of diverse individual learners.

Box 4.1 College and Career Readiness Anchor Standards for Reading

Key Ideas and Details

1. Read closely to determine what the text says explicitly and to make logical inferences from it; cite specific textual evidence when writing or speaking to support conclusions drawn from the text.

2. Determine central ideas or themes of a text and analyze their development; summarize the key supporting details and ideas.

3. Analyze how and why individuals, events, and ideas develop and interact over the course of a text.

Craft and Structure

4. Interpret words and phrases as they are used in a text, including determining technical, connotative, and figurative meanings, and analyze how specific word choices shape meaning or tone.

5. Analyze the structure of texts, including how specific sentences, paragraphs, and larger portions of the text (e.g., a section, chapter, scene, or stanza) relate to each other and the whole.

6. Assess how point of view or purpose shapes the content and style of a text.

Integration of Knowledge and Ideas

7. Integrate and evaluate content presented in diverse media and formats, including visually and quantitatively, as well as in words.

8. Delineate and evaluate the argument and specific claims in a text, including the validity of the reasoning as well as the relevance and sufficiency of the evidence.

9. Analyze how two or more texts address similar themes or topics in order to build knowledge or to compare the approaches the authors take.

Range of Reading and Level of Text Complexity

10. Read and comprehend complex literary and informational texts independently and proficiently.

Key Ideas and Details

Anchor Performance 1: Making Logical Inferences

Making inferences is a process of drawing conclusions from various pieces of information. When teachers ask students to infer meaning from a text, they expect students to go beyond the surface of the printed words and discover suggested meanings or make judgments. In order for students to make inferences, they need to activate their prior knowledge.

For this anchor performance, kindergarten and first-grade students are expected to ask and answer questions about key details in the text. In contrast, second and third graders are directed to ask and answer Wh-questions (who, what, where, etc.) about the text and describe the relationships between a series of ideas or events, and those students in fourth and fifth grade need to refer to details and examples given in the text and explain what the text conveys explicitly.

Essential Strategy to Support Anchor Performance 1: Activate Prior Knowledge/Build Background

Teachers need to provide students with opportunities to tap into their prior knowledge in order to connect what they already know with the new information they will be learning. When students make these connections, their comprehension increases. Good readers automatically activate their prior knowledge to make sense of what they read. The following are some approaches that can start students thinking about what they already know about a topic:

Brainstorming. With the teacher as facilitator, students offer their information and ideas about a particular topic or question and the teacher writes them down on chart paper or a whiteboard. There are no judgments given by the teacher or the students about the information received. A set time limit allows all students to share yet contains the activity to make it a good prereading strategy. To help struggling learners, teachers should present the topic and give students sufficient wait time to process the information before eliciting ideas.

Visual Images. One way to preview content, introduce new vocabulary, and build background knowledge is to use photographs, drawings, charts, video on DVD or through video-sharing websites such as YouTube. Diverse students benefit from having some exposure to the content through visual means before they are asked to uncover meaning from the text.

Semantic Mapping. A strategy that helps students to expand their vocabulary, semantic mapping can draw upon students' prior knowledge or build schema. It displays the relationship between vocabulary words or similar concepts. One way to build a semantic map is to write a concept word on the board and elicit from students words that are connected or similar in some way to the concept. Figure 4.1 is an example of semantic mapping.

Semantic mapping can be combined with visual representations to give students the background knowledge and the vocabulary they need to participate in creating the map.

Anticipation Guides. Anticipation guides can build student interest about a subject and establish a purpose for reading, as well as tap into learners' prior knowledge. Before reading, students respond to a series of statements about the text by indicating whether or not they think they are true or false. Students make predictions about what the text will reveal. As the text is read, students are able to verify their predictions. Figure 4.2 is an example of an anticipation guide written for a text about windstorms.

Through the process of using anticipation guides, students are often better able to remain focused on more difficult texts. To help struggling learners, teachers can project the image of the anticipation guide to the class and read each statement aloud. Instead of asking students to respond

Figure 4.1 Semantic Mapping: American Revolution

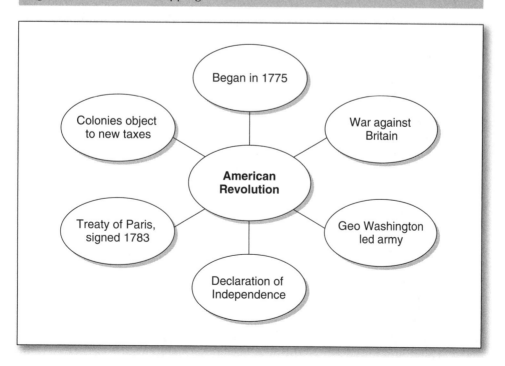

Figure 4.2 Anticipation Guide

Storm Chasers: Tracking Twisters (Herman, 1997)

Directions: Read the following sentences about what happens during a windstorm. Write "T" if you think the sentence is true. Write "F" if you think a sentence is false (not true).

———— Tornadoes happen when the weather is very warm.
———— Hailstones the size of your fist might fall to the ground.
———— People should hide under their beds for safety.
———— The noise of a tornado can sound like a roller coaster.
———— A tornado lasts for many hours.
———— Some people do not run and hide from tornadoes; they chase them.
———— There are three different kinds of windstorms.
———— To find out about a hurricane, a pilot might fly a plane into the storm.
———— Tornado winds are faster than hurricane winds.
———— Tornadoes can strike in any state in the United States.

with a paper and pencil activity, students might be surveyed by asking them to raise their right hand if they think an answer is true or their left hand if they think it is false. Additionally, individual, hand-held whiteboards can be used to log student answers.

Anchor Performance 2: Identify and Summarize Key Themes and Supporting Details

Helping students organize the main ideas and details contained in informational texts aids in their overall comprehension and their ability to read more deeply as prescribed by the CCSS. Diverse learners often find grade-level text difficult to navigate. Therefore, text information becomes more accessible when it is arranged in an organizational chart during reading. With practice, students become more skilled with identifying the main idea and supporting details and are better able to understand specific content. For this anchor performance, kindergarteners and first graders are expected to identify the main topic and key details in the text, whereas upper elementary youngsters are directed to determine the main idea of the text and explain how it is supported by key details.

Essential Strategy to Support Anchor Performance 2: Utilize Summary Organizers

Summary organizers help students sort and categorize information during active reading. They create a simple framework for diverse learners to identify and process pieces of text, most often with a teacher's guidance, as well as to demonstrate their understanding. Summary organizers can be adapted to suit the needs of individual learners and may be completed independently, in student pairs, or in small groups. They may be differentiated to already contain some of the text information with the task remaining for students to find the details to complete the summary. The following are two types of summary organizers:

Two-Column Notes. The main purpose of a two-column note organizer is for students to sketch out a text's main ideas and their corresponding details. Teachers can begin using this method by modeling the completion of the organizer on chart paper or other writing surface displayed to the class during a shared reading. Providing ongoing opportunities for students to complete two-column notes in class will strengthen their ability to recognize text features that lead them to the main ideas and details of the text. Below (Figures 4.3 and 4.4) are examples of a fully and a partially completed two-column note organizer based on the book *Alligator at Saw Grass Road* (Halfmann, 2006). Providing students with the main ideas and asking them to fill in all the details or by first presenting the details and having students determine their corresponding main ideas are two ways to further modify this organizer.

Figure 4.3 Fully Completed Two-Column Notes

Two-Column Notes	
Title: Alligators at Saw Grass Road (Halfmann, 2006)	
Main Ideas	**Details**
The alligator makes a nest.	She pushes plants and mud to make a nest above the water.
	She digs a hole on top of the nest to lay her eggs.
The alligator lays many eggs.	She covers them with plants.
	She keeps them safe and warm.
	She chases away other animals from her nest.
The eggs hatch at the end of the summer.	The alligator uncovers the nest.
	The alligator helps some of the babies come out of their shells.
	They are nine inches long.
The alligator protects her babies.	The babies sit on the alligator's head and back.
	They stay with their alligator mother for two years or more.

Figure 4.4 Partially Completed Two-Column Notes

Two-Column Notes	
Title: *Alligators at Saw Grass Road* (Halfmann, 2006)	
Main Ideas	**Details**
The alligator makes a nest.	She pushes plants and mud to make a nest above the water. _____ _____
The alligator lays many eggs.	She covers them with plants. _____ _____
The eggs hatch at the end of the summer.	The alligator uncovers the nest. _____ _____
The alligator protects her babies.	The babies sit on the alligator's head and back. _____ _____

Summary Wheels. A somewhat simplified version of the two-column notes in a different format, the summary wheel is a graphic representation to help student identify one main idea at a time along with its corresponding details. This organizer may be more suitable for earlier elementary grades or for students who do not have a strong facility with Standard English. As an alternative to writing text, students can illustrate the details surrounding the main idea or use a combination of both text and drawings. Figure 4.5 is an example of a summary wheel developed from the same text as above, *Alligator at Saw Grass Road* (Halfmann, 2006).

Anchor Performance 3: Analyze Cause and Effect

Cause-and-effect text structures are common in many printed materials in subjects such as history or science, which often contain descriptions of certain events or phenomena coupled with their determining factors. In order for students to understand causal relationships, they must first comprehend the overall information in the text. Giving diverse students a general overview of what the text contains increases their understanding while they are reading the text and allows them to make better connections between cause-and-effect relationships.

Figure 4.5 Summary Wheel

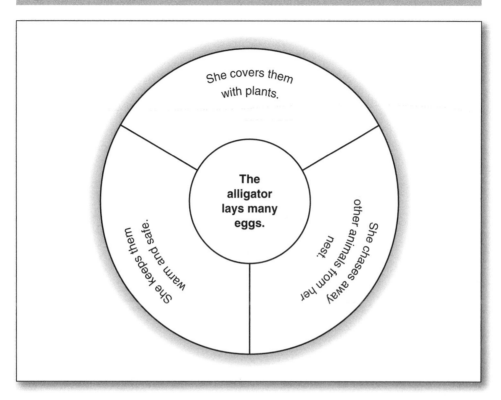

For this anchor performance, kindergarteners and first graders are expected to make connections between two story events, ideas, or pieces of information, whereas second and third graders are directed to make connections between a series of events and ideas, and fourth and fifth graders must take it one step further and explain the interactions between individuals, events, and ideas supporting their assertions with specific text information.

Essential Strategy to Support Anchor Performance 3: Create Structured Overviews

A structured overview is the process of organizing and arranging topics to make them more comprehensible. It identifies the major ideas and important details contained in the text. With a structured overview, students are better able to become familiar with new concepts. The simplified format allows students to clearly focus on the main ideas of the text before they read. Two types of structured overviews are a *One-Pager* and a *Graphic Representation*.

One-Pager. This type of overview identifies the main ideas and some details contained in the text in a list of complete sentences that follow the order the information is revealed during reading. Students have the opportunity to examine and comprehend smaller amounts of text that contain important concepts and vocabulary that can be discussed before the text is read. As suggested previously, teachers can project the image of the one-pager and read aloud each statement, pausing to discuss the more difficult vocabulary and paraphrasing the information to verbally scaffold instruction. Take a look at the sample one-pager (Figure 4.6) written for an article titled *Forgive Billy the Kid?* (Walters, 2010):

Figure 4.6 One-Pager

One-Pager: *Forgive Billy the Kid?*

- Billy the Kid was a notorious outlaw in the late 1800s.
- New Mexico Governor Bill Richardson is considering granting him a pardon— an official forgiveness for his crimes.
- Historical documents show that before he died, Billy agreed to testify in court about a killing he had seen to receive a pardon.
- The pardon never happened.
- Many people are upset about the possible pardon because they believe any governor should not pardon such a criminal.
- No decision has yet been made.

Graphic Representation. This type of structured overview includes various visual depictions, such as diagrams, maps, graphs, photo displays, for example, that represent ideas contained in the text. It may be more appealing to some students who are overwhelmed by a full page of text. Figure 4.7 shows one possible graphic representation of the *Forgive Billy the Kid* text.

Craft and Structure

Anchor Performance 4: Determine Meaning of Words and Phrases

Explicit vocabulary instruction and frequent repetition of the use of targeted vocabulary are essential practices for students to expand their comprehension of increasingly complex reading selections. Students need multiple opportunities to draw on new vocabulary not only through reading, but also while engaged in the other three language skills: listening, speaking, and writing. For this anchor performance, students are directed to accomplish different tasks according to their grade level. Kindergarten

Figure 4.7 Graphic Representation

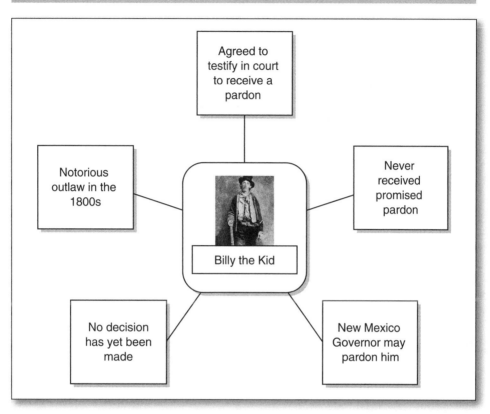

and first-grade students are prompted to ask and answer questions about general unknown words or phrases contained in informational text, whereas students in second through fifth grade determine the meaning of general academic (Tier 2) and content-specific (Tier 3) words or phrases specific to their grade level.

Essential Strategy to Support Anchor Performance 4: Build Vocabulary Sense

In the previous chapter on Reading Strategies for Literary Texts (see chapter 3), many suggested strategies for teaching vocabulary are also applicable to informational texts. In addition to those strategies, we have compiled several approaches to learning words and phrases to better help students understand informational texts.

List-Group-Label. A combination of brainstorming and semantic mapping, List-Group-Label activates students' prior knowledge, increases vocabulary, and helps students understand the relationship between groups of words. Students are asked to brainstorm a list of words about a topic within a particular time frame set by the teacher. Using critical thinking skills, students then group the words according to categories that they recognize. Last, they devise labels or titles for each of their word groups. This strategy is often completed in student pairs, trios, or small groups and can be used before, during, or after the text is read. Lists can be generated in a whole-class setting with students partnering to complete the rest of the task. Two variations of this strategy to differentiate instruction are as follows:

- Word Sorts. Teachers prepare printed lists of words along with titled categories. With partners, students cut out the words and sort them according to the teacher-specified categories.
- Photo Sort. No words are involved with this activity. Students are given a small stack of photos (generated from Google Images) that they must group and categorize. Category labels may be teacher-specified or student-devised.

Morphing Words. Here is one strategy that is helpful for students, particularly for English language learners, to understand the connections between words that are built from the same root word. Students need to recognize various words generated from common root words to increase their reading comprehension. This strategy gives students practice with frequently used words found in expository texts and offers them the opportunity to generate and identify the different forms these words can take. It works well as a timed game in which students are challenged to generate as many morphed words as they can either alone, in pairs or small groups within a certain time frame.

Table 4.1 gives an example of *Morphing Words*.

Table 4.1   Morphing *Inform*

Root Word:	*inform*
Morphed Words:	*informs* *informed* *informing* *information* *informative* *misinform* *misinforms* *misinformed* *misinforming* *misinformation* *uninformed* *uninformative*

Figure 4.8 Concept Map

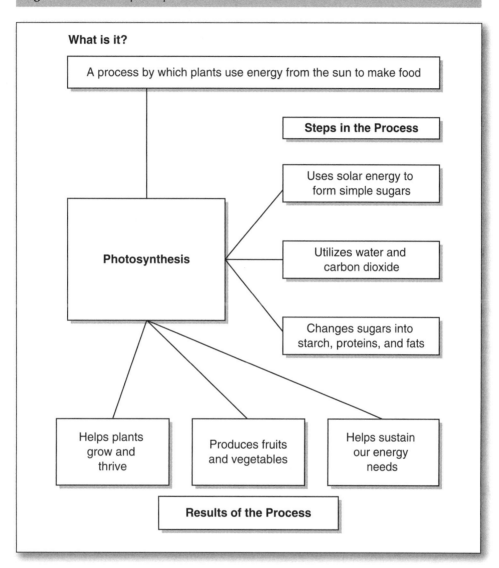

(Adapted from Echevarria, Vogt, & Short, 2012)

Concept Maps. To organize text information, students utilize a concept map (Novak & Cañas, 2008) to identify key words and phrases about a topic. This during-reading or after-reading strategy helps students make meaningful connections between the main idea and its supporting details. These organizers can be completed individually, with partners, or in full-class settings with a projected image (see Figure 4.8). The concepts they contain are generally new material for students, and teacher modeling and guidance in their completion is particularly helpful with diverse learners.

Anchor Performance 5: Know Informational Text Features

Students need to know and use the features of informational texts to be able to find key information contained in the text. Identifying simple text features, such as headings, subheadings, table of contents, and other supporting elements of informational texts help students to locate information and more readily answer text-based questions. For this anchor performance, kindergarteners are expected to identify the basic features of a book (e.g., front and back cover), whereas first and second graders become increasingly aware of other text features (e.g., table of contents, glossaries, bold print, and subheadings). Third graders are expected to use text features to find information in the text, in contrast to fourth and fifth graders who are anticipated to describe the overall structure of information in a text as well as compare and contrast the structures of two or more texts.

Strategy to Support Anchor Performance 5:
Identify The Elements of Informational Texts

We have found that elementary youngsters more often can cite the elements of literary texts (characters, setting, plot, etc.) than they can the features of informational texts. These features frequently are taught individually rather than as a set of elements necessary for understanding printed information. The following are identified as elements of informational texts (Marinak & Gambrell, 2009):

- *Author's purpose.* The reasons why the author is writing the text, whether it is to provide information, persuade or convince the reader of a particular point of view, or entertain
- *Major ideas.* The major concepts, convictions, or thoughts expressed by the author
- *Supporting details.* Information that verifies or further illustrates the main ideas in the text
- *Visual support.* Graphic representations that offer helpful information including charts, drawing, photographs, and tables
- *Vocabulary.* Words that are pertinent for understanding and writing about the text

Activities to promote understanding the features and elements of informational texts include an informational text exploration, a scavenger hunt, or a text-feature search. The purpose of each is to engage students in game-like, low-anxiety tasks that encourage text skimming and risk-taking.

Informational Text Exploration. Students can direct their attention to the key elements of informational texts using the organizational chart in Table 4.2. This activity can be teacher led and completed in student pairs. This organizer can be differentiated by having part of the information completed in the chart before the students engage in the task.

Table 4.2 Informational Text Exploration Template

Informational Text Exploration Text Title: _____	
What is the author's purpose? ❑ to entertain ❑ to inform ❑ to persuade ❑ other _____	How do you know the author's purpose? What evidence can you find in the text? _____ _____ _____ _____
What are the main points the author wanted to make? What information supports each main idea?	Main point #1_____ _____ Details _____ _____ _____ Main point #2_____ _____ Details _____ _____ _____ Main point #3_____ _____ _____ Details _____ _____ _____
What vocabulary words are most important to know and tell about the main ideas and details?	

Scavenger Hunt. In preparation for an engaging scavenger hunt, teachers create a list of instructions students will follow to explore select informational text elements. This type of activity can focus on the organizational features of the text, such as finding the page numbers of the table of contents, the index, and the glossary, or text features that give informational clues to the content, such as chapter titles, headings, subheadings. Students might "hunt" for photographs or tables and share the information they contain.

Text Feature Search. In this version of the activity, students complete a text feature chart which allows them to see a concise summary of all the key features and identify their purpose (see Table 4.3 for a blank template).

Table 4.3 Text Feature Search Template

Text Feature	Location (Page number)	Purpose	Notes
Table of Contents			
Headings			
Subheadings			
Key Vocabulary (bolded, highlighted)			
Sidebars			
Textboxes			
Tables			
Charts			
Diagrams			
Time Lines			
Maps			
Captions			
Glossary			
Index			
Other			

Anchor Performance 6: Understanding Point of View

Informational texts may be written with the intent of informing or persuading the reader. Therefore, students must be able to understand the role of the author and distinguish between various viewpoints and sources of information. Additionally, they must be aware that events and how they are interpreted can be viewed in more than one way. As such, the point of view expressed in a selection may be subjected to critical review even by young learners or students who might be struggling with text comprehension when the task is carefully scaffolded. For this anchor performance, kindergarteners and first graders are expected to identify the author and illustrator of the text and contrast information provided by illustrations and text, whereas second and third graders identify the main purpose of the text and distinguish their own point of view from the author. In addition, fourth and fifth graders are directed to compare and contrast first- and second-hand reports of information and analyze various accounts of the same event.

Essential Strategy to Support Anchor Performance 6: Question the Author

Questioning the Author (McKeown, Beck, & Worthy, 1993) is a protocol that invites students to critically think about a shorter selection of text and evaluate the author's intent: Was the message clearly communicated? Could the author's point of view be better presented? Try the template in Table 4.4 on one key sentence (an intriguing or inspirational quote such as "There is more treasure in books than in all the pirates' loot on the Treasure Island" by Walt Disney or "The best way to destroy your enemy is to make him your friend" by Abraham Lincoln), a paragraph, or a short passage (such as the Pledge of Allegiance) depending on the students' language proficiency or literacy readiness level.

Table 4.4   Question the Author (QTA) Protocol

Question the Author Prompts	Student Responses
What is the author trying to tell you?	
Why is the author telling you that?	
Does the author say it clearly?	
How could the author have said things more clearly?	
What would you say instead?	

Integration of Knowledge and Ideas

Anchor Performance 7: Analyzing Text Aids to Support Meaning

Informational texts are often supported by illustrations, diagrams, charts, and other text aides, which tend to offer the same information as the text in an alternative format. Students need to understand and be able to make meaningful connections among multiple modes of information. For this anchor performance, kindergarteners are prompted to connect illustrations with text and first graders use both illustrations and text to identify key ideas; second and third graders use illustrations and images to clarify and gain information to answer questions, and fourth and fifth graders interpret information displayed visually and are asked to draw information from multiple sources.

Essential Strategy to Support Anchor Performance 7: Text Aid Tour

Similar to a picture walk of a literary selection, invite your students on a text tour. Put on your straw hat, hold up a flag, and pretend to be a tour guide as you take your students on a journey through the target text highlighting all the key illustrations that support the text. Briefly discuss the purpose and key features of each illustration, while eliciting scaffolded questions from your students that you could respond to:

- *Who is in the photograph?*
- *What does the caption say?*
- *What country (city) is in the map?*
- *What kind of illustration is that?*
- *What type of diagram is that?*

After modeling this activity, make sure your students take on the role of the tour guide and explain the key text aides that appear in the same and additional nonfiction books.

Anchor Performance 8: Describing and Explaining Logical Text Connections

In order to make logical connections, students need to have the skills to make comparisons, identify cause and effect, or retell the order of main ideas and details in sequence. They must be able to find evidence that supports the author's assumptions or identify the reasons why an author has a particular point of view. In order to support these complex tasks, teachers need to scaffold instruction for diverse learners. For this anchor performance, students in kindergarten and first grade are encouraged to identify the information an author gives in connection with particular points made in the text, whereas second and third graders are expected to describe how author's reasons support certain points and make logical connections between particular sentences and paragraphs. Students in fourth and fifth grade must be able to tell how the author uses evidence and identify which reasons support which evidence.

Essential Strategy to Support Anchor Performance 8: Scaffold Instruction

In the process of scaffolding, the teacher helps the student master a task or concept that the student is initially unable to grasp independently. According to McKenzie (2000), scaffolding

- increases student understanding by providing clear explanations and step-by-step scaffolding instructions to complete the intended task;
- makes students clearly aware of the purpose and importance of the activity; and
- assures students remain on target and keep focused to improve their understanding.

General Scaffolding Approaches:

- Specifically connect students' prior experiences with target concepts.
- Build student knowledge with visual images of the text.
- Devise prereading and postreading questions or prompts.
- Model think-aloud techniques to showcase the use of multiple strategies while reading.
- Use graphic representations to organize information and retell the main ideas of the text.
- Scaffold linguistically to emphasize key vocabulary in multiple, meaningful ways.
- Paraphrase information or invite students to do so.
- Reinforce the meaning of new words in context.
- Highlight key text features such as recurring sentence patterns.
- Comprehend-aloud (Zwiers, 2008) by allowing the students' insights into your own thought process of meaning making.

Anchor Performance 9: Compare and Contrast Information Between Two Texts

Students must be able to draw and compare information from separate texts and identify key ideas and supporting details. To this end, they need to develop the organizational skills to connect the ideas of each text and eliminate unnecessary information. Students also need to learn specific vocabulary words and phrases to express comparisons of texts, such as *similarity, difference, in contrast to, alike, both,* for example. To develop the written and verbal expression of compare and contrast, certain graphic organizers can help arrange information for students to better relate these comparisons. For this anchor performance, students in kindergarten and first grade are expected to identify the basic similarities and differences between two texts on the same topic, whereas second and third graders compare and contrast information on the same topic present in two different texts, and students in fourth and fifth grade merge information from two or more texts in order to write or tell information about a particular topic.

Essential Strategy to Support Anchor Performance 9: Model Compare/Contrast Organizers

When students engage in compare/contrast activities, they shift their focus from the main ideas and pay closer attention to details. Graphic organizers such as the Venn-diagram or variations of the T-Chart allow students to successfully extract and manipulate essential information from the text. Graphic organizers are ideal tools to be differentiated for multilevel classes, since they can be presented blank or with some or a lot of information preentered in them. Below are our preferred ways of presenting these two commonly used tools:

Venn Diagram. The overlapping circles create three writing areas. Students review the reading selections and write information that is exclusive to each text on the top and on the bottom parts of the organizer (Figure 4.9). In the middle, students identify information that is contained in both texts.

T-Chart. An organizer used for identifying two separate topics or viewpoints, a T-Chart can include any two topics that can clearly be contrasted and compared. Some contrasting or opposite concepts for using such a chart might include fact and opinion, past and present, wonder and know, and advantages and disadvantages. It may also be used to contrast the attributes of two separate animals such as indicated on the T-Chart in Table 4.5.

Range of Reading and Level of Text Complexity

Anchor Performance 10: Reading Informational Texts Independently

Encouraging students to read independently is a challenging task for teachers of struggling learners. Although reading a wide range of informational texts can increase reading achievement, students who lack reading fluency are reluctant to read independently and often do not read frequently enough to gain facility with their literacy skills. Furthermore,

Figure 4.9 Making the Venn Diagram More Conducive to Writing

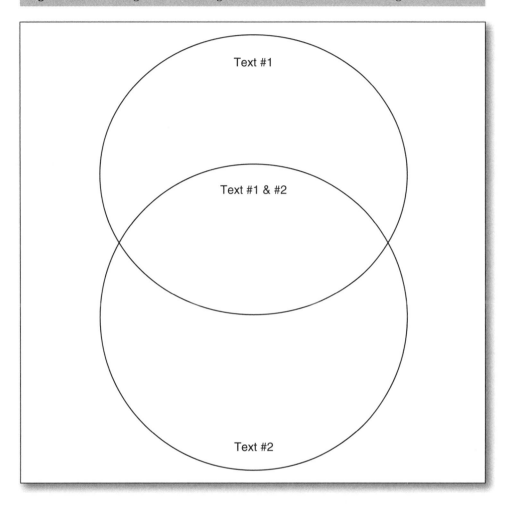

Table 4.5 Partially Completed T-Chart

Alligators	Polar Bears
✔Live in a warm climate	✔Live in a cold climate
✔Can swim	✔Can swim
✔Lay eggs	✔Give birth
✔Protect their young	✔Protect their young
✔Are reptiles	✔Are mammals
✔Have scales	✔Have fur
✔_____	✔_____
✔_____	✔_____
✔_____	✔_____

struggling learners do not know that they must be actively engaged with the text to make meaning. Teachers can help students become actively engaged in reading tasks by identifying commonly used strategies employed by competent readers and modeling them during shared readings of text.

Essential Strategy to Support Anchor Performance 10: Identify and Model Reading Strategies

Although numerous cognitive processes are employed during comprehension, competent readers generally use only a few of them consistently to make sense of what they read (Block & Pressley, 2002). Here are some of the more common strategies taught to elementary readers (also identified in Chapter 3):

Experienced readers
- Think about what they are reading
- Reread when they do not understand
- Make predictions
- Make personal connections
  o Text to self
  o Text to text
  o Text to world
- Jot down words they do not know
- Use context clues to find meaning
- Picture text ideas in their minds
- Ask questions about what they read
- Can summarize the main idea of the text
- Evaluate and form opinions about what they read

To help struggling learners, teachers need to introduce each of these strategies, perhaps one strategy every few weeks, to give students time to observe them being used during shared readings and to practice using them. In addition, students often benefit from being assigned a task while reading independently that incorporates one of these strategies. One such activity is asking thick and thin questions (Fang, 2010).

Thick and Thin Questions. Competent readers generate their own questions while reading to make sense of new information and ideas. This activity introduces students to the difference between asking thick questions, which focus on broad topics and are not right there in the text, and thin questions, which often are used to clarify information and are easily answerable. Here are some characteristics of each of these types of questions:

Thick question:	Thin question:
• Deals with large concepts • Leads to deeper discussion • Answers are long and involved • Not right there in the text • Often begins with "Why?" "How come?" or "I wonder."	• Most often is right there in the text • Clarifies information • Helps figure out the meaning of a new word • Makes sense of confusing section of the text

To begin this activity, students are asked to jot down questions on sticky-note papers, one question per note while reading the same text. After reading, students volunteer to read their questions aloud and place each of their sticky notes on a divided chart, one side for thick questions and the other for thin questions. Through discussion of each question, the class determines whether the questions were placed correctly on the chart (Table 4.6).

Table 4.6 Thick and Thin Question Examples

Thick questions	Thin questions
• Why do we have so many microbes in our bodies? • Are people today becoming more at risk for dangerous diseases? • What might happen if we did not have microbes in our bodies?	• How many cells are in the human body? • What is the most common microbe called? • How do microbes play a role in the food we eat?

Teaching students how to ask thick and thin questions helps them relate their prior knowledge to the text. It stimulates their engagement with the reading task, encourages monitoring of their own comprehension process, and promotes inquiry and active learning. This strategy requires extensive modeling and practice for it to be most effective.

ANTICIPATED OUTCOMES

Access to informational text content is expected to be challenging for English learners and academically struggling readers. The strategies presented above are designed to accomplish the following:

1. Increase students' prior knowledge for more meaningful connections.

2. Provide access points to the target nonfiction text.

3. Enhance text comprehension with appropriate scaffolds and supports.

4. Expand students' receptive and productive vocabulary.

5. Engage struggling learners with texts they could not successfully handle independently.

INSTRUCTIONAL CHALLENGES

Requiring academically and linguistically diverse students to read the same texts as their on-grade-level-reading peers seems counterproductive in some respects, and many teachers believe the practice will only result in frustration on the part of the students. However, the main goal of teachers dealing with informational texts should be to expose all students to grade-level material. Although it certainly seems more prudent to implement lessons at an instructional level somewhat above a student's level of independent learning, it is still necessary to expose all students to grade-appropriate texts and various levels of text complexity, not for these texts to be read independently, but to be an overall part of shared reading and instruction on the subject matter.

Shared reading introduces students to a variety of authors on a particular subject whose writing they most likely would not be able to read independently; it creates a low-anxiety environment for discussing the text, promotes an enjoyable learning experience, and is the perfect opportunity for teachers to discuss vocabulary and content more deeply. As a part of shared reading practices, teachers may follow these general guidelines for providing reading instruction for students with various language and academic challenges:

- Focus on teaching comprehension strategies to students, providing repetitive modeling of strategy use and class time for students to practice them.
- Provide both low-tech and high-tech visual and auditory aids for students by displaying photographs, realia (real objects), graphic organizers, and other print media that support reading content, as well as making available multimedia technology including video, personal computers, and iPod/iPad applications to build background knowledge and motivate students to read.
- Promote the use of Standard English and content vocabulary through cooperative and collaborative group activities focused on reading and interpreting informational texts. Structured conversations that focus on analyzing and categorizing topic data, jointly creating information summaries or text-based inferences, and finding key details that match main ideas are just some of the ways students might have an opportunity to use oral language and check their general and specific understanding of the targeted text.

PROMISING CLASSROOM PRACTICES

Third-grade teacher Lilly Moffat selected the text *Face to Face with Polar Bears* (Rosing & Carney, 2009) for a shared reading with her students as part of a unit from the district science curriculum titled *Habitats: How People Affect Plants and Animals*. She collaborated with the ESL and literacy teachers as to how she could best accommodate those students with language and reading challenges. Together, they came up with a plan to incorporate various strategies into a series of lessons and several readings of the text.

Lilly began the initial lesson with a five-minute brainstorming session about polar bears. She listed information obtained from her students on chart paper. Lilly explained and illustrated vocabulary on the same chart paper to clarify information that was shared. Soon after, she displayed four illustrations she had copied from the text, described each of them, and modeled how students might infer certain information about the text from one of the illustrations. She invited students to turn and talk with a partner to share their own inferences about each illustration displayed and had a few pairs of students share their ideas with the whole class. Next, the teacher projected the text with a document camera and began to read the text aloud asking students to follow along. She scaffolded the reading by frequently pausing to explain key vocabulary and paraphrase information. As she read, she asked students questions about the text to check for understanding. After the shared reading, students were grouped in pairs or trios and asked to complete a graphic organizer, which highlighted the main idea of the text and identified three supporting details (see Figure 4.4 for a similar example).

Subsequent lessons involved the classroom teacher rereading the text aloud to the class, and students using the following strategies:

- Writing *Thick and Thin Questions* on sticky notes and posting them on chart paper
- Completing a class chart on the elements of informational texts using the target text
- Morphing the word *manage*

The ESL and literacy teachers also "pushed in" to the class to assist students during Reader's Workshop, an activity that involved students reading texts about polar bears at their independent reading levels, and Writer's Workshop, in which students wrote summaries about their readings.

COMMON CORE READING STANDARDS— UN(COMMON) REFLECTION QUESTIONS

1. Which of the ten anchor standards or the grade-appropriate equivalents will present the greatest departure from your previous literacy instructional practices regarding teaching informational texts?

2. Which of the ten anchor standards or the grade-appropriate equivalents will present the greatest challenge to your students?

3. How are you planning to strategically address the difficulties your students will face with select standards?

KEY RESOURCES

Professional Resources

DK Eye Witness Books, published by Dorling Kindersley Ltd.

Duke, N. K., & Bennett-Armistead, S. V. (2003). *Reading and writing informational text in the primary grades: Research-based practices.* New York, NY: Scholastic.

Harvey, S. (1998). *Nonfiction matters: Reading, writing, and research in Grades 3–8.* Portland, ME: Stenhouse.

Kletzien, S. B. (2003). *Informational text in K–3 classrooms: Helping children read and write.* Newark, DE: International Reading Association.

Online or Print Nonfiction Magazines for K–5 Readers

- *OWL* magazine
  http://www.owlkids.com
- *National Geographic Explorer* and *NG Little Kids* magazines
  http://magma.nationalgeographic.com/ngexplorer
- Your Big Backyard, Ranger Rick, and Ranger Rick Jr.
  www.nwf.org/Kids/Your-Big-Backyard.aspx
- *Time for Kids* magazine
  http://www.timeforkids.com/
- Great Websites for Kids
  http://gws.ala.org

5 Reading Foundational Skills

I find television very educating. Every time somebody turns on the set,
I go into the other room and read a book.

— Groucho Marx

OVERVIEW

Consider your memories and experiences with reading as a young child. What do you remember most vividly? When we ask people this question, they rarely identify the drills that they were subjected to in school as children—reciting the alphabet, matching letters and sounds, memorizing sight-word lists. Most often, they share with us a favorite story that was read to them at bedtime, the illustrations in a memorable storybook, or the first book they were able to read on their own.

Now consider your diverse learners and imagine what one of their reading memories might be. Many of these youngsters may come from homes where suitable reading material is not readily available. English learners often may not have easy access to storybooks in their home language, and their parents frequently are unable to read to them in English. Some students with disabilities have difficulty attending to books read aloud or cannot easily connect spoken words with written text. Children of poverty often come from homes devoid of print material as well as technology. It is easy to assume that most of these students have different memories of learning to read than their teachers.

When we recall our own reading memories and compare them with what we assume diverse learners might recall, it is important to remember not to assume anything about the literacy experiences of these youngsters. This notion is particularly important when dealing with older elementary school students whose cognitive abilities, lack of English skills, or other circumstances may have led them to miss out on important foundational reading instruction. Although two of the four anchor standards in this section are identified for K–1 students only, keep in mind that some diverse youngsters in Grades 2–5 may also benefit from work with print concepts and phonological awareness skills.

Another lesson to be learned from recalling reading memories is that in these stories, meaning making invariably trumps skills instruction. If teachers plan and execute foundational skills instruction in isolation, solely using workbooks or photocopied sheets in which students trace letters, match letters and sounds, copy spelling patterns or sight words, color groups of pictures with the same beginning sound, etc., all without story text support, their skill instruction most likely will be less memorable and not transferable to authentic reading and writing tasks. However, in comparing our observations in classes with the most effective instruction, we found teachers who were

- acutely aware of the needs of their individual students;
- prepared and executed highly engaging activities;
- differentiated instruction so that challenging lessons were accessible to all learners; and
- and kept skills instruction anchored by the use of authentic text.

Cunningham and Allington (2011) further suggested that exceptional teachers integrate reading and writing in all subject matter, use a wide variety of materials as well as class configurations and collaborative learning groups for students to meet with success, and most important, teach reading and writing skills explicitly along with time for students to practice them.

WHY EXPLICIT INSTRUCTION IN BASIC LITERACY SKILLS IS NECESSARY

According to the National Assessment of Educational Progress (1999) Black and Hispanic youngsters score below the reading levels of their White counterparts. Likewise, reading difficulties persist among disadvantaged youngsters. Most encouraging, however, is that despite students' lack of exposure to print concepts in the home, intensified, explicit reading instruction at school coupled with a literacy-rich environment can help struggling learners keep pace and catch up with their on-target peers (Cunningham & Allington, 2011).

In order to accommodate diverse learners, curriculum and teaching methods should be differentiated and learning strategies explicitly taught to meet students' distinct learning needs. In many ways, the CCSS can be the catalyst for such accommodations, establishing a set of curricular goals, yet leaving educators the freedom to determine how best to achieve them. According to the National Institute for Urban Improvement (2000), collaborative teaching arrangements help teachers develop the necessary expertise to create lessons in order to individualize instruction. Working alongside and in consultation with other teachers allows for a thorough examination of the standards, identification of effective teaching strategies, and ideas for how to best execute instruction to reach all learners.

The overarching goal of explicitly teaching basic literacy skills is to plan focused instruction that integrates the standards and provides the necessary strategies and supports for all students to learn academic content. In this way, diverse youngsters will have the advantages of a challenging curriculum yet benefit from developing their basic reading skills through tailored instruction.

CORE READING STRATEGIES

The strategies identified in this chapter are aligned to the four College and Career Readiness Anchor Standards (CCRAS) for Foundational Skills (Box 5.1). These standards are categorized according to *Print Concepts, Phonological Awareness, Phonics and Word Recognition,* and *Fluency*. Both *Print Concepts* and *Phonological Awareness* are designated for Grades K–1 only. However, we recommend that teachers of students in Grades 2–5 review them along with their related strategies to determine if they may be beneficial for some diverse learners in these grades. This type of review is also referred to as back mapping or spiraling back the curriculum to reinforce basic skills. As stated in previous chapters, a series of related *Anchor Performances* accompany each of these four standards along with related strategies for diverse students.

Print Concepts

Anchor Performance 1: Demonstrate an Understanding of the Basic Features of Print

All learners benefit from explicit literacy instruction, and some diverse students in particular need reinforcement in general reading skills and

Box 5.1 College and Career Readiness Anchor Standards for Foundational Skills

Print Concepts (K–1)

Demonstrate understanding of the organization and basic features of print.

Phonological Awareness (K–1)

Demonstrate understanding of spoken words, syllables, and sounds (phonemes).

Phonics and Word Recognition (K–5)

Know and apply grade-level phonics and word-analysis skills in decoding words.

Fluency (K–5)*

Read with sufficient accuracy and fluency to support comprehension. (*The standard for Kindergarteners reads: Read emergent-reader texts with purpose and understanding.)

concepts as a result of their limited exposure to written English. Although this standard is most applicable to Grades K–1, diverse learners in other grades may need basic information about text before they begin to read. Generally speaking, that information is categorized as print concepts, fundamental understandings about printed information that students must know in order to learn to read successfully. These concepts include the following knowledge of print:

- Spoken words can be written;
- The location of the title, front cover, and back cover of a book;
- Where a story begins and ends;
- Where a sentence begins and ends;
- The ability to point to words as they are read;
- How to follow words from left to right and top to bottom;
- The beginning and ending of individual words;
- The identity of the letters of the alphabet and the difference between capital and lower case letters; and
- The identity and purpose of punctuation marks.

Essential Strategy to Support Anchor Performance 1: Explore the Conventions of Print Through a Variety of Reading and Writing Activities

It is critical that teachers explicitly identify and reinforce the meaning of each convention of print through demonstration and modeling.

Additionally, have students explore conventions through learning centers, working cooperatively with other students to uncover the purpose of reading and writing. By way of various classroom activities that incorporate reading and writing and foster guided practice, students will be able to demonstrate their knowledge of conventions of print.

Shared Reading. With this strategy, the teacher engages students in different types of text—short stories, poetry, rhymes, proverbs—that are read aloud and analyzed for print concepts.

- Begin by selecting an appropriate text, either fiction or nonfiction, and display it so students have easy access to its contents via interactive whiteboard, chart paper, or big books. When working in small groups, copies of the text can be provided for each student.
- Conduct a *book walk* in which you preview the contents of the book, beginning with the cover, the title, the author, and moving through the book page by page reviewing the contents and illustrations as you solicit predictions about the text from students.
- Read the text aloud, pointing to the words as students follow along. Pause periodically to discuss word meaning, paraphrase information, and check for student comprehension.
- Elicit from students their favorite parts and reread them with purpose. Explicitly identify particular concepts of print according to lesson objectives. Point out how the text is read from left to right, analyze the parts of a sentence or word, and help students identify capital and lower case letters as well as punctuation marks.

Shared reading is an appropriate strategy not only for all K–1 youngsters, but is also an effective approach with small groups of select diverse learners in other grades as well.

Shared Writing. This activity gives students the opportunity to write in unison with other students to complete a group-created text. The teacher sets the writing task, solicits information from individual students, and writes the shared information either on chart paper or whiteboard. As the teacher copies the information, he or she demonstrates different print concepts or asks students to make decisions about how sentences should be written. Some questions the teacher might ask include the following:

How do I begin writing the first word in the sentence?

How do I spell _____?

What punctuation mark should end the sentence?

Why did I indent this sentence?

Together, students can create brief letters, short stories, notes, cards, or nonfiction pieces about a topic being studied in class, compare and contrast the different organizational styles of each type of writing, and thereafter practice composing their own writing pieces.

Word Labels. Identifying classroom objects and subject-specific artifacts with word labels helps students connect *realia* (real objects) to printed text, develop print concepts related to individual words, and assists English learners in developing basic vocabulary. We recommend introducing one new word per day. To begin, compose each word label together with students, having them sound out and spell selected words, and post them according to their corresponding objects. Refer to the words displayed throughout the room often, or play games having students guess one of the words you have selected by giving them clues. It is important to refer to the words labels frequently; these posted words should be an active reference source for all youngsters to help them develop letter-sound correspondence as well as additional reading and writing skills.

Choral Reading. This strategy involves students reading the same text in unison, either as a whole class or in small groups. Choral reading builds students' fluency, use of sight vocabulary, and develops their understanding of where sentences begin and end as well as the purpose of each punctuation mark. Students learn to read with expression, pausing for commas and periods and altering their voice inflection with question marks and exclamation points. Choral reading also provides English learners the opportunity to pronounce words orally with increased comfort and less embarrassment. As with shared reading, make sure all students have access to the printed text, and model reading the passage first before inviting students to join in.

Reader's Workshop. A multistep activity, reader's workshop generally begins with a minilesson in which a concept or particular reading strategy is introduced to students. The teacher models and demonstrates the skill and gives students a brief period of time for guided practice. After the minilesson, students are directed to apply what has been taught by reading books at their independent reading level either alone or in pairs. Other reader's workshop activities include students writing about what they have read in a journal, sharing the journal writing with a partner, reading aloud to or conferencing with the teacher, and participating in guided reading groups. Teachers generally end the reader's workshop by meeting with the whole class once again to review the minilesson concept and gather feedback from students about their various reading activities.

Writer's Workshop. A valuable activity for students to practice and demonstrate their knowledge of the basic features of print, writer's workshop provides students with opportunities to practice writing in genres independently. One way to introduce writer's workshop is with a read-aloud which might serve as a mentor text for student writing. Teachers may choose to continue with a minilesson to teach a particular writing concept. With young learners or diverse students of any age, lessons might focus on some print convention such as beginning sentences with capital letters, indenting when starting a new paragraph, or ending sentences with the correct punctuation marks. Most of the time spent during writer's workshop should be on student writing. Students may begin this task by completing a graphic organizer such as a Four Square (see Figure 5.1) to plan and organize their writing. During this independent writing time, students write a first draft and then confer with the teacher. Afterward, they spend time revising their writing. Teachers also set some time aside for students to share their finished piece of writing with the whole class or a peer.

Writing Centers. Teachers set up center activities for exploring a variety of writing tasks. These tasks can help young learners experiment with various genres and practice using concepts of print. Tasks can be assigned by the teacher or self-selected by the student from a list of writing activities. Some of these activities might include the following:

- Draw a picture and write a sentence that describes it.
- Compose and illustrate a journal entry.
- Create a greeting card.
- Design a bookmark.
- Write and illustrate a storybook.

Figure 5.1   Four-Square Graphic Organizer

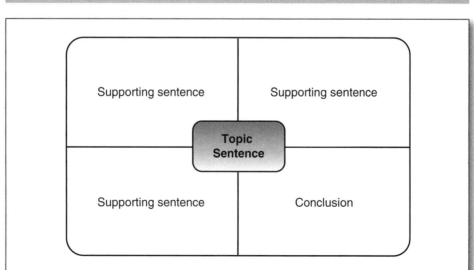

- Write a letter to a family member, famous person, or story character.
- Author an acrostic poem.
- Create an advertisement for your favorite toy.

Students may self-select or be assigned specific writing tasks. Writing buddies might be assigned to assist students who need extra support in completing writing tasks.

Phonological Awareness

Anchor Performance 2: Identify the Parts of Spoken Words Including Sounds, Syllables, and Rhymes

Phonological or phonemic awareness is the ability to understand that words are made of individual sounds or *phonemes*, and that these sounds can be combined in different ways to make new words. Before children are able to read, they not only need to be aware of individual sounds, but also how the sounds in spoken words can be translated into print. A weakness in this skill is a hindrance in learning to read (Liberman, Shankweiler, & Liberman, 1989) and a predictor of reading difficulty. However, teachers need to be cautious when making judgments about diverse learners if they present with weak skills in this area.

If the sounds of Standard English are unfamiliar to students, they may have difficulty distinguishing them auditorily. It is important to remember that words and their associated sounds taught in isolation will be more difficult for these students to grasp. It is always a better practice to imbed the development of phonemic awareness with these youngsters in meaningful context including familiar or just-read stories, real-life experiences, *realia* or real objects in the immediate environment, and language-learning games and activities, which focus on manipulating letters and sounds.

Essential Strategy to Support Anchor Performance 2: Explore the Sounds, Syllables, and Rhymes Through Oral/Aural and Tactual Activities

In order for students to become familiar with the individual sounds words contain, have students participate in a variety of activities that help them to identify beginning and ending sounds, blend words together, and manipulate sounds to change one word into another. Take time to discuss different sounds and how these sounds may be altered to change words or create new ones. There are literally dozens of activities that teachers can incorporate into phonological skills lessons. The activities specified below are only a few of our suggestions.

Talk Like A Ghost. Teachers can help students discover the phonemes in words by having them stretch out word sounds, imitating the way a ghost might speak. Begin by asking students if they know how a ghost might say something, and after having some volunteers share their ghostly imitations, demonstrate your own rendition of what a ghost might sound like speaking particular words or phrases. Make sure words are spoken in a way in which each phoneme is clearly and distinctly audible. Share the spelling of words or phrases by writing them together on a chart or whiteboard. This activity may be used as a strategy for students to spell their own words when writing.

Object Sort. Compile a collection of real objects that can be sorted in various ways according to their beginning and ending sounds, number of syllables, words that rhyme, for example. Have students work in small groups or at learning centers to sort the items accordingly. One variation of this activity is to have each student in a small group select one item, identify it, then tell another word that begins or ends the same or rhymes with the selected object. Another variation, *Object Toss,* can be accomplished as a game with the whole class. Select an item and have students toss it from one to another, naming the item and sharing another word with matching sounds or rhymes.

Finish My Rhyme. Using familiar poetry, books, or made-up rhymes, have students complete rhyming patterns aloud either individually or chorally. To encourage student participation, pause at the end of a phrase or sentence being read and have students orally complete the rhyme. Use unfamiliar text with students and have them guess words that might belong in the sentence to complete the rhyming pattern, and additionally assess student comprehension. Many Dr. Seuss books, for example, are good choices to execute this strategy with young learners. This activity may be used with older students as part of an overall lesson using a selection of poetry. Some poetry for children is identified in Box 5.2, which can be easily found on the Internet.

Box 5.2 Poetry for Children

"About the Teeth of Sharks" by John Ciardi

The Adventures of Isabel by Ogden Nash

"The Dentist and the Crocodile" by Roald Dahl

"Daddy Fell Into the Pond" by Alfred Noyes

"The Quarrel" by Maxine Kumin

"My Shadow" by Robert Louis Stevenson

The Tiger Who Wore White Gloves: Or What You Are You Are
  by Gwendolyn Brooks

Inventive Spelling. Teachers can help students develop phonological awareness and become independent writers by supporting students' inventive spelling. Instead of spelling words for students when asked, demonstrate how youngsters can sound out words and write the sounds they hear to approximate spelling. Have students practice this strategy individually to complete simple writing tasks. Do not be concerned if all the sounds are not represented accurately. According to Cunningham and Allington (2011), "As phonics instruction continues, their phonics spelling will more closely match the actual spelling of the word" (p. 41).

Phonics and Word Recognition

Anchor Performance 3: Apply Grade-Level Phonics and Word Analysis Skills in Decoding Words

All students need to be able to figure out words they are unable to read. For this reason, they need to know the "mechanics" behind word building to develop the skills to cognitively manipulate letters into sounds and sounds into words that have meaning. "All proficient readers have the ability to look at regular words they have never seen before and assign probable pronunciation" (Cunningham & Allington, 2011, p. 66). Yet, diverse learners often struggle with this task even if they have developed adequate phonics skills. The problem generally lies in the fact that although they may have adequate probable pronunciation of an unknown word, no meaning for the word is activated by their pronunciation attempts. For this reason, it is vital to remember to embed phonics instruction within a context that supports meaning making for diverse students. The more predictive the text, the better able students will be to decode unknown words.

Essential Strategy to Support Anchor Performance 3: Participate in Word Analysis

Explicit phonics instruction more frequently occurs in early elementary grades; yet, the CCSS through this standard recognizes this set of skills warrants instruction to develop them incrementally throughout each grade level. Although participation in word analysis activities helps all students advance their facility to decode unknown words, the expectation of student ability is different for each grade level.

Kindergarten students are expected to develop basic knowledge of sound-letter correspondence as well as read high-frequency words whereas first graders are anticipated to decode one-syllable as well as some two-syllable words that follow basic patterns. Second graders work toward regularly decoding two-syllable words and those with common prefixes and suffixes, whereas third graders are instructed to identify and understand most grade-appropriate prefixes and suffixes and decode multisyllabic words. By fourth and fifth grade, students are expected to use their knowledge of phonics to decode a variety of multisyllabic words both in and out of context.

No matter what grade level, all students need to be assessed for their ability levels in this skill area, and word analysis instruction needs to be differentiated to meet individual learning needs. The following strategies help diverse learners as well as all students work toward developing their phonics and word recognition skills (see Patricia Cunningham's [2008] work for further examples).

Word Walls. Creating a word wall is an activity that requires careful attention to the words selected in order to build the recognition of common sight words as well as the building blocks to develop decoding skills. Selected words are generally displayed alphabetically. For youngsters in Grades K–3, introduce five or six new, grade-appropriate words each week to the wall and practice them via spelling chants, clapping each letter as it is orally spelled, writing them, or both. For Grades 4–5, word walls may be theme based and focused on a particular content area or have a divided word wall that displays words from various labeled content areas—math, science, social studies, ELA. Many teachers focus on building word walls that have Tier II vocabulary words—academic vocabulary that is common across grade levels.

It is important to recognize that the word wall is not just a classroom display. It is a source for multiple daily literacy-learning activities and a reference to inform student writing. A word wall must be helpful and useful to all students, displayed in an area of the room where it can be clearly seen, and employed on a daily basis with review activities so that its words can be easily and automatically read as well as its contents inform the reading of new and unknown words.

Guess the Covered Word. This activity teaches students to identify what words make sense in context as well as to carefully focus on and learn to spell the beginning sounds of words. One way to begin is to write five to seven sentences on the board that focus on a particular theme. For young learners, sentences should follow a pattern such as the following:

Jenny likes to eat pizza.

Max likes to eat hamburgers.

Sara likes to eat carrots.

In the above example, the underlined words are covered. Read each sentence aloud without saying the covered word. Ask students to guess words that might fit in the sentence and write four or five of their guesses on the board. Next, reveal the beginning of the covered word (the first letter of the word if it begins with a single consonant or the first two or three letters if the word begins with a diagraph or blend). Return to the list of student guesses, and, based on the initial spelling, cross out words that could not be the covered word; circle any remaining words that are still possibilities. Finally, uncover the entire word. Repeat the process with each of the sentences. Additionally, *Guess the Covered Word* can be used with Big Books, poetry posters, rhyming patterns, and particularly for older students, with prepared content area summaries.

Making Words. This activity helps students become aware of various spelling patterns and allays the perceived mystery held by some youngsters about spelling Standard English words. Students manipulate from six to eight reproduced, small letter cards in order to create words with the given letters as directed. The teacher has a matching set of large letter cards displayed on a card chart in front of the class. Lessons begin by asking students to form two- and three-letter words. As the lesson continues, longer words are chosen for students to produce. Students are given time to spell each word, and the teacher circulates the room to assess students' abilities. Soon after, the teacher invites one student to the card chart to form the word after all students have attempted to spell it individually. The culminating activity is for students to guess the *secret word* by trying to form one word with all the given letters.

During this activity, it is important to give students clues about how to transform one word to another. Some suggested clues are to identify how many letters are in each word, how many letters students need to change to create a new word, or what specific letters they have to remove from the current word to create the new one. An example of a making words lesson can be found in Box 5.3.

Box 5.3 Making Words Lesson

Distribute the following letters to each student: *a, a, e, c, k, n, p, s.* Ask students to follow these directions.

1. Take two letters and make the word an.
2. Add one letter and make the word pan.
3. Change the first letter, and turn pan into can.
4. Don't change any letters and don't take any away. Just add one letter and make the word cans.
5. Change one letter and turn cans into caps.
6. Change one letter and turn caps into naps.
7. Don't change any letters and don't take any away. Add one letter and make the word snaps.

8. Now take away all the letters and let's start again. Take three letters and make the word can.

9. Add one more letter to can and make the word cane.

10. Add one more letter to cane and make the word canes.

11. Take away the letter in the middle of canes, and add one letter in the middle, and change canes into cakes.

12. Now use all the letters to find the secret word (pancakes).

An easy away to distribute the letters is to have rows of letters reproduced, cut into strips, and distributed to each child who must separate the letters with a scissor. See Figure 5.2 for an example.

Figure 5.2 Rows of Letters for Making Words Lesson

a a e c k n p s

a a e c k n p s

a a e c k n p s

a a e c k n p s

a a e c k n p s

Changing a Hen to a Fox. In this activity, students manipulate the three-letter names of animals to change one animal name into another. Using pencil and paper begin by asking students to write the word *hen*. Next, ask students to change *hen* into the word *pen* by altering only one letter. The "metamorphosis" continues with students being asked to change one letter to create new words until the word *fox* is written. The following is the word sequence to complete the task: *hen pen, pin, pit, sit, six, fix, fox*. This is a great activity to use in conjunction with the story *Hattie and the Fox* (1992) by Mem Fox. Other lessons can be developed in this fashion to have students in all grade levels change one word into another.

Fluency

Anchor Performance 4: Read Grade-Level Texts With Sufficient Fluency to Support Understanding

Fluency, an essential reading skill, is the ability to read most text aloud with relative ease and proper expression. To read fluently, the reader must be able to recognize high-frequency words quickly and accurately. According to Cunningham and Allington (2011),

> It is critical to reading comprehension because of the attention factor. Our brains can attend to a limited number of things at a time. If most of our attention is focused on decoding the words, there is little attention left for the comprehension part of reading. (p. 49)

Developing fluency with diverse learners requires more support and careful attention to developing sight words as well as time for guided practice. They often need assistance to work on the rhythm, stress, and intonation of spoken Standard English as well as additional guidance to enhance their comprehension of text. For this reason, they need multiple opportunities to listen and speak in order to develop the patterns of Standard English.

Essential Strategy to Support Anchor Performance 4: Frequent Exposure and Practice to Identify High-Frequency Words and Read Aloud with Expression

Diverse learners need multiple opportunities to listen to stories as well as informational text read aloud to them, particularly in Grades 4 and 5, where such practices in elementary schools often wane. Students need to follow along in the text while they hear it being spoken with expression in order to absorb the sounds and rhythms of Standard English. They also need frequent opportunities to practice what they see and hear by rereading aloud passages both individually and chorally.

As with other Common Core anchor standards, the expectation for each grade level to meet this standard differs. Kindergarten children are expected to become increasingly aware of fluency skills to support their reading comprehension. First and second graders will read on-level text with understanding, accuracy, and expression, and will learn to self-correct and reread as necessary. Expectations for third, fourth, and fifth graders are similar to those for first and second, with the addition of being able to read both poetry and prose orally with accuracy.

General strategies to develop reading fluency include the use of predictable books that contain easily learned patterns for younger students to repeat. Poetry with predictable rhyming schemes or repetitive word patterns might be more suitable for older students. Additionally, the following strategies support students across grade levels in the development of their reading fluency.

Modified Guided Reading. Guided reading was first introduced as a part of a balanced literacy reading program or Four-Blocks framework (Cunningham, Hall, & Defee, 1991) that supports student reading using small-group instruction. Students participate in the group by reading the same text and are directed by the teacher with prompts, strategies, context clues, background knowledge, previewed vocabulary, and discussion of anything that may be unfamiliar related to the text. Guided reading is designed for students to transfer the skills and strategies they learn in the group to their independent reading; it supports students to become fluent, skilled readers.

Modified guided reading (Avalos, Plasencia, Chavez, & Rascón, 2007) was developed with English learners in mind, but we believe it is applicable with most diverse learners. It suggests an increase of the average time of a guided reading session to 30 minutes and the use of culturally relevant texts that connect both content and language structure to students' personal experiences. In addition, it advises teachers to read the text aloud rather than have students read silently to model reading fluency for diverse learners and have them "vocalize softly as they read the text" (p. 320). Modified guided reading also emphasizes vocabulary development as a key factor for building reading comprehension and fluency.

Readers Theatre. A strategy to develop reading fluency, Readers Theatre provides students the opportunity to read aloud from scripts in ways in which rereading is a large part of the activity. After a script is selected, students first engage in listening to the script read by the teacher and then participate in reading together through echo reading (teacher says a line and the students repeat it) and choral reading as a whole class to develop reading accuracy, prosody (rhythm, stress, and intonation), and overall fluency. Eventually, students are divided into small groups and assigned parts in the script, which can be altered according to students' language proficiency. For more information and step-by-step instructions for using this strategy, please see Chapter 3.

Movie Scripts. Children as well as some adults enjoy watching their favorite films over and over again. Take advantage of this inclination by using some of these films to develop reading fluency. Survey the class for their favorite movies and plan to show short scenes from them. Have the dialogue from these scenes prepared for students to read along as the film clip is shown. After showing the same scene several times, invite students to recreate the scene using the prepared scripts. Involve the whole class in rating students' individual performances by developing a simple rubric that evaluates reading fluency and expression.

Word Walls. In addition to supporting word analysis skills, building a word wall is an excellent strategy for learning high-frequency words. According to Cunningham and Allington (2011), "approximately 100 words make up half of the words we read and write" (p. 59), so it is most important for students to learn to read these words easily to build their reading fluency. For more about Word Walls, please see the information concerning strategies to support Anchor Performance 3 in this chapter.

ANTICIPATED OUTCOMES

The standards presented in this chapter will help diverse learners build the necessary foundational skills in reading to meet with academic success. Working with the accompanying strategies will foster students' understanding and ability with conventions of print, phonological awareness, word recognition, reading fluency, and other basic reading concepts. These foundational skills are an essential component to every reading program and need to be a particular focus of instruction to somewhat older struggling readers as well as those who lack English language proficiency. For this reason, upper elementary grade teachers need to set aside time in their schedule to develop foundational skills in their classes to reach all learners.

INSTRUCTIONAL CHALLENGES

Early acquisition of literacy skills is essential to school success. Yet diverse learners often have not had the opportunities to fully develop basic reading skills. When students from kindergarten through second grade are learning elemental concepts of literacy, some diverse learners are unable to totally grasp essential foundations of reading due to interrupted schooling, learning disabilities, and lack of proficiency in English. Teachers therefore need to tailor their instruction for these youngsters, particularly in third, fourth, and fifth grades to cultivate these underdeveloped skills.

Finding the time to individualize instruction to foster basic skills is another challenge for teachers. We recommend devising different classroom management techniques such as working with small, flexible groupings. A departure from full-class lessons will support teachers to differentiate instruction and create the necessary time for basic literacy learning to take place.

PROMISING CLASSROOM PRACTICES

Anna Owen, a first-grade teacher, combines a number of strategies to teach her students basic reading concepts. For one, she coteaches part of her day with the ESL teacher, Erin Gruwell. Together, they follow a Four-Blocks framework for their students' reading program, which helps to support the development of their cotaught lessons. Anna and Erin teach together a double period of literacy daily.

Their lesson generally begins with a Word Wall activity, which both Anna and Erin take turns leading. On Mondays, new Word Wall words are introduced. For this activity, students are asked to number a piece of paper from 1 to 6. As the new words are told one at a time, students are asked to spell the words as best they can, using their knowledge of letters and sounds. After all the new words are introduced, the correct spellings are revealed, and the words are then placed on the Word Wall. Students then practice the new words with an activity called *Clap, Snap, Stomp, and Cheer*, in which students spell words by clapping their hands, snapping their fingers, stomping their feet, and cheering each letter as the word is spelled. As the week progresses, other Word Wall activities take place daily such as *Guess the Covered Word* (see Anchor Performance 3) or *Pencil Tap* in which students use their pencils to tap out word wall words.

One of Erin's favorite Word Wall activities is *Be A Mind Reader*. Before the activity begins, she puts on a fancy-looking turban (a cloth turban that has been decorated with sequins and glitter) and instructs students to number a piece of paper from 1 to 5. Then she closes her eyes, touches her forehead with the tips of her right-hand fingers and says the following:

- *I'm thinking of a Word Wall word.*
- *It has four letters (hold up four fingers).*
- *The first sound you hear in the word is [g] (tell the sound not the letter).*
- *Last sound you hear in the word is [d].*
- *If you can read my mind, write the word next to number one on your paper (the word is later revealed to be good).*

The activity progresses until students have guessed all five words using the Word Wall.

After Word Wall activities, Anna and Erin generally divide the class into small groups for guided reading lessons and center activities, into pairs for partner reading, or the class remains together for a miniwriting lesson before writer's workshop begins. The framework of this type of literacy block supports diverse learners because not only do they have the attention of two teachers, they also have more opportunities for differentiate instruction with the varied activities presented for literacy learning.

COMMON CORE READING STANDARDS— (UN)COMMON REFLECTION QUESTIONS

1. How can we ensure that skills practice is embedded in meaningful texts so that students' decoding skills don't progress faster than their ability to comprehend complex text?

2. Since developing decoding skills, fluency in oral reading, and reading comprehension interact in complex ways, how can these three elements be effectively integrated into the same lessons using the same text so each element may help build and reinforce the other?

KEY RESOURCES

Professional Books

Cunningham, P. M. (2008). *Phonics they use: Words for reading and writing*. Boston, MA: Allyn & Bacon.

Cunningham, P. M., & Allington, R. L. (2011). *Classrooms that work: They can all read and write* (5th ed.). Boston, MA: Allyn & Bacon.

Cunningham, P. M., Hall, D. P., & Heggie, T. (2001). *Making words: Multi-level, hands-on phonics and spelling activities*. Columbus, OH: Good Apple.

Diller, D. (2003). *Literacy work stations: Making centers work*. Portland, ME: Stenhouse.

Israel, S. E. (2008). *Early reading first and beyond: A guide to building early literacy skills*. Thousand Oaks, CA: Corwin.

Nevills, P., & Wolfe, P. (2009). *Building the reading brain: PreK–3* (2nd ed.). Thousand Oaks, CA: Corwin.

Online Resources

- Choral Reading
  http://www.readingrockets.org/strategies/choral_reading/
- Foundations for Literacy: Canadian Language and Literacy Network
  http://foundationsforliteracy.cllrnet.ca/index.php/Foundations_For_Literacy
- Modified Guided Reading
  http://centereducationpolicy.illinoisstate.edu/initiatives/ell/guidedreading.pdf
- Poetry for Children
  http://www.writersdigest.com/whats-new/poems-for-kids
- Reader's Workshop
  http://www.thelearningpad.net/readersworkshop.html
- Word Walls
  http://www.readingrockets.org/strategies/word_walls/
  http://www.teachnet.com/lesson/langarts/wordwall062599.html
- Working with Words
  http://www.wfu.edu/education/fourblocks/block4.htm
- Writing Center Menu
  http://01fa982.netsolhost.com/Centers/WritingMenu.pdf
- Writer's Workshop
  http://busyteacherscafe.com/literacy/writing_workshop.html
- Writer's Workshop Mini-lessons
  http://www.tooter4kids.com/classroom/possible_minilessons_for_writing.htm

6 Writing Strategies

Children want to write. They want to write the first day they attend school. This is no accident. Before they went to school they marked up walls, pavements, newspapers with crayons, chalk, pens or pencils . . . anything that makes a mark. The child's marks say, "I am."

—Donald Graves, 2003, p. 3

OVERVIEW

Many primary and elementary schools have a common writing program or follow a curriculum map or curriculum guide for writing which offers a scope and sequence of genres and skills that students at each grade level are expected to master. Whether your school has these resources available or not, the Common Core State Standards (CCSS) provide a framework for writing instruction to which all other initiatives could be aligned. When commenting on the CCSS and writing instruction in the opening chapter on *Finding the Pathway to the Common Core*, writers' workshop expert Lucy Calkins and her colleagues Mary Ehrenworth, and Christopher Lehman (2012) suggested that

> once students become fluent, fast, structured, and proficient writers across a range of genres, it is easy to take those skills on the road, using writing as a tool for thinking across all the disciplines. When students write across the curriculum, it not only escalates their engagement in other subjects but also makes teachers more accountable and more responsive. When students write about their fledgling understandings, teachers can't help but take students' ideas into account and to adapt instruction so that it has real traction. (p. 14)

The goal of this chapter is to offer numerous ideas on how to make the CCSS for writing meaningful and accessible for our not-so-common learners, so they, too, will grow to be *fluent, fast, structured, and proficient writers*.

WHY SCAFFOLDING AND EXPLICIT STRATEGY INSTRUCTION IMPROVE THE WRITING OF DIVERSE LEARNERS

We concur with Nancy Akhavan (2009), who observed that "writing is rarely taught. Writing is often *assigned*, but children are not taught *how* to write. Writing is often pulled apart into bits and pieces of skills but not taught as an integrated, organic process" (p. xii). Students who struggle at school will especially find writing tasks daunting when they are simply assigned to them without appropriate instruction. Based on reviewing current research, Goldenberg and Coleman (2010) pointed out that structured writing instruction and specific teacher or peer feedback has improved linguistically diverse students' writing. Supporting diverse learners as first they develop and then hone their writing skills through a variety of ways is imperative. Scaffolding is one critical way to offer the necessary support to all students in all English language arts (ELA) skill areas but especially to struggling writers. Though scaffolding has been previously discussed (see Chapter 4), here we quote Gibbons (2009), who identified its three major characteristics as follows:

> It is *temporary* help that assists a learner to move toward new concepts, levels of understanding, and new language.

> It enables a learner to know *how to do something* (not just what to do), so that they will be better able to complete similar tasks alone.

> It is *future oriented*: in Vygotsky's words, what a learner can do with support today, he or she will be able to do alone tomorrow. (p. 15)

Teaching writing—as one of the most challenging skills for diverse or struggling learners—then must focus on carefully designed temporary supports that could and should be adjusted and removed as students develop each new writing skill; it must be centered around the process of writing with ample opportunities for structured direct instruction and guided practice with revisions; and it must be developmentally appropriate and engaging while being progressively more and more challenging.

CORE WRITING STRATEGIES

The strategies contained in this chapter follow the expectations of the ten College and Career Readiness Anchor Standards (CCRAS) for writing. These standards are divided into four subcategories: (a) text types and purposes, which are designed to ensure that students know how to produce opinion and argument pieces, and that both informational and narrative writing structures are practiced; (b) production and distribution of writing, which focuses on the writing process and the product, as well as the use of technology across all genres; (c) research to build and present knowledge, which ensures that students learn to take an analytical approach to both literature and nonfiction; and finally (d) range of writing, which parallels a similar anchor standard for reading reminding teachers to expand the types of writing experiences students should have grade after grade (see Box 6.1). What is unique about this chapter is that it has its own organizational pattern—more than one essential strategy is presented for several anchor standards because of the broad reach of writing across literature and informational texts.

Box 6.1 College and Career Readiness Anchor Standards for Writing

Text Types and Purposes

1. Write arguments to support claims in an analysis of substantive topics or texts, using valid reasoning and relevant and sufficient evidence.

2. Write informative/explanatory texts to examine and convey complex ideas and information clearly and accurately through the effective selection, organization, and analysis of content.

3. Write narratives to develop real or imagined experiences or events using effective technique, well-chosen details, and well-structured event sequences.

Production and Distribution of Writing

4. Produce clear and coherent writing in which the development, organization, and style are appropriate to task, purpose, and audience. (Begins in Grade 3)

5. Develop and strengthen writing as needed by planning, revising, editing, rewriting, or trying a new approach.

(Continued)

(Continued)

6. Use technology, including the Internet, to produce and publish writing and to interact and collaborate with others.

Research to Build and Present Knowledge

7. Conduct short as well as more sustained research projects based on focused questions, demonstrating understanding of the subject under investigation.

8. Gather relevant information from multiple print and digital sources, assess the credibility and accuracy of each source, and integrate the information while avoiding plagiarism.

9. Draw evidence from literary or informational texts to support analysis, reflection, and research. (Begins in Grade 4)

Range of Writing

10. Write routinely over extended time frames (time for research, reflection, and revision) and shorter time frames (a single sitting or a day or two) for a range of tasks, purposes, and audiences. (Begins in Grade 3)

Text Types and Purposes

Anchor Performance 1: State Opinion in Writing While Offering Age-Appropriate Reasons

Though Anchor Standard 1 listed in Box 6.1 identifies writing arguments, in the K–5 classroom, a critical CCSS-based anchor performance is formulating opinions and offering acceptable explanations for those beliefs. Students might be able to express simple likes and dislikes commonly associated with everyday choices, but they frequently need guided, carefully structured learning activities to be able to communicate more complex ideas orally and to put their thoughts into writing using academic language.

Essential Strategy #1 to Support Anchor Performance 1: Opinion Choice Prompts

Below we present a number of brief strategies that are structured and scaffolded, may be directly connected to the topic or text the class is exploring, and frequently tied to enhancing other language skills, such as reading, listening, or speaking. Important word of caution: have students share what they have written, so they can see "(1) that writing is part of learning, (2) that such writing assignments are integral to the lesson and not merely busywork, and (3) that what they write is valued" (Walling, 2009, p. 19).

Scaffolded Opinion Chart. When students seem to be stuck on simply stating an option but are not readily able to elaborate, model the three steps in Table 6.1 and also offer this scaffolded opinion chart for students to see how to organize their ideas surrounding a target topic or text. This makes a great classroom poster as well to remind students on how to contribute a more thoughtful answer to some questions!

Table 6.1 Scaffolded Opinion Chart

1. What do you think?	Opinion
2. Why do you think so?	Reasons
3. How do you know it?	Evidence

Take a Stand. At the completion of a lesson or after having read and discussed a text that presents multiple perspectives, provide students with a list of Agree–Disagree prompts. Invite them to select one to which they will respond by (a) *taking a stand* at a designated area in the classroom (one wall or corner can be labeled *Agree*, the other *Disagree*), (b) sharing their own arguments and listening to their classmates' ideas, or (c) responding in writing by using sentence stems and word boxes. Box 6.2 has some possible prompts about friendship appropriate for second graders:

Box 6.2 Agree–Disagree Prompts About Friendship

Friends have to tell everything to each other.

You cannot have more than one best friend.

Friends are forever.

The only way to have a friend is to be one.

Anticipation Guide Extensions. As we discussed in Chapter 4, anticipation guides help build student interest about a subject, establish a purpose for reading, and tap into learners' prior knowledge. As students agree or disagree with a few carefully written anticipation guide statements that are closely aligned to the upcoming lesson or text, they get a quick preview of what is about to be taught. For oral language development, Doug Fisher, Nancy Frey, and Carol Rothenberg (2008) suggested that students read the statements individually and also discuss them with a partner. To connect these anticipatory guides to writing, have students write a brief explanation for their choices. Ask them to revisit the guide at the end of the unit or lesson to note any changes in their thinking. At this time, they may write a statement explaining the change in their thinking and cite evidence from the text (see samples in Box 6.3).

Box 6.3 Anticipation Guide Extension Samples

Now I know that wolves are good parents because they take care of their young.

First I thought wolves were very dangerous, but I learned that they almost never attack humans.

Essential Strategy #2 to Support Anchor Performance 1: Questionnaires and Surveys

In order to engage students in authentic writing experiences, introduce questionnaires and surveys as a genre. First, have students respond to teacher-generated questionnaires based on a text or a topic studied in class (see Box 6.4).

As a next step, create questionnaires and surveys collaboratively as a class or in small groups. Finally, engage students in pair-work activities to share questions and answers to their questionnaires. A sample questionnaire generated in a kindergarten class looks like this:

1. *Do you have any pets?*

2. *What kind of pet is it?*

Box 6.4 Sample Topics

Kindergarten

Family life

Animals and pets

Fire safety

Feelings

Seasons

Holidays

Senses

Grades 1–2

Classroom and school rules

Families and responsibilities

Neighborhoods and communities

Likes and dislikes

Wants and needs

School areas, personnel, and activities

Use of resources and recycling

Grades 3–5

Foods and nutrition

Cross-cultural experiences

Goods and services

Health and safety

Needs of groups, societies, and cultures

Weather patterns

Source: Based on the *English Language Proficiency Standards for English Language Learners in Pre-Kindergarten through Grade 5* (WIDA, 2007)

3. *Where did your pet come from?*

4. *How do you take care of the pet?*

Anchor Performance 2: Write Informative/Explanatory Texts Related to Grade-Appropriate Content

Before students are ready to generate their own informational texts, they need to see clearly the difference between expository and narrative texts (compare Anchor Standards 2 and 3). Karen Donohue and Nanda Reddy (2006) suggested using structured minilessons during which students complete a series of *prompt dissections* to better understand how prompts help writers approach the task successfully.

During the prompt dissection portion of a writing lesson, explicitly teach students that a writing prompt typically has three parts: "The first part tells the topic: the No-Brainer. The second part asks you to think: the Brain. The last part tells you exactly what to do: the Boss" (p. 11). For example, take the following prompt and analyze it using the three-part dissection method:

> *In some schools, students are forbidden to use any personal electronic devices. Imagine that the school board of your district is considering the use of cell phones, iPods, iPads and other gadgets during school hours. Write a five-paragraph essay either supporting or opposing the idea of using personal electronic devices at school for learning.*

You will probably produce the following structural analysis or dissection with your students:

No Brainer:

In some schools, students are forbidden to use any personal electronic devices.

The Brain:

Imagine that the school board of your district is considering the use of cell phones, iPods, iPads, and other gadgets during school hours.

The Boss:

Write a five-paragraph essay either supporting or opposing the idea of using personal electronic devices at school for learning.

To further enhance students' skills regarding understanding of expository and narrative writing, generate a *prompt differentiation* chart and display it as a poster to remind students about the characteristics of these two types of writing (see Table 6.2).

Table 6.2 Prompt Differentiation Summary Chart

With Expository Writing, you will	With Narrative Writing, you will
Explain or describe something.	Tell a story.
Discuss real life.	Pretend or make believe something happened.
Tell what you would do.	Discuss what happened.
List information or reasons in any order; you choose the order.	Tell something in the order it happened.

Source: Adapted from *180 Days to Successful Writers: Lessons to Prepare Your Students for Standardized Assessments and for Life* by Karen Donohue and Nanda N. Reddy, 2006. Thousand Oaks, CA: Corwin.

Essential Strategy #1 to Support Anchor Performance 2: Writing Power

Many readers might be familiar with Fearn and Farnan's (2001) *power writing* defined as "a structured free-write where the objective is quantity alone" (p. 501), which is an excellent strategy for building writing fluency and overcoming writer's block and fear of writing. In contrast, what we mean by *writing power* is a group of scaffolding techniques in which teachers use published, high quality texts as models for student writing, thus *empowering* students to express their ideas at the word, sentence, paragraph, and text level based on their grade, readiness, and language proficiency levels.

A power word is the most important word in a sentence, paragraph, or even a text. After some modeling and lots of think-alouds, invite students to find one power word in informational text titles, in introductory sentences, and later in carefully selected short paragraphs. We have found that—with lots of practice—a *really powerful* power word gets a close to unanimous vote by any group of children! Identifying *power words* teach students to use essential words or precise academic vocabulary in their own writing as well.

A power sentence is a student-friendly definition or summary account that often follows an established pattern. A power sentence can frequently be derived from the text. It may be the topic sentence or summary statement that also tends to offer a good linguistic model for analyzing and imitating. Alternately, the teacher may model sample sentences following a pattern and students collaboratively—and later independently—write their own power sentences about the text or topic (see samples in Box 6.5).

Box 6.5 Power Sentence Samples

Sentence Frames

(Verb+ing) IS _____ BECAUSE _____.

(Verb+ing) + noun phrase IS ADJECTIVE BECAUSE _____.

Examples:

Playing with matches is dangerous because they can cause fire.

Having a fire safety plan at home is helpful because it can save lives.

Reading about fire safety is important because you learn fire safety tips.

A power paragraph is a well-constructed paragraph students will create from a target text. After selecting a model paragraph, subject it to student analysis both for content and paragraph development and allow students to see the choices the author made and can emulate in their own writing. Model writing a paragraph on a different topic using the same language patterns in the paragraph. Guide students to write sentences using a part of the paragraph. Finally, have students write a paragraph of their own. See if you can guess where the power paragraph that *empowered* this student to write so well came from in Box 6.6?

Box 6.6 A Student-Generated Excerpt Based on a Power Paragraph

The most important thing about my mom is that she goes out of her way to make things fun for me. When we go to the shopping mall or TJ Maxx (my mom's favorite store) she knows that I don't like staying there too long so she lets me look for cool stuff. In the store I look for cool things alone because sometimes I find a computer game for ten dollars that is worth fifty. She turns shopping for food into a game, where I find things in the supermarket like hot dogs and soy sauce. But the most important thing about my mom is that she goes out of her way to make things fun for me. (Lee, 5th grade student)

If the structure of the sample paragraph written by Lee, a multilingual fifth grader seems familiar, it is because prior to completing this writing assignment, the class read and studied the craft and structure of a classic, *The Important Book* by Margaret Wise Brown (1949), and it was used as a mentor text to guide the student's writing. Here is the first page of that book:

> The important thing about a spoon is that you eat with it. It's like a little shovel, you hold it in your hand, you can put it in your mouth, it isn't flat, it's hollow, and it spoons things up. But the important thing about a spoon is that you eat with it.

Power texts come from high quality authentic resources that are both engaging in content and language, as well as presentation: Select an age-appropriate complete text such as an article published in *Scholastic News* (http://classroommagazines.scholastic.com). *Times for Kids* (www.timeforkids.com/), *Big Backyard or Ranger Rick* (www.nwf.org), or *National Geographic Kids* (http://kids.nationalgeographic.com/kids). On a large chart paper or on the SMARTBoard, work collaboratively as a class or in smaller groups to generate a visual representation of the entire text by mapping out both the main ideas the author presented in the article and the structure of how those ideas were organized.

First seeing the text structure as a skeleton or frame with the majority of the text removed and then imitating the text structure will allow students to understand the explicit organization of the text and will also prepare them "to write like an investigative reporter" (Coleman, 2011, p. 4). See Box 6.7 for a Power text sample based on a *National Geographic Kids* article on "Winter Celebrations" (n.d.). Each subheading and the first sentence of each paragraph are given in the box to show that this article is organized by listing (and elaborating on) each of the major or most commonly known winter holidays alphabetically to avoid bias or preferential treatment.

Box 6.7 Power Text Sample Based on "Winter Celebrations"

Winter Celebrations

Chinese New Year

Chinese New Year is the most important of the traditional Chinese holidays.

Christmas

Christmas is celebration of the birth of Jesus Christ.

(Continued)

(Continued)

Eid Al Adha, the Festival of the Sacrifice

Eid Al Adha is celebrated by Muslims on the 10th day of the month Dhu al-Hijjah of the lunar calendar.

Hanukkah

Jewish people celebrate Hanukkah, a holiday honoring the Maccabees victory over King Antiochus.

Kwanzaa

From December 26 to January 1, Kwanzaa is celebrated. It is a holiday to commemorate African heritage.

New Year's Day

New Year's Day is the first day of the year in the Gregorian calendar on January 1.

Three Kings Day

At the end of the Twelve Days of Christmas comes a day called the Epiphany, or Three Kings Day.

Winter Solstice

The Winter Solstice occurs around December 21st. It is the shortest day of the year.

Essential Strategy #2 to Support Anchor Performance 2: Visual Frameworks for Expository Writing

Getting students ready for writing and helping them plan their work is a critical step to success. Visual frameworks, select graphic organizers, or manipulatives can aid in the writing process by offering the necessary support for all students.

Fact Strips. Students can organize information they have gleaned from nonfiction text by completing Fact Strips (Florida Center for Reading Research, 2005). After reviewing the text that was shared or read independently, invite students to write the topic in the first box. Next, have them identify key facts (see Figure 6.1), each of which they can write or illustrate separately in the remainder of the squares.

Figure 6.1 Fact Strip About Washington, DC

Washington, DC	Washington is the capital of the United States.	It does not belong to any state.	It is the home of the federal government.	The President lives here.

Fact Cards. Distribute index cards to students to record one important fact per card. Have them read their cards in pairs. After they agree on five (more or less) facts about the topic, have them arrange the cards so they could collaboratively write a summary using the cards as scaffolds.

Time lines. Following a read-aloud or shared-reading session, have students summarize the key events by first mapping the sequence on a scaffolded time line. For example, *A Thanksgiving Story* by Jane Hollander (1991) would have the following simple time line to aid students in organizing their ideas and jotting down key notes connected to each season (see Figure 6.2).

Figure 6.2 Time Line for *A Thanksgiving Story*

| Winter | Spring | Summer | Fall |

After reading the biography *Who Was Rosa Parks?* by Yona Zeldis McDonough (2010), have students review the key events in Rosa Parks's life and create an annotated time line of the major details. Based on the readings, students develop a concise biography offering facts and concrete details, quotations, or other relevant information and examples. A partially completed time line is shown in Figure 6.3.

Summary Chart. A summary chart assists students in categorizing all key ideas related to a topic and supporting details and aids them in developing language chunks into complete sentences and paragraphs (see Figure 6.4).

Signal Word Poster. A poster-size version of the chart presented in Figure 6.5—based on Barbara Moss's (2004) work—offers a quick reference to the five most common expository text structures, their definitions, the most frequently occurring signal words, and the most common graphic organizers associated with each. A printable version of this poster maybe used in the students' writer's notebook or in the writing center to remind them of the differences found in the five genres.

Figure 6.3 A Partially Completed Time Line for *Who Was Rosa Parks?*

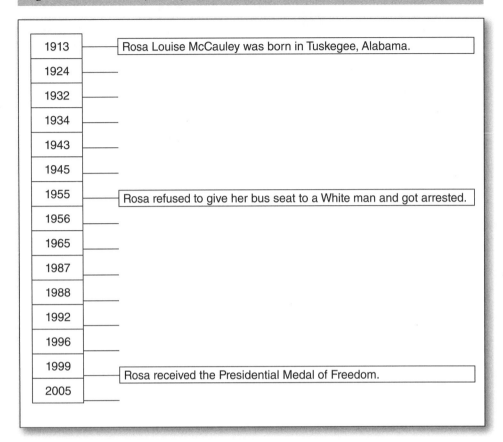

1913	Rosa Louise McCauley was born in Tuskegee, Alabama.
1924	
1932	
1934	
1943	
1945	
1955	Rosa refused to give her bus seat to a White man and got arrested.
1956	
1965	
1987	
1988	
1992	
1996	
1999	Rosa received the Presidential Medal of Freedom.
2005	

Figure 6.4 Partially Completed Summary Chart on Climate Change

	Main Idea The Greenhouse Effect	Main Idea Extreme Weather	Main Idea Possible Solutions
Details	Pollution adds carbon dioxide to the air	Heat waves, droughts	
Details	Cutting down trees Burning rain forests	Blizzards and extreme cold weather	
Details	Heat is trapped in the atmosphere	Dangerous tornadoes and hurricanes Heavy downpours and flooding	

Figure 6.5 Signal Word Poster

Expository Text Structures, Definitions, Cue Words, and Graphic Organizers			
Pattern	**Description**	**Cue Words (Signal Words)**	**Graphic Organizer**
Description	To describe a topic by listing characteristics, features, attributes, and examples	• for example • characteristics • for instance • such as • is like	
Sequence	To list items or events in numerical or chronological sequence	• first • second • third • later • next	1. _____ 2. _____ 3. _____ 4. _____
Comparison	To present how two or more events, concepts, theories, or things are alike and/or different	• however • nevertheless • on the other hand • but • similarly	Topic 1 | Similarities | Topic 2
Cause and Effect	To present ideas, events in time, or facts as causes and the resulting effect(s) or facts that happen as a result of an event	• reasons why • as a result • therefore • because • consequently	Effect 1 / Cause / Effect 2
Problem and Solution	To show the development of a problem and one or more solutions	• problem is • dilemma is • if/then • because • so that	Problem → Solution

Anchor Performance 3: Write Narratives About Real or Imaginary Events and Use Descriptive Writing

Although most students have had considerably more experience writing personal narratives and developing their writing skills through descriptive genre, struggling learners and English learners will continue to rely on scaffolding techniques to perform these writing tasks successfully until they have had ample practice and success.

Essential Strategy #1 to Support Anchor Performance 3: Visual Frameworks for Narrative Writing

Similar to Anchor Performance 2 above, visual frameworks also support learners as they develop their narrative and descriptive writing skills. These frameworks assist students in determining pertinent details to include in their writing and in presenting story events in a logical fashion. Select graphic organizers that match the narrative and descriptive genres are presented below.

Sequencing Flowcharts. Flow charts are effective graphic organizers to represent the order or sequence of events. Pictures, key words, short phrases, or sentences may be used depending on the students' readiness and language proficiency levels. A sequencing activity can easily be created on an interactive whiteboard: it will allow students to move around and order events on the board and indicate the beginning, middle, and end of a story by manipulating language chunks on the whiteboard. Alternately, they can also be challenged to figure out the order of a more detailed sequence of events. See http://exchange .smarttech.com for numerous ready-to-go examples created by fellow educators. Figures 6.6 and 6.7 are examples of a vertical and a horizontal flowchart.

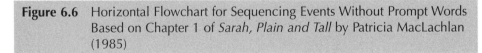

Figure 6.6 Horizontal Flowchart for Sequencing Events Without Prompt Words Based on Chapter 1 of *Sarah, Plain and Tall* by Patricia MacLachlan (1985)

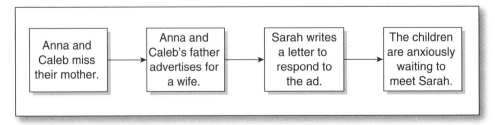

Figure 6.7 Vertical Flowchart for Sequencing Events with Prompt Words

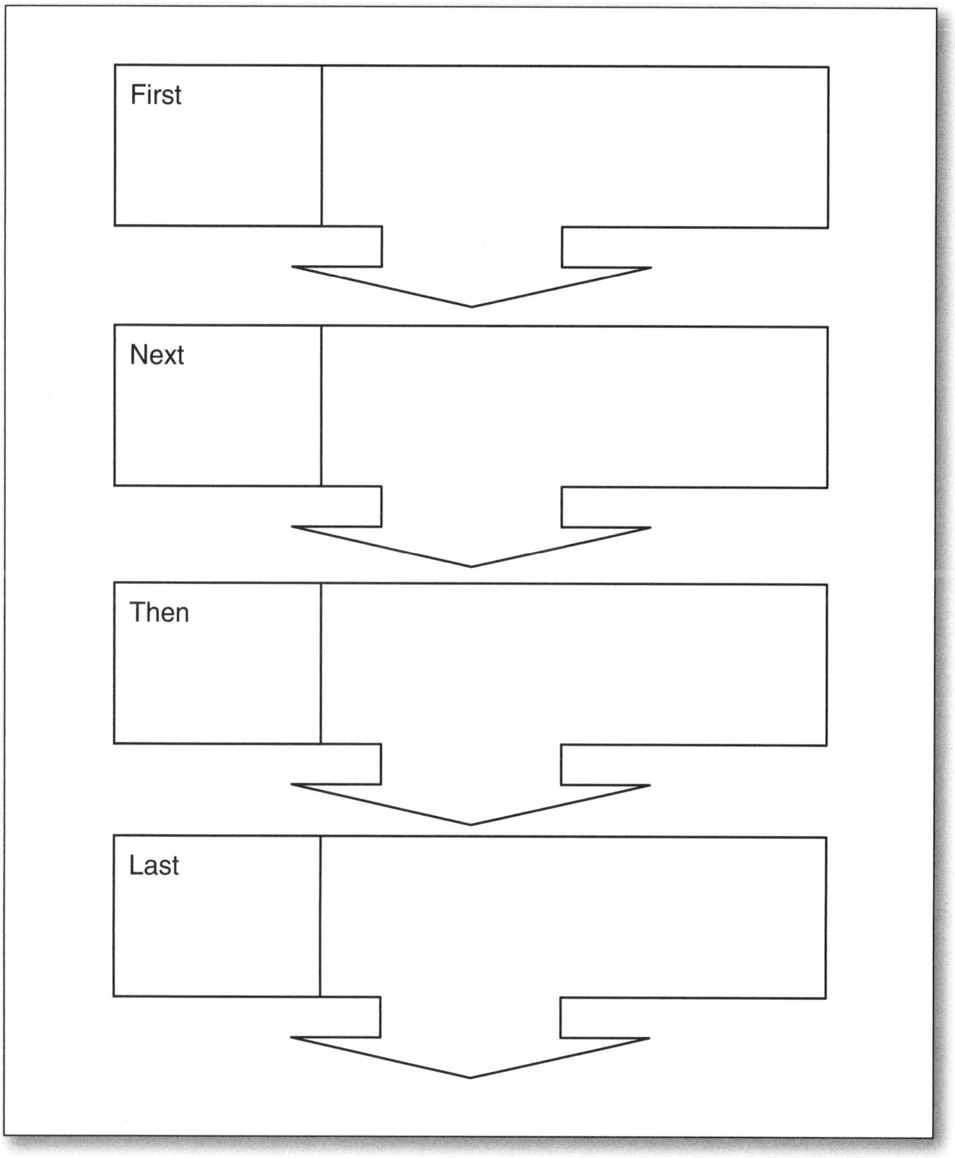

First

Next

Then

Last

Story Lines (Time Lines). To encourage students to see the sequence of events in historical fiction or chapter books, have them map the story on a time line showing the key dates (or times) and abbreviated events associated with each time segment. For example, a kindergarten-first grade favorite of ours, *Jasper's Beanstalk* by Nick Butterworth and Mick Inkpen (2008), would have the following time line (see Figure 6.8):

Figure 6.8 Time Line for *Jasper's Beanstalk*

Monday	Tuesday	Wednesday	Thursday	Friday	Saturday	Sunday	Monday

Story Maps. Also referred to as story grammar, story maps (see Figure 6.9) contain the key elements of narratives: characters, setting, conflict, sequence of events, and resolution. When presented visually and used frequently, students recognize and remember the essential components of narrative texts more easily and are therefore better able to plan their own writing.

Figure 6.9 Story Map Template

Characters	
Setting	
Conflict	
Sequence of Events	
Resolution	

Essential Strategy #2 to Support Anchor Performance 3: Multisensory Writing

We agree with Fitch and Swartz (2008), who claimed "those who teach poetry with passion and joy know it is one of the richest learning experiences students can have. We journey to worlds and peer into spaces in our hearts and minds and soul through poetry" (p. 4). Writing a multisensory poem based on factual information is one such rewarding experience. Have students work in groups to create lists or thematic word maps related to what they see, hear, taste, feel (touch), and smell during a particular season, holiday, or on a field trip. Generating a sensory chart (a five-column graphic organizer) would also work as a prewriting activity to prepare students for developing a descriptive paragraph or a highly sophisticated poem as illustrated in Box 6.8.

Box 6.8 A Collaboratively Written, Scaffolded, Sensory Poem*

How to Write a Scaffolded Sensory Poem

Present a topic (such as summer in this example) and have students work in groups to brainstorm nouns and adjectives associated with the season. Have them jot down the words and phrases that come to mind or create thematic word maps. Begin the shared writing experience by completing five sentence starters (I see . . . ; I hear . . . ; I feel . . . ; I smell . . . : I taste . . .). The final line—*I know summer is here*—should be given. Create simple sentences by using only two nouns per line from the thematic word maps leaving blanks for editing, so the first draft of your poem should look like this:

I see	*fireflies*	*and*	*gardens*
I hear	*seagulls*	*and*	*waves*
I feel	*sand*	*and*	*sunburn*
I smell	*sunblock*	*and*	*BBQs*
I taste	*ice cream*	*and*	*watermelon*

I know summer is here!

After completing this initial first draft, follow up with three additional steps: First, select appropriate adjectives to describe each noun (*I see bright fireflies and colorful gardens, etc.*). Then add adverbials to elaborate on the location or present participles to offer details (*I see bright fireflies flickering and colorful gardens blooming, or I feel hot sand between my toes and itchy sunburn on my shoulders, etc.*). Finally, remove the sentence starters and produce the following sensory-rich poem filled with sophisticated language chunks:

Bright fireflies flickering and colorful gardens blooming

Hungry seagulls yapping and big waves crashing

Hot sand between my toes and itchy sunburn on my shoulders

Coconut sunblock in the air and yummy BBQs in the backyard

Chocolate ice cream on my tongue and juicy watermelon dripping down my arm

Summer is here!

---

*Note: Special thanks to the Patchogue-Medford first-grade teachers who collaborated on this poem and gave permission to include it here.

Essential Strategy #3 to Support Anchor Performance 3: Identity Text

Most struggling students need to develop personal connections to academic literacy tasks to make meaning from difficult content and to be motivated. To this end, Calkins et al. (2012) analyzed not just what is in the CCSS but also what is missing from the document. They concluded that "Common Core deemphasizes reading as a personal act and emphasizes textual analysis" (p. 24), thus placing text-to-self connections, accessing or building students' prior knowledge, exploring personal responses, or relating the reading to one's own life into less prominent position. Considering diverse learners' needs to make personal connections to text, Jim Cummins (2001), a strong proponent of a powerful, personally meaningful literacy project, suggested that students be invited to generate written, spoken, visual, musical, or multimodal artifacts for what he refers to as identity texts—*cognitive engagement and identity investment.* Since students invest their identities in them, they write or produce multimedia texts about their cultural identities and take ownership and great pride in these products. See www.multiliteracies.ca or Jim Cummins and Margaret Early's (2011) edited volume *Identity Texts: The Collaborative Creation of Power in Multilingual Schools* for examples.

We would like to remind our readers that they need to reach beyond the Common Core—the CCSS are the basics; "they focus on what is most essential, they do not describe all that can and should be taught: A great deal is left to the discretion of teachers and curriculum developers" (CCSS, 2010, p. 6). Infusing students' cultural capital is one such area where we believe educators can and should go beyond what is in the standards.

Production and Distribution of Writing

Anchor Performance 4: Produce a Written Response With Grade-Appropriate Organization and Development

With carefully planned guidance and support from teachers, students are expected to produce writing that shows the development and organization of ideas that are appropriate for the assigned task and the purpose of the written work. Since the CCSS also emphasizes the need for support and guidance, we concur that many youngsters may not be able to achieve this without outside help initially.

Essential Strategy to Support Anchor Performance 4: Scaffolding Writing Tasks

Scaffolding writing can take numerous forms and can offer various degrees of support. One purpose of scaffolding instruction might focus on the actual outcome or product of the writing, thus offering students fully or partially developed examples at the sentence, paragraph, and text level. Another approach to scaffolding writing instruction assists students with the entire writing process.

Sentence Starters With or Without Word-Level Support. For producing written responses at the sentence level, have students complete sentence starters either independently or with additional support using mentor texts, word lists, glossaries, word walls, or word boxes.

Paragraph Frames and Essay Outlines. Another way to scaffold student expository writing is by offering them paragraph frames or essay outlines that will help students further their understanding of the most frequently encountered expository text patterns, which include: (a) description; (b) sequence, (d) compare-contrast; (e) cause-effect, and (f) problem-solution—or narrative text. For example, to help students present the steps in a science experiment, the following paragraph frame could be used (see more examples in Jean Pottle's [1998] *Writing Frames*):

In today's science experiment, there were three important steps. First, ___

_____

_____ *. Second,* _____

_____*.*

Last, _____

_____*. These three steps*

*allowed us to see how*_____

_____*.*

Guided Writing. In order to assist students with most-needed writing strategies, guided writing lessons give small groups of students or whole classes the time to craft their writing with teacher guidance. Sharan Gibson (2008) suggested conducting a guided writing lesson in four steps: (1) start with a brief shared experience and discussion, (2) introduce a writing strategy, (3) offer students time to write a new text based on the shared experience and the new strategy with immediate teacher guidance, and (4) leave time for students to share their work.

Collaborative Text-writing. Nancy Cloud, Fred Genesee, and Else Hamayan (2009) recommended using the text structure found in a story shared in class to conduct collaborative text writing. Students are invited to work together to produce their own stories in small groups on chart paper. Students may illustrate sections of their writing and sign their names to show shared ownership of the writing.

Anchor Performance 5: Edit and Revise Written Work

Students who are not yet proficient writers will rarely know how to edit and revise their own work. To prepare them for such a challenging task, model how you edit and revise your own writing and gradually release the responsibility to students through guided and collaborative practice (Fisher & Frey, 2008).

Essential Strategy #1 to Support Anchor Performance 5: Explicit Instruction in the Editing and Revising Steps of the Writing Process Through Modeling and Guided Support

The expectations for students to engage in the writing process expand across all grade levels; kindergarten through fifth-grade learners are all expected to plan, revise, and edit their written work. What varies is the level of independence and the complexity of revisions and edits that are required. To help diverse learners become successful with the writing process, they need explicit instructions in each step of the process, with special emphasis on the revising and editing steps.

Write Aloud. Similar to read-alouds and think alouds, the purpose of *writing aloud* for and with students is to model the entire writing process by showing not only the thoughts that go into planning the written piece but also how a writer handles false starts, rewrites, reading and revising at the word, sentence, paragraph, and text level. Such modeling will help develop metacognitive awareness in students about the editing and revising process.

Interactive Editing. Similar to interactive writing defined as "an instructional context in which a teacher shares a pen—literally and figuratively—with a group of children as they collaboratively compose and construct a written message" (McCarrier, Pinnell, & Fountas, 2000, p. 4), interactive editing allows for collaborative rereading of the group-written piece, while checking for meaning and form, looking for errors in conventions, and editing or revising at the word, sentence, or text level.

Feed Forward. After modeling writing in the target genre, allow students to work in small groups to generate similar drafts collaboratively. The collaboration may take place in various forms: students can produce one piece of writing on a large piece of paper, or each write their own versions of the written piece. During the process, circulate the room and teach on purpose, offer immediate personalized assistance—or *feed forward*—to each student or group in anticipation of what they might be struggling with. Feed forward can take any of the following shapes: remind students of writing strategies you previously introduced, guide them with word choice, help with sentence structure, offer transition words choices, and so on.

Rubrics and Checklists. Use editing and revising tools, such as checklists and rubrics that are age and grade appropriate and are written at the students' cognitive and linguistic levels. Best way to approach implementing the use of such tools is to collaboratively generate them with your students. Franklin (2005) proposed placing the set of child-generated criteria on a poster that hangs on the wall throughout the year. The example developed by her class reads as follows:

> *"Excellent writing . . .*
> - *has lots of details*
> - *puts a picture in your head*
> - *is really exciting or interesting*
> - *makes you feel like you are there*
> - *tells exactly*
> - *is easy to read" (para. 11).*

For sample rubrics and for templates to develop your own rubrics, see one of these sites: www.rubrics4teachers.com/ or www.teachnology.com/web_tools/rubrics/.

Essential Strategy #2 to Support Anchor Performance 5: Prepare Students to Engage in Self- and Peer-Editing Tasks

When students learn to edit their own writing, they develop increased awareness of how well their ideas are developed and how closely they have observed writing conventions. Focusing on specific features helps students become more self-directed, independent learners and more confident writers. Peer editing helps create both a community of engaged writers and a supportive learning environment in which mistakes are accepted and feedback and comments are welcome.

Self-assessment/Reflection Tools. Make self-assessment and reflection on students' own writing a regular practice. Start with star stickers or star-shaped Post-it notes and have students attach their stickers to a section (sentence or paragraph) that contains a *stellar idea*. Move on to creating self-reflection checklists such as the one in Figure 6.10.

Figure 6.10 3-2-1 Self-Assessment Reflection Tool

3 ideas I successfully expressed
2 ideas/sections I improved upon with a friend's help
1 idea I still need to work on

Peer Feedback. At the K–5 level, teachers could invite students to comment on any aspect of each other's writing—idea development, organization, conventions—as long as students have had explicit instruction, ample modeling, and readily available, appropriate sentence starters on how to offer constructive feedback. Additionally, see examples in Adele Fiderer's (1998; 1999) two books, *35 Rubrics & Checklists to Assess Reading and Writing (Grades K–2)* and *40 Rubrics & Checklists to Assess Reading and Writing (Grades 3–6)*, which offer some helpful assessment tools both for self- and peer-editing.

Anchor Performance 6: Use Computers or Digital Devices to Register Ideas

Information technology standards are incorporated into the CCSS, so students will be expected to use computers and web-based resources as well as other nonprint-based media to access information and to communicate their own ideas. Though technology and digital devices are more and more widely available, do not assume that all children have easy, routine access to them outside the school. Familiarize your students with technology since many ELLs or students living in poverty may not have had access to digital devices, even though they are often labeled the digital natives (Prensky, 2010). If you give homework assignments that require access to computers, make sure there are accommodations made (use of library, after school access to computer lab, etc.) so all students will be able to complete the task. Yet, other learners might have multiple digital devices and advance computer skills; thus preassessing students' level of access and experience with computers and digital technology is essential.

Essential Strategy to Support Anchor Performance 6: Provide Access to Technology

Based on the preassessment data, we suggest that you not only use the existing classroom computers, the school computer lab, and the digital devices available in the school library, but also teach students about the available resources in their communities (such as the local library). Also, advocate for lending technology to students; if you work on grant proposals, make sure you include allocations for building up technology resources to enhance all students' chances for using technology. Finally, initiate a COW (Computers on Wheels) program, which consists of a class set of laptops on a cart that may be shared by multiple members of the faculty as teachers sign up for computer use regularly.

Research to Build and Present Knowledge

Anchor Performance 7: Participate in a Grade-Appropriate Research Project

Whether completed as a shared endeavor or, in the upper grades as an independent task, gathering and organizing information for a research project may be rather challenging for most K–5 students, thus initially they will need opportunities to work under your guidance and collaboratively with classmates.

Essential Strategy to Support Anchor Performance 7: Collaborative Writing Projects

Collaboration is one key strategy that is anticipated to permeate all literacy instruction. Developing group writing tasks will not only make writing instruction more engaging but it will also help develop a critical 21st century skill, which is collaboration.

Collaborative Collages. Young learners will benefit greatly by participating in an authentic learning experience, such as a neighborhood walk, a visit to the local fire department, or a trip to the supermarket. Supplemented with student-or-teacher-gathered library or Internet-based research or interview data, these activities can be followed by a collaborative writing activity that also invites artistic expression. Have your students contribute pictures, photographs they have taken, diagrams, written descriptions, and so on to a collaborative collage. It may be planned as a whole group or small group project. Christy Hale (2006) suggested "the diverse buildings, people, and activities portrayed will inspire young writers to rich explorations of point of view" (p. 21). Similar projects may focus on the school building itself, a field trip location such as the zoo or farm, or any hands-on science experiments.

Class Books. Students of any age may successfully participate in a collaboratively developed book project, which invites each student to contribute one page. The structure and contents of the class book may be modeled on a shared reading experience (e.g., Who cares about the weather?) or a content-based topic study (rainforest animals, animals and their habitats, etc.).

Group Explorations. Author, topic, and genre studies lend themselves to a guided group-research activity, in which the entire class or smaller groups of students read a selection of related books or other materials by the same author, on the same topic, or written in the same genre. As a follow up, students collaboratively generate a report to summarize and evaluate their experiences. To support the collaborative writing process, students could either work in a jigsaw fashion, where each person is responsible for a well-defined portion of the project, or specific roles must be assigned (cover designer, reporter, illustrator, editor). Helen Hoffner (2010) made a point to connect literacy activities not only to standards but to students' communities as well. A group exploration she suggested is called the Hometown History Project, with the following three possible objectives:

1. The students will gather facts about their hometowns by consulting print and electronic references as well as by interviewing residents.

2. The students will write a report about an interesting building.

3. The students will write a work of historic fiction set in the local area. (p. 12)

Group explorations also allow for students' funds of knowledge and expertise to be recognized and nurtured—acknowledging that there might be a disconnect between the taught curriculum and the students' own knowledge. Students bring varied backgrounds and knowledge bases to the class that should be valued and utilized. A word of caution: cooperative group structures must be explicitly taught and practiced for students to work together well. (See, for example, Kagan, S.[1994] *Cooperative, learning*. San Clemente, CA: Kagan Publishing).

Anchor Performance 8: Take Notes and Organize Information

Jane D. Hill and Kathleen M. Flynn (2006) recommended three critical research-based note-taking strategies for diverse, multilevel classrooms:

1. Offer students teacher-prepared notes to model good note-taking and to differentiate based on students' language proficiency level.

2. Introduce and practice a variety of note-taking formats such as webs, outlines, and combination notes that contain both words and images.

3. When using combination notes, demonstrate how to use linguistic and nonlinguistic notations to ensure student comprehension, organization, and retention of key information.

Essential Strategy to Support Anchor Performance 8: Structured Note-Taking

Note-taking is one of several essential skills that cannot be expected to develop without appropriate instruction and scaffolded support. If left to their own devices, some students may write down everything they hear or copy from the target text extensively without sorting relevant and nonessential information. Others may randomly select details that might not be instrumental for content area learning. Structured note-taking, on the other hand, helps all learners to develop the skill of selecting the main ideas and important details, synthesizing some essential points while omitting the less essential ones, and being able to gather just the right amount information to work independently on a subsequent task.

Field Notes. During field trips and other authentic learning experiences, such as science experiments or school building tours visiting less frequently seen parts of the building (boiler room, etc.), students should be invited to observe their environment, describe people and places with words, take pictorial notes, and sketch graphic representations of what they see to be able to recall and report on their findings back in the classroom.

To further support the experience, set up note-taking buddies who share a note pad. Or provide a graphic organizer such as a map of the location that you are visiting to indicate key places on which students should be taking notes. Additionally, students can try guided note-taking by stopping at strategic points and jotting down key information at appropriate places during the trip together as a class.

Scaffolded Note-taking. A note-taking organizer (Figure 6.11) can be a useful tool to help diverse learners take pertinent notes. As students watch a news report, half the class completes the first column of the organizer by focusing on and capturing actual quotes from the subject of the news report. The other half of the class takes notes on the person's actions as portrayed in the video clip. After students watch the video two or more times, they work in small groups with others who took notes in the same column of the template to make their own notes more complete. As a final step, students are paired up to complete an information gap activity, during which they give one and take one piece of information by sharing their own notes orally and take notes as they listen to their partner.

Figure 6.11 Collaborative Note-Taking with Complementary Prompts

What was said (Quotes)	What was done (Descriptions of actions)

Graphic Organizers for Information Gathering and Organization. Graphic organizers not only help students become familiar with different text structures through a range of reading and writing activities presented in this book previously, they also aid learners in applying their understanding of how ideas are organized in different genres when they start building knowledge on a topic by gathering information and organizing ideas using a visual tool. (See, for example, www.thinkingmaps.com, www.smartdraw.com, or www.dinah.com for unique graphic organizers.)

Anchor Performance 9: Offer Text-Based Answers Using Grade-Appropriate Literary and Informational Texts

Students who are learning English as a new language or struggle with linguistic expression must have additional support with text-based answers, also dubbed as one of the six shifts the CCSS bring to our instruction (see http://engageny.org/resource/common-core-shifts/).

Essential Strategy #1 to Support Anchor Performance 9: Connect Questions and Responses

Students need to understand that there is an intricate system of connections between questions and answers. The more metacognitive strategies they develop about how to approach a simpler text, the easier they can handle responding to more complex readings or assignments as they progress through the grades.

QAR (Question Answer Relationship). In the early 1980s, Taffy Raphael (1982, 1986) introduced this strategy to help students categorize the types of questions (depicted in Table 6.3) they are asked and gave them a tool to discover where to look for the answers. If the answers are *In the Book*, students will either find them in a specific place in the text (*Right There*), or they will have to look in several places in the text (*Think and Search*). The two subcategories of the *In My Head* category include *Author and You* questions, which refer to when students need to use a combination of textual information and their background knowledge and experiences and *On My Own* questions, in which students rely merely on background experiences and knowledge to come up with the answer (a question type not promoted by the CCSS) (see Raphael, Highfield, and Au, 2006).

Table 6.3 QAR (Question Answer Relationship) Template

IN THE TEXT	IN MY HEAD
RIGHT THERE	AUTHOR AND YOU
THINK AND SEARCH	ON MY OWN

Read Something, Write Something. Working in small groups, have students read short amounts of text—from one paragraph to one full page. After reading silently or aloud, ask them to write one sentence that responds to a text-based question, such as having students identify the main idea of what was read (with or without sentence starters or other scaffolds provided if needed). This activity may continue until a summary paragraph is complete and students share their summaries in a small group. For subsequent tasks, vary the prompt and allow for a range of text-based questions to be practiced.

Essential Strategy #2 to Support Anchor Performance 9: Create Structured, Collaborative Opportunities for Students to Write From Multiple Sources About a Single Topic

The activities we describe here—jigsaw writing, the I-Chart, and gallery walk—are all strategies that pave the way for students to write independently from multiple sources. Since both are collaborative, students have an opportunity to practice using multiple sources in a less threatening or overwhelming way.

Jigsaw Writing. Before each student can tackle complex writing tasks independently, structure the writing assignments that require the use of multiple sources for input in the form of a jigsaw activity. Each group of students (or each individual student) will be responsible for providing answers based on the reading assigned to them only. For example, divide up a selection into several paragraphs and assign each paragraph to a different student to respond. Once the independent jigsaw-writing segment is done, bring the whole class together to see how the entire task fits together. Later on, expand the writing-response activity to a page, an article, a webpage, a book or other resource, making the individual writing task more complex, thus increasing the individual accountability of each student.

I-Charts (Inquiry Charts) were developed by James Hoffman (1992) to encourage critical reading across the content areas. The adapted template presented in Table 6.4 invites students to use multiple sources to answer the same three questions. This template is also conducive to collaborative or jigsaw writing in which each group of students focuses on one source only and completes one column of the chart.

Table 6.4   I-Chart Template Adaptation

Topic	Source 1	Source 2	Source 3	Source 4
Title and Author				
Question 1				
Question 2				
Question 3				
Summary				

Gallery Walk. In this strategy, kinesthetic learning is coupled with pair work. Select and place around the classroom five or six reading and image selections related to the topic the class is studying. Make sure to include a variety of sources and types of *exhibits,* such as brief poems, songs, proverbs, famous sayings, images with or without text, photographs, and cartoons, for example. Invite students (in pairs first, then later in the year, alone) to walk around and study at least three selections they find in your gallery. Ask them to fill out a scaffolded gallery-response sheet that invites students to reflect on the exhibits and make connections to their own experiences. (See sample gallery walk response questions in Box 6.9.)

Box 6.9 Sample Questions

Which 2 or 3 exhibits were the most meaningful to you? List them and explain why.

Which two exhibits are connected?

How are those two connected?

What evidence can you cite from the exhibits for the connection?

Range of Writing

Anchor Performance 10: Express Ideas and Thoughts in Writing Through a Variety of Tasks Ranging From Very Short to Extended Writing Assignments

As required by the Common Core and as suggested by common sense, for students writing to improve, they need opportunities for sustained, extensive involvement in multiple, meaningful writing tasks. For writing to become a powerful tool for learning, it must become an integral part of every class. To expand the daily independent writing tasks, we also suggest inviting diverse learners to produce writing that is collaboratively generated over a period of time and edited and published for a real audience including parents and the entire school community.

Essential Strategy #1 to Support Anchor Performance 10: Structured and Unstructured Daily Writing Opportunities

We cannot take this challenge lightly. Writing only develops when students have nonthreatening opportunities for sustained, ongoing, nongraded practice, so writing every day for a variety of purposes and in a variety of genres should become an integral part of every classroom. Some writing experiences should be naturally flowing, fitting with a favorite motto of ours: "Writing is thinking with a pencil" (anonymous). Other writing tasks should be structured to help students master craft elements (text structure or character development), writing skills and mechanics (spelling or punctuation), and process strategies (planning, drafting, and revising tactics).

Quick Write and Quick Draw. Nancy Frey, Douglas Fisher, and Sandi Everlove (2009) proposed using quick writes not only for inviting students to jot down some key ideas they have but also to practice writing quick responses to literature or content learning. Quick writes serve as a starting point as well for student-to-student dialogues, pair work, or small group interactions during which students engage in a discussion with one another more successfully since they have previously collected their thoughts and are more prepared to share their ideas.

Use the following quick write or quick draw prompts and invite students to offer their ideas:

Today we learned about _____.

Tomorrow we will learn about _____.

I enjoy learning about _____.

Alternatively, make up prompts that are specifically aligned to the lesson you are teaching:

My favorite character is _____ because _____.

What do you think will happen next in the story?

What does [key concept from lesson/text] mean? What evidence leads you to think so?

Why should we protect endangered animals?

Journaling. Experiment with a variety of journal writing tasks to engage students in a range of brief forms of response to a topic or text. *Dialogue journaling* allows two students or the teacher and a student to exchange ideas in writing in the same journal, passing the journal back and forth periodically, and in essence creating a personal written "dialogue" between them. *Response journals* invite students to share the most important word/idea/sentence/or piece of information they encountered in a text and offer their opinions/feelings/personal reactions/connections they made. *Word journals* encourage students to collect, organize, illustrate, and regularly review newly acquired vocabulary. *Learning logs* help students develop ways to reflect on and organize what they have learned.

Placemat. Used most frequently as a collaborative writing task, the placemat (Bennett & Rolheiser, 2001), a divided paper sectioned for writing multiple responses (see Figure 6.12) requires each student to individually reflect upon and jot down their ideas related to a selected topic or text in their designated writing space on the mat at the same time. After each section is filled with age- or grade-appropriate responses (drawings, single-word answers, short phrases, sentences, paragraphs, or longer units of thought), students share and compare what each group member has written and identify the common items in the center of the paper. Students

Figure 6.12 Placemat Template

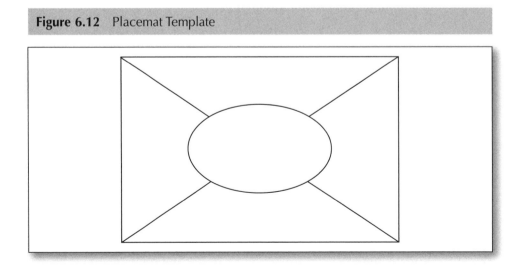

should sit around the rectangular-shaped placemat to be able to write in their own sections.

Essential Strategy #2 to Support Anchor Performance 10: Writing Process

Follow the steps of the writing process with special attention to the initial stages; most ELLs and struggling learners will need a considerable amount of time and support given to the prewriting and drafting stages. One possible framework for teaching how to assess writing is the 6 + 1 Trait Writing model which is made up of 6 + 1 key qualities that define strong writing (see Box 6.10 for basic definitions adapted from http://educationnorthwest.org/traits). Features of the 6 + 1 Trait Writing aligned to the appropriate stages of the writing process will be helpful in keeping the process focused on essential skills (See Table 6.5).

Box 6.10 Features of the 6 + 1 Trait Writing Model

- **Ideas:** What is the main message?
- **Organization:** How is the writing internally structured?
- **Voice:** What is the author's personal tone like?
- **Word Choice:** How does the writer choose the vocabulary to convey the intended meaning?
- **Sentence Fluency:** How does the language flow on the page?
- **Conventions:** Are the writing mechanics observed? and
- **Presentation:** How does the writing look on the page?

ANTICIPATED OUTCOMES

When students have opportunities to develop and enhance their craft of writing, and their development of writing skills are well supported with other rich literacy experiences such as reading and discussing engaging literary and nonfiction texts, they are likely to be more successful academically in all subject areas. Though not limited to only these outcomes, the strategies presented above are designed to accomplish the following:

1. Introduce students to writing as a form of learning.

2. Help students explore and internalize the stages of the writing process.

3. Motivate and engage students in a variety of writing tasks.

4. Improve students' overall language skills in the domains of reading, speaking, and listening as well, through integrated language arts lessons.

Table 6.5 Stages of the Writing Process Aligned to the 6 + 1 Trait Writing

Step	Main Focus	6 + 1 Traits
Prewriting	Build background; gather information; establish purpose, audience, and form	Ideas, Voice
Drafting	Generate first version of the written piece Organize ideas, make choices about word selections and sentence structures	Ideas, Organization, Word choice, Voice
Sharing and Responding	Receive feedback on draft	Ideas, Organization, Word Choice
Revising	Revise for content and clarity of expression	Voice, Ideas, Organization, Word Choice, Sentence Fluency
Editing	Make corrections to language usage, grammar, conventions	Conventions
Publishing	Finalize the piece Prepare it for sharing in print	Voice, Presentation

Generally speaking, when students' learning needs are accommodated, they reap benefits that are rarely quantified. Writing lessons made accessible to diverse learners through scaffolding and other supports create actively engaged learners who can accomplish academic tasks they were unable to complete previously. From these positive learning experiences, diverse learners gain self-confidence, self-esteem, and a sense that they are able to succeed academically.

INSTRUCTIONAL CHALLENGES

It is widely recognized that writing is the most challenging to teach of the four language skills (listening, speaking, reading, and writing). Nancy Akhavan (2009) insightfully noted:

Writing is a gatekeeping skill. Those students who write well do well in the upper-elementary grades, in high school, and beyond.

Those who are never given the opportunity to learn to write never get the chance to think, connect, and excel in classes that demand of them the ability to show what they know. (p. xii)

For diverse learners, writing in one's second or third language, in a range of academic genres, and on demand in response to prompts are just a few of the major challenges. Additionally, some students are less than motivated to tackle them. Teachers we know who have successfully overcome these challenges shared one common characteristic with us also recognized by Amy Mazur and Patricia Rice Doran (2010). They refused to fall into a "deficit" model of thinking and turned what others might have perceived as limitations of students' linguistic, cultural, physical, cognitive, and other diversities into opportunities: Opportunities to express themselves in writing every day; opportunities to write about meaningful, engaging topics; opportunities to learn cooperatively in a safe supportive environment; and opportunities to be guided and mentored personally and through the great writings of others.

PROMISING CLASSROOM PRACTICES

Maria Segura, a Grade 3–5 ESL teacher, thinks that an effective way to make nonfiction texts accessible to learners of any skill level is to carefully craft lessons that provide opportunities to fully understand not only text features but also text structure, signal words, and the possible types of questions involved with each kind of text so all her students have a solid foundation for reading and writing nonfiction genres.

She explores five main types of text structure (sequence, problem and solution, compare and contrast, description, cause and effect) students will encounter while reading and emulate while writing. A *working mat* that includes multiple visual scaffolds and graphic organizers guides students to analyze these texts and also provides a supportive working space for students to write their own examples of each type of text structure. See Figure 6.13 for a sample working mat template.

Maria incorporates the use of what she calls 3-D graphic organizers to define the purpose of each text type. To accomplish this, students employ a layered book word template to write their definitions of each text structure using their computer skills. They insert visual mnemonics as well as the types of signal words found in various text structures. The layered books are printed, stapled, and used as a supportive tool (see more on *Foldables* in Chapter 3).

Figure 6.13 Sample Workmat Template

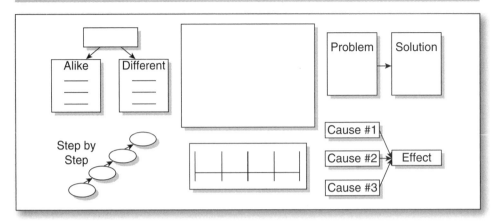

She directs her students to examine and identify different types of texts as a class. Students take turns reading sample texts aloud, and subsequently, the class is encouraged to use the center box of their working mats to identify the structure of the text and to highlight the signal words contained in the text in pairs. All findings are reviewed as a group.

Finally, Maria introduces a new element by asking students to predict, in writing, the kind of essential questions they could be asked for each of the five text structures. She also gives the students a chart that displays the kinds of questions per text structure that are more commonly found in textbooks and on state assessments. She concludes the lesson by giving the students their layered books, two working mats, and the essential questions chart so they can practice writing paragraphs with their choice of two types of text structure. She advises her students that upon completion, they will present their paragraphs to the whole class as well as teach others about the text structures in the paragraphs they constructed.

COMMON CORE WRITING STANDARDS— (UN)COMMON REFLECTION QUESTIONS

1. Which of the ten anchor standards or the grade-appropriate equivalents will present the greatest challenge to your students and why?

2. Which of the strategies presented in this chapter will help your students overcome the difficulties they may face?

3. How will you differentiate writing instruction in multilevel classes while keeping the common goals of the anchor standards in mind?

KEY RESOURCES

Professional Books

Moss, B., & Loh, V. S. (2010). *35 strategies for guiding readers through informational texts.* New York, NY: Guilford.

Pottle, J. L. (1998). *Writing frames: 40 activities for learning the writing process.* Portland, ME: J. Weston Walch.

Online Resources

- National Writing Project
  http://www.nwp.org
- National Gallery of Writing
  http://galleryofwriting.org
- CCCC Statement on Second Language Writing and Writers
  http://www.ncte.org/cccc/resources/positions/secondlangwriting
- Into the Book
  http://reading.ecb.org/
- Florida Center for Reading Research
  http://fcrr.org/
- Education Northwest (Home of 6+1 Trait Writing)
  http://educationnorthwest.org/
- *NCTE Beliefs about the Teaching of Writing*
  http://www.ncte.org/positions/statements/writingbeliefs
- Teachers College Reading and Writing Project website:
  http://www.readingandwritingproject.com

7 Speaking and Listening Strategies

Children's speaking and listening skills lead the way for their reading and writing skills, and together these language skills are the primary tools of the mind for all future learning.

—Roskos, Tabors, and Lenhart, 2005, p. v

OVERVIEW

When discussing the needs of beginner English language learners, Denise D. Nessel and Carol N. Dixon (2008) cautioned that these students

> need to use the new language in supportive, nonthreatening environments in which mistakes are accepted. For example, the novice benefits by talking with friends who ignore errors, focus on the intent of the communication, and encourage further speech. The novice must also have many opportunities to listen without being forced to respond, a situation that affords the chance to become familiar with the sound of the language; grasp as much as possible; and benefit from seeing gestures, intonation, and facial expressions as well as hearing words. Free to concentrate on listening rather than formulating a response, the language learner has a better chance of comprehending. (p. 6)

We would concur that it is not just beginner level language learners but all diverse students who need a supportive, nonthreatening learning environment in which they can safely experiment with finding and using their voices, make mistakes, and be encouraged to continue trying to express themselves, as well as have ample opportunities to listen to, interact, and collaborate with peers, teachers, and other members of the classroom and school community without being hampered by outside scrutiny or judgment. Yet, we must add that diverse learners need also to be engaged in structured, meaningful interactions and challenged to reach the next level of their language acquisition or expressive language development.

WHY SPEAKING AND LISTENING SKILLS IMPROVE THE OVERALL ACADEMIC PERFORMANCE OF DIVERSE LEARNERS

During their school years, students must develop complex speaking and listening skills so they can make themselves understood and understand others at increasingly higher levels of complexity as demanded by grade appropriate academic tasks. Many researchers have examined the relationship between oral language and literacy and found that they are interdependent. Among others, Diane August and Timothy Shanahan (2006) (National Literacy Panel) found that strong oral language skills enhance the development of literacy in second-language learners. Most interestingly, Genesee, Lindholm-Leary, Saunders, and Christian (2006) reported that "ELLs make use of L1 oral proficiency to draw on prior knowledge and experience, either in the absence of or in addition to similar levels of L2 oral proficiency, in the service of L2 literacy tasks" (p. 82). In other words, oral language proficiency in the native language and second language both contribute to literacy development.

It has also been found that children who grow up in a home where using the language in meaningful conversations abound and who have opportunities to develop rich conceptual backgrounds are at a definite advantage when they enter school because they have larger vocabularies and more knowledge about the world that surrounds them (Gillanders, Iruka, Ritchie, & Cobb, 2012). The Common Core State Standards (CCSS) must be used as a vehicle to provide equitable opportunities for all learners to enrich their receptive and expressive oral language skills, expand their vocabulary, and build new knowledge in literacy and the content areas.

CORE SPEAKING AND LISTENING STRATEGIES

There are only six Speaking and Listening Anchor Standards, which are organized into two subgroups. The first three standards emphasize listening comprehension and student collaboration, whereas the last three standards require students to hone their presentation skills or their oral language skills to formally deliver an age-appropriate speech or report (see Box 7.1). The use of multimedia—both for listening and speaking or presentation—are incorporated into these standards indicating that 21st century technology skills must be an integrated part of any classroom.

Box 7.1 College and Career Readiness Anchor Standards for Speaking and Listening

Comprehension and Collaboration

1. Prepare for and participate effectively in a range of conversations and collaborations with diverse partners, building on others' ideas and expressing their own clearly and persuasively.

2. Integrate and evaluate information presented in diverse media and formats, including visually, quantitatively, and orally.

3. Evaluate a speaker's point of view, reasoning, and use of evidence and rhetoric.

Presentation of Knowledge and Ideas

4. Present information, findings, and supporting evidence such that listeners can follow the line of reasoning and the organization, development, and style are appropriate to task, purpose, and audience.

5. Make strategic use of digital media and visual displays of data to express information and enhance understanding of presentations.

6. Adapt speech to a variety of contexts and communicative tasks, demonstrating command of formal English when indicated or appropriate.

From each of the six College and Career Readiness Anchor Standards (CCRAS) for Speaking and Listening, we derived and aligned a series of related Anchor Performances—skill sets that all students need to develop—and suggest strategies to help diverse learners build these skills in order to meet the standards. Some strategies may be more appropriate than others depending upon the grade levels or language proficiency levels of the students. To that end, we also include suggestions on how to adapt strategies to meet the needs of diverse individual learners.

Comprehension and Collaboration

Anchor Performance 1: Participate in a Range of Small and Large Group Discussions

The speaking and listening anchor standards emphasize the need for students to interact with each other based on the content they are learning. In order to become successful collaborators, they need frequent, meaningful opportunities to work in groups of all sizes to accomplish the following oral language development tasks: to exchange ideas, to consider input from others, to express themselves clearly and coherently, to defend or adjust their own point of view, and many others as demanded by the curriculum. The first speaking/listening standard spans across all six grades revealing a clear shift in third grade. Kindergarten and first-grade students are expected to participate in collaborative conversations about grade-appropriate topics and texts both with their diverse peers and adults in small and larger groups, whereas, third- to fourth-grade students are expected to be more proactive and able to engage others in a range of collaborative discussions (one-on-one, in groups, and teacher-led) on grade-appropriate topics and texts. A special emphasis is placed on "building on others' ideas and expressing their own clearly" for these upper elementary grades. An increased complexity of the conversation and participation skills are further explained by the many subpoints introduced below each grade-level standard all the way from kindergarten through Grade 5.

Essential Strategy to Support Anchor Performance 1: Support Student Participation Through Collaborative Practices

Using flexible grouping with diverse learners ensures they will work with varied groups of peers, rather than seeing themselves and one another belonging to set groups. Thus, all students should be grouped both heterogeneously and homogeneously, both with their friends and with others with whom they do not have any social contact outside school, both with the highest performers and the struggling learners. If you simply assign students to pair work or small group work without any guidance or support, some conversations will take off, whereas others may falter or become less than fruitful. We are not suggesting that specific roles are always necessary to be assigned for productive conversations to take place, though they could be helpful scaffolding tools in some cases. Rather, we promote a few effective structures below for oral language development that authentically engage all those involved.

Buddy System. Just as you may pair struggling students with a reading buddy, or a writing buddy, the buddy system also works for oral language support. A language buddy may serve as a supportive partner who can model participation in small and large group discussions, offer opportunities to share ideas, as well as rehearse answers with before volunteering in front of a class. Teachers sometimes place high-performing students with low-performing students when they utilize the buddy system. To make sure that there is no stigmatism associated with this strategy, we suggest considering varied partner possibilities. Students can also be paired by shared interest, by native language, by learning styles, or by any other meaningful characteristics.

Turn-and-Talk. Prior to inviting students to offer a response in front of a larger group, have them turn to a partner and briefly share some ideas. Other versions of this strategy involve some personal planning time as in **Think-Pair-Share** or writing down some ideas as in **Think-Jot-Pair-Share.** Soto (2012) claimed that one of the most basic yet powerful techniques for enhancing ELLs' academic oral language development is **Think-Pair-Share**. Students are invited to individually read a selection or reflect on a question posed by the teacher, then pair up and share their ideas. Even at lower levels of language proficiency, students can participate when sentence starters or oral language-development stems are offered. To present additional opportunities for students to evaluate another speaker's ideas, pairs double up and form "squares" or groups of four: In this set up, students first complete the Think-Pair-Share portion of the task and then summarize their own discussion with another pair as well as compare both of their conclusions. One more type of pair-work activity is called **Pair-Plus-One;** a third person observes the two conversing students in order to offer feedback on how effective their interaction is (Zwiers & Crawford, 2011).

Instructional Conversations. A unique form of interaction between the teacher and a small group of students is what Goldenberg (1992) first called *Instructional Conversation,* the purpose of which is to promote complex language development and afford opportunities for more authentic interactions. During these conversations, students listen and respond to not only the teacher's but also their fellow students' input in an open-ended dialog about a select topic. Since participants build upon each other's ideas, turn taking, risk-taking, respectful disagreement, active and interactive listening skills are all acquired in a unique way that encourages extensive discussion, complex learning, and multiple solutions to a question and problem.

Instructional conversations are in contrast to the typical sequence of (1) teacher asks a question—(2) student answers (typically with one or two words)—(3) teacher evaluates student response (*Good!* or *Correct!*). If teachers choose to continue to use this Initiate, Respond, Evaluate (IRE) sequence, students in their classrooms will give "truncated responses with limited opportunities for extended conversation or divergent thought"

(Powers, 2011, p. 202). Instructional Conversation is a strategy that needs demonstration, modeling, and some scaffolded supports in the form of sentence starters to be most successful with diverse learners.

Literature Circles. Among many others, Harvey Smokey Daniels (2002) recommended the use of literature circles for student-directed discussions of literature. The teacher presents the class with an initial selection of three to five books and offers the class a brief oral overview or introduction to each. Next, students select a book they want to read individually and then form small groups with others who have selected the same book. As it is a highly student-centered activity, groups must agree on their own time line for reading the book and completing the assignments (or projects) based on the book. Most recently, Harvey and Daniels (2009) summarized the current status of literature circles after they have been embraced in US schools for over 25 years. Some of the most important new developments they mentioned happen to be closely aligned to the CCSS:

- Implement literature circles in all content areas, with all types of texts, using multiple genres and multiple texts for greater critical engagement.
- Allow for a more authentic engagement in the discussion by all participants using Post-it notes, text annotations, and graphic responses.
- Teach the social and collaboration skills necessary for successful participation by all.

Inquiry Circles. Similar to literature circles, students can also engage in meaningful, deep conversations focused on content area topics (also based on shared readings). Stephanie Harvey and Harvey Smokey Daniels (2009) suggested a sequence of three guiding questions to help students discuss content-based readings. They named the three types of questions as (a) definition, (b) consequence, and (c) action questions. See generic and content-specific examples in Table 7.1.

Anchor Performance 2: Listen to and Discuss a Read-Aloud or Multimedia Production

In Grades K–1, the second speaking/listening standard requires students to understand key ideas, whereas starting in Grade 2, students are expected to do the following:

- Recount and describe main ideas and details (Grade 2).
- Determine the main ideas and supporting details (Grade 3).
- Paraphrase a portion of a text (Grade 4).
- Summarize the text (Grade 5).

Table 7.1 Guided Questioning for Inquiry Circles

Question Type	Guiding Questions	Examples From Grade 4 Lesson on Climate Change
Definition Questions	What is it? What is taking place?	*What is climate change?* *What is happening to the weather in our region?*
Consequence Questions	Why does it matter? Why is it important?	*Why should we learn about climate change?* *Why does it matter if weather patterns change?*
Action Questions	What can be done? What actions should be taken?	*What actions can we take as individuals? What actions can our community take together?*

What is common in all the grades is that the standard does not stop at read-alouds or written texts, but emphasizes students' skills to interact with and comprehend information presented through multimedia channels, thus this standard should be considered a critical example of and opportunity for technology integration.

As Vanessa Morrison and Lisa Wlodarczyk (2009) noted, "having students listen to a read-aloud then participate in an engagement activity relevant to the text is one context in which to keep conversation focused on a target learning goal" (p. 112). We have also found that when teachers expose their students to more complex texts than the children could read independently or when they share carefully selected, short movie clips, or other nonprint-based literary or nonfiction selections such as podcasts, radio reports, songs, and so on that are engaging and challenging, they can use these experiences as catalysts for rich discussions. Such shared explorations frequently lead to increased student motivation to read or to further explore the curricular topic.

Essential Strategy to Support Anchor Performance 2: Connect the Read-Aloud or Multimedia Viewing to Previous Learning and to Students' Cultural Backgrounds, Interests, and Prior Knowledge Through Structured, Interactive Tasks

It has been carefully documented that language and culture are intertwined entities and they not only influence each other but student learning as well. Take the opportunity this standard affords to engage diverse students in personal meaning-making through rigorous, content-based and literature-driven conversations. How to achieve that? Encourage active processing by making connections to what students already know— whether that knowledge originated in the class or outside of it.

Predictions. Predictions made about a reading or multimedia selection can take place before, during, and after the read-aloud or listening/ viewing. One way of activating student prediction and engaging the whole class prior to a reading or media presentation is by asking them to share their **First Impressions**, their own ideas about the selection based on some preliminary input presented by the teacher (Buehl, 2001). For this strategy, carefully select words, phrases, audio snip-its, or images that represent critical information about the reading or presentation and have students create their own version of what they think they are going hear or see based on the preliminary input.

After students share and discuss their predictions, and after they have heard or seen the selection, they can be asked to compare their versions with the original one. During the read-aloud or multimedia viewing, stop once or twice and ask students to make predictions about the selection. Strategically target essential concepts in nonfiction selections or pose "big picture" questions in literature rather than ask for less important details. After the read-aloud or multimedia viewing, engage students in discussions centered around extension and evaluation questions or prompts that invite them to (a) make connections to their own out-of-school literacies and experiences, and (b) elaborate on what could happen next in a story or what consequences may be predicted based on the information.

Visualization. Forming images in their heads and then describing what they see with their mind's eyes will help students not only to enhance their comprehension but also to improve their oral expressions. Start by asking students to pretend that they are at the movies and try to imagine what they would be seeing just as when they go to see a film and watch a movie scene after scene. Next, have students listen to an audio recording while you share your personal visualization with them. By sharing your own visualization, students learn how to form mental images in their heads. Then, have students listen to a read-aloud and practice visualizing. Pause the reading periodically and have students turn and talk to a partner to share their visualizations.

Listen and Sketch. A possible follow up to visualization is to have students draw a quick sketch of what they hear. Start small. Just read one sentence or one short paragraph for students to draw a quick image of what they gathered from the material.

Interactive Read-Aloud/Interactive Viewing. Students must make connections to the material they are studying, thus a variety of interactive structures can support such reflections and discussions. In **Partner Reading** (Fuchs, Fuchs, & Burish, 2000), students take turns reading assigned short sections aloud; after one student reads a paragraph of the selection, the other summarizes what their partner has read. Some teachers call this strategy **Buddy Summary**, though the shared literacy experience does not have to be limited to reading aloud to each other and summarizing the selection. Students can be supported with a range of prompts to encourage discussion (see Box 7.2).

Box 7.2 Discussion Starters to Enhance Partner Reading

My favorite _____ was _____ because _____.

What was your favorite _____?

I didn't understand when _____.

One important thing I learned is _____.

What did you learn about _____?

Reader/Writer/Speaker Response Triads. In addition to pair work, students can be placed in groups of three to work cooperatively while taking turns having three different roles: One student reads aloud the assigned selection (a portion of the text the entire group is going to tackle); the next student writes responses to questions about the text based on a small group discussion. It is critical that the writer does not take sole responsibility for providing the answers; instead, that role is to be the note-taker or scribe who gathers information from the others in the triad and jots down the important details. Finally, the third student will report the answers to the whole class. A most effective way to set this activity up is to ensure that each member of the triad takes one of the three possible roles; thus all language skills are practiced within the context of the lesson (Vogt & Echevarria, 2007).

Sound Off, Sound On. In an intriguing video-viewing activity, students watch a short excerpt of a video with the sound turned off. Their task is to predict what the characters who appear on the video or the narrator who presents the material depicted in the video might be saying. Have students work in pairs or small groups to share and consolidate their ideas before playing the video again with the sound on. Ask students to compare and contrast the differences between what they predicted would be said on the video and what they actually heard. The segment you show must be short, visually rich in detail, yet not too obvious to generate a considerable amount of discussion among students.

Anchor Performance 3: Ask and Answer Questions With Scaffolded Support

From kindergarten to third grade, the main focus of this standard is for students to be able to ask and answer questions and thus engage another speaker in a dialogue. Fourth and fifth graders, however, have more challenging goals; not only will they engage with a speaker, but they also will have to try to identify the reasons and evidence a speaker provides to support particular points. By fifth grade, students are required to summarize the points a speaker makes and explain how each claim is supported by reasons and evidence. An anchor performance we selected—ask and answer questions—is one that teachers have always used in their classroom. The shift we are suggesting is to engage students in a student-centered, increasingly student-directed dialogue that is structured and scaffolded appropriately based on the grade-level complexity of the CCSS expectations and the topic or content the students are exploring.

Essential Strategy to Support Anchor Performance 3: Kinesthetic Discussion-Based Activities

Many teachers have shared with us that when their students partake in a discussion or other interactive learning tasks while they are also encouraged or expected to move around the room—rather than merely sitting at their desks—the level of participation, engagement, and even productive noise, increase. This seems to be particularly the case with many diverse learners who perform instructional tasks more readily when removed from traditional classroom seating arrangements and are engaged in up-on-your feet activities. Not just for diverse learners, Gardner (1999) identified kinesthetic activities as vital for all elementary-age youngsters to learn and that "merely passive experiences tend to attenuate and have little lasting impact" (p. 82). The suggested strategies that follow are simple yet powerful examples of kinesthetic activities.

Four Corners. This activity begins by the teacher assigning each corner of the room a category related to the curriculum. Depending on the grade level and the specific learning objective, the four corners might be labeled as the four seasons (for kindergarten), four characters in a story (any grade), or as *Agree, Strongly Agree, Disagree,* or *Strongly Disagree* (Grade 3–5). In preparation for the discussion and the kinesthetic component of the activity, students are given a specific task to be completed independently. For example,

- Kindergarteners will be given pictures or word cards identifying a different clothing article. The task is to first decide which season the clothes on their cards belong to and then move to the corner labeled with the correct season.

- Students receive short descriptions of one of four characters of a story, or some key lines the characters have or could have spoken in the story. After careful consideration, each learner will move to the corner labeled with the name of the character to create a match with the description or the quote.
- Assigning values such as *Agree, Disagree, Strongly Agree,* or *Strongly Disagree* to each of the four corners lends itself well to forming an opinion about any topic presented in the upper-elementary curriculum. Once the teacher identifies a topic statement such as "The president of the United States should be allowed to serve more than two terms in office," students express their ideas by moving to the corner of the room aligned to their opinion.

It is critical that students are prepared to ask each other questions and share their decisions through scaffolded sentences, sentence starters, or model responses. Once they are in their chosen corners, a small group discussion takes place, where participants take turns asking each other to explain their choices and share their answers along with their arguments for those choices.

Inside Outside Circle. This strategy may be used with any grade level and any curricular topic. First, each student generates a set of notes on index cards (with questions regarding the assigned topic on one side and key ideas as possible answers on the other side). For those who need assistance, structured, partially completed notes will have to be made available. Then the class is divided into two equal parts. One-half of the class forms an inner circle with students facing outward; the other half forms a second circle surrounding the inner circle with the students facing inward. Students are then partnered up, one from the inside circle with one from the outside circle (see Figure 7.1). The index cards are used to scaffold the interaction between the randomly assigned partners. The students in the inside circle start with a question to their partners; outside-circle students answer the question and then the roles are reversed. After a few minutes of discussion, the outside circle is signaled to move down one person while the inside circle stays in place. When new pairs are formed, the process is repeated.

Line Up and Fold. For another way for students to engage in active conversation and discussion on their feet, first have students line up in a particular order; ask them to line up in order of birthdays, alphabetically by first names or last names, or give them cards with information to sequence themselves. Once students have formed a straight line, the first student at one end of the line is directed to walk down to face the last student at the other end of the line, followed by the other students until the line is "folded in half" and everyone has a partner. Similar to the **Inside Outside Circle,** index cards or notes may be used to scaffold the interaction between the

Figure 7.1 Inside Outside Circle

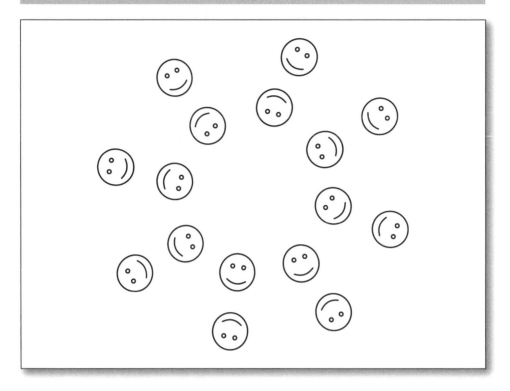

partners. The line closer to the teacher may start with a question, and the students on the opposite line will answer, and then the roles are reversed. After a few minutes of discussion, students in one of the lines are signaled to move down two people while the other line stays in place. When new pairs are formed, the process is repeated.

Stand Up, Hand Up, Pair Up. In this final kinesthetic, discussion-based activity also suggested by Kagan and Kagan (1998), students are given a literacy or content-based task to prepare prior to the three steps outlined here:

1. Stand up holding your index card or note sheet in one hand.

2. Raise your other hand and look around the room for a partner.

3. Pair up with someone from another table (someone you do not talk to regularly).

Once students self-select their partners in this fashion, they engage in the discussion about the prepared topic. For example, they may have been given a sentence or paragraph from a target text and had to generate a key question to ask their partners. Fifth graders exploring Chapter 1 of *Hatchet* (Paulsen, 2007), for example, will each have a short excerpt from the novel which they will study very closely to make sure they understand the meaning of their assigned selection as best as they could without the larger context of the entire chapter. Then they generate an authentic question or two related to their selection, which they write on the back of the card (see Figure 7. 2).

Figure 7.2   Quote and Questions for a Stand Up, Hand Up, Pair Up Based on *Hatchet* (Paulsen, 2007).

Brian felt his eyes beginning to burn and knew there would be tears. He had cried for a time, but that was gone now. He didn't cry now. Instead, his eyes burned and tears came, the seeping tears that burned, but he didn't cry. He wiped his eyes with a finger and looked at the pilot out of the corner of his eye to make sure he hadn't noticed the burning and tears. (Paulsen, 2007, p. 9)	*Why do you think Brian felt like crying? Why did he want to hide his tears?*

When paired up, the first student reads his or her selection aloud and asks the question prepared ahead of time. Students take turns asking and answering questions or discussing the meaning conveyed in the reading selections. If the selections lend themselves to it, students should be asked to make connections between the short reading passages assigned to them. Once their exchange is complete, they raise their hands and look for new partners with whom they will repeat the verbal exchange further exploring the topic or the text.

Presentation of Knowledge and Ideas

Anchor Performance 4: Give an Oral Account of Events, an Oral Description, or an Oral Report

Korn (1998) noted that

encouraging children to tell stories is important not only for its role in enhancing communication skills, but also for its part in helping children develop a sense of who they are as active participants in the world and as social beings in culturally significant interactions with others. (p. 225)

Telling stories or giving an oral account of events is a skill that serves as a common thread for this K–5 speaking/listening standard. However, in the early grades (K–1) students are mostly expected to describe people, places, and things by adding more accurate details. As they start second grade, the expectation to speak clearly emerges. In third through fifth grade, students are also required to be able to give an oral report based on a topic or text and to be able to offer a factual oral account with relevant information, thus showing more advanced planning and organization skills.

Essential Strategy to Support Anchor Performance 4: Scaffolding Oral Language Expression

The most critical support teachers can offer diverse learners to be successful with this standard is to scaffold their oral language production. Since scaffolding any task begins with strong teacher modeling, it is no different for oral language development. Model how to use extended academic language and rich vocabulary even when students do not understand every word or phrase. In other words, do not oversimplify your own language; instead, take advantage of the opportunity every interaction with your students provides to introduce and reinforce more complex sentence structures and more sophisticated word choices for your students to produce on their own. Regardless of their linguistic and academic background, their receptive language skills (or listening comprehension) will always be more advanced than their productive skills (such as speaking in complete sentences using academic discourse). Modeling will not be enough though. Scaffolding oral language also includes the following practices:

- Use questions and prompts that invite students to extend what they have said.
  - *Ask open-ended questions, ones that begin with* why *and* how *to encourage students to add more details.*

- Expand students' thoughts by adding new vocabulary or using more complex syntax while recognizing their contribution to the discussion.
  - *For example, if a student describes his first experience with a tornado saying, "It went around and round like this and was very loud," while gesturing with his hands, you can comment by adding, "Tornados form a funnel and often sound as if a train were coming. It must have been very frightening when you first encountered one."*

- Request clarification and teach them how to ask for clarification when they do not understand someone else.

  o *What do you mean? Could you explain that again, please? How did you get your answer?—are some possible model sentences to use and explicitly teach.*

- Provide frequent constructive feedback on students' language output to encourage, interpret, and evaluate their responses or their participation in small group or class discussions.

  o *Instead of simply praising a student with a generic "Good job!" or even "Nicely stated," try be more specific with your feedback and say "When you said _____, I was able to paint a picture in my mind because you used such a vivid adjective." Or, "First, I was not sure what you meant by _____, but when you gave an example from your own life, I realized you were talking about _____."*

Anchor Performance 5: Create a Visual, Audio, or Multimedia Illustration that Supports An Oral Presentation

Elementary school students are expected to develop visual literacy—demonstrated by the end-of-year expectation in all grades that students are to add visual displays to their oral presentations. Kindergarten and first-grade students are encouraged to draw to support the details of their oral presentations. In Grades 2–4, students learn to create audio recordings of stories and poems, and finally, in fifth grade, students add multimedia components as well to their presentations.

Essential Strategy to Support Anchor Performance 5: Collaborative, Art-Based Activities

A notable proponent of art-based literacy instruction, Beth Olshansky (2008) observed that "the language of pictures can be enlisted to support writing and enhance reading and writing practice" (p. 26). Students can be encouraged to look deeply at their drawings and other artwork and learn to *read their pictures* by using details and enriched vocabulary in response to reading or prior to writing. We also want to recognize the immense possibility of maximizing the use of artistic expression and multimedia technology to support oral literacy development. Beth Olshansky also noted that by intertwining art and literacy, students "develop a heightened sense of visual interest, awareness, and purpose" (p. 53), and also enhance their skill of visualizing, creating pictures on paper and in their minds. As their artistic expression becomes richer in detail, so does their verbal expression or *oral rehearsal* describing their artwork. When the artistic expression or multimedia creation precedes the oral presentation, visual language and visually expressed thoughts are translated into descriptive words.

Wordless Book Making. Just as commercially published wordless picture books may be used to develop students' oral expression, creating wordless books using a variety of illustration techniques allows students to tell a story first through visual tools and then use words when they present their books to each other. To enhance students' oral language development, consider this book-making activity to be collaborative so students will have to create a plan, discuss details, negotiate critical elements, and build on each other's ideas.

Collaborative Poster. Based on the topic or text the class is studying, small groups of students work together on a collaborative poster that represents any of the following:

- Main ideas and supportive details
- Causes and effects
- Main and supportive characters
- Time line of key events

Students within the team agree on using images that represent key ideas in response to the task, not merely decorate their poster. Poster images can either be drawn, cut out from magazines, printed off the Internet, or a combination of all three, appealing to the preferences of individual team members.

Slideshow Presentation. The need for integrating technology into English language arts (ELA) instruction is apparent throughout the CCSS. As students develop language and literacy skills, their access to and development of proficiency with digital tools must be ensured. Developing a PowerPoint (Microsoft), Keynote (Apple), or Prezi (Internet-based) presentation may prove to be both a challenge and a source of satisfaction for upper elementary students. They learn to accompany their oral reports with slides that come alive with images, sounds, perhaps even animation, and just the right amount of text or with a new digital storytelling tool that consists of a single canvas the user may pan and zoom in and out of while including video clips, images, and short text among other digital components. The overall goal here is for teachers to develop their personal knowledge of these presentation tools well enough to direct students to use them. Keep in mind that diverse learners sometimes have less access and savvy with technology and may need preliminary lessons or a *technology buddy* to complete such assignments.

Anchor Performance 6: Express Ideas Clearly and Appropriately (by Speaking in Complete Sentences)

By the end of the kindergarten year, students are expected to speak audibly and express thoughts and feelings clearly. From first grade on, there is an emphasis on producing complete sentences when appropriate based on the assigned task and situation. The end-of-year expectations for fourth and fifth graders reveal that students in these grades are also expected to differentiate between formal and informal English (Grade 4) and adapt their speech to the level of formality required in various contexts (Grade 5). These standards parallel the language standards discussed in Chapter 2.

Essential Strategy to Support Anchor Performance 6: Engage Students in Purposeful Talk

Purposeful Talk. Nichols (2008) defines this as "focused, collaborative talk; a social process that requires children to actively engage with ideas, think out loud together, and work to a co-construction of those ideas" (p. 10). Not all students are readily able to engage in these types of conversations. Most young students and some diverse learners need particular structures in place to facilitate purposeful talk. Many strategies already identified in this text have detailed cooperative learning activities that assist student to engage in active and meaningful conversations. The following activities are just a few more examples of how to create learning situations in which worthwhile conversation can be fostered.

Circle Time or Morning Meeting. This favorite in early childhood classrooms provides an opportunity to share personal narratives, oral accounts of individual or group experienced events, news of the day, or descriptions of personally relevant objects and experiences. Upper-elementary teachers can also use Circle Time successfully to afford students a democratic forum to share concerns (the test given the day before was too challenging) or to discuss issues openly (bullying happening during recess).

Show and Tell, Brown Bag, and Object of Interest. Another frequently seen activity in the younger grades that contributes to oral language development as well as vocabulary building is **Show and Tell.** Encourage students to select and name an object, describe it using varied, precise vocabulary, and offer explanations for choosing the object for sharing. To help diverse learners, have students brainstorm possible words to describe the object before an individual student is expected to speak. Variations on this activity is naming and describing teacher provided materials or participating in **Brown Bag**, a guessing game in which students reach into a paper bag, touch, feel, but do not see certain objects related to the lesson. By gathering sensory clues, students take turns guessing the objects the bag contains. For older grades, we learned an activity from Ellen Tournour, North Bellmore UFSD teacher, who invites a different student each week to present an **Object of Interest** (personal communication, June 17, 2012). Students take turns bringing in an unusual household item that has a unique purpose or special significance, thus each child's heritage or family customs are also celebrated. The class has a week to figure out what the object is, what it is used for, and what it might be called. Describing the object, predicting its use, asking questions about it, and making an attempt to name it all successfully contribute to an authentic conversation that includes an enriching vocabulary building experience as well.

Wordless Picture Books. Based on the topic and complexity of ideas expressed in selected wordless picture books, use them with younger grades or lower language proficiency students to encourage oral expression. Wordless picture books in Box 7.3 lend themselves both to describing objects and people, sequencing events, predicting what might happen next, discussing cause and effect, and many other oral language and literacy skill development.

As Tammy McGregor (2007) also reminded us "mistakenly considered by some to be baby books, wordless books provide a rich, authentic place for readers of all ages to rehearse strategic thinking" (p. 6). We would add that they also provide a forum for talking about events, characters, settings, problems and solutions while ensuring that multiple perspectives are validated. Each child will describe what he or she sees and how he or she interprets the pictures differently.

ANTICIPATED OUTCOMES

"Academic language is part of a cognitive tool for undertaking real content area tasks in the same or analogous ways to experts"(Wilhelm, 2007, p. 44). More specifically, oral language use, the type of formal, content-based, and academic task-driven interaction that leads to active, engaged school participation, is critical for student success. All learners—not just students with diverse academic and linguistic needs—benefit from explicit instruction in and ample opportunities with academic English in all their classes. Yet, in more recent years, the explicit teaching of oral language, even in the earliest elementary grades, has fallen by the wayside, replaced in many classrooms by more direct instruction in reading and writing. However, explicit teaching in oral language skills is paramount, particularly for diverse learners who may have had limited exposure to Standard English. When such learning opportunities prevail, students incorporate newly acquired academic vocabulary in their speech, use more complete sentences rather than merely

Box 7.3 Wordless Picture Books

Title	Author
Time Flies	Eric Rohmann
The Gray Lady and the Strawberry Snatcher	Molly Bang
Good Dog, Carl	Alexandra Day
The Red Book	Barbara Lehman
Pancakes for Breakfast	Tomie dePaola
The Hunter and the Animals: A Wordless Picture Book	Tomie dePaola
Flotsam	David Wiesner
The Lion and the Mouse	Jerry Pinkney
A Ball for Daisy	Chris Raschka
Home	Jeannie Baker
Octopus Soup	Mercer Mayer
The Chicken Thief (Stories Without Words)	Beatrice Rodriguez (Contributor)
The Boys	Jeff Newmann
A Boy, a Dog, a Frog and a Friend	Mercer and Marianna Mayer
Is it rough? Is it Smooth? Is it Shiny?	Tana Hoban
Is it Red? Is it Yellow? Is it Blue?	Tana Hoban

sentence fragments, and acquire more complex grammatical structures. In turn, strong academic oral language skills will support the acquisition of advanced reading comprehension and writing proficiency.

INSTRUCTIONAL CHALLENGES

Designing and implementing discussion-based activities that support the six Speaking and Listening Standards may appear to be easy and simple at first. Most students like to talk, so put them in small groups and give them a task (a prompt or a question) to discuss and the lesson is on its way, right? Not always so! Students with diverse learning needs also demonstrate varied classroom participation patterns and comfort level with speaking in public, even if that public speech means turning and talking to one another. Thus the following overall recommendations will help overcome the challenges of involving reluctant speakers:

- Create a supportive learning environment, one in which risk-taking is fostered and part of the class culture.
- Allow for mistakes and struggles as class community members learn to express themselves.
- Model ways for students to communicate with one another, and how students should respond when they do not understand a classmate who is speaking.
- Scaffold, scaffold, scaffold, and then release responsibility to students.
- Integrate listening and speaking with reading and writing, artistic expression, and technology use.

PROMISING CLASSROOM PRACTICES

Park Avenue School in the Westbury Public Schools in New York is the proud host of the first early childhood TV studio run by kindergarten through second-grade students on Long Island. As their website notes,

PBC News is a bi-weekly student news broadcast featuring the talented kindergarten, first, and second grade students from Park Avenue School in Westbury, NY. Our students hone their reading, writing, listening, and speaking skills as they assist in the creation and production of each broadcast. Our call letters are PBC which stand for Park Bear Cubs.

The TV broadcasts are also available as Vimeo podcasts so students and their families can enjoy them over and over (see samples at http://vimeo.com/channels/parktv). Engagement in this type of authentic, collaborative literacy activities that lead to practicing all four language skills is an exemplary way to ensure that students have opportunities to share their own learning and explorations, learn to speak clearly and listen attentively to each other, and at the same time, engage the local—and even wider—community in their learning experiences.

COMMON CORE SPEAKING AND LISTENING STANDARDS—(UN)COMMON REFLECTION QUESTIONS

1. Which of the six anchor standards or the grade-appropriate equivalents will present the greatest challenge to your students?

2. How will you help your students overcome the difficulties they may face?

3. How will you support oral language development when reading and writing skills receive so much more attention due to the typical tasks on standardized tests?

4. How do you perceive the relationship between the speaking/listening standards and the reading and writing standards?

KEY RESOURCES

Professional Books

Buehl, D. (2001). *Classroom strategies for interactive learning* (2nd ed.). Newark, DE: IRA.

Daniels, H. (1994, 2002). *Literature circles: Voice and choice in the student-centered classroom.* Portland, ME: Stenhouse.

Online Resources

- Chapter books to read aloud
  http://kinderkorner.com/readalouds.html
- Reader's Theater Editions
  http://aaronshep.com/rt/RTE.html
- Reader's Theater scripts and plays
  http://www.teachingheart.net/readerstheater.htm
- Connecting artistic expression to literacy development
  http://www.picturingwriting.org/
- Learning to create a Prezi
  http://www.prezi.com
- Student-generated comic strips
  http://www.makebeliefscomix.com/

8 Key to Successful Implementation

Collaborative Strategies

Information age rest in pieces. This is the age of collaboration.

— Grace Rubinstein

OVERVIEW

The goal of this chapter is to explore the collaborative practices that English-as-a-second language (ESL), bilingual, special education, and general education teachers engage in to implement the Common Core English language arts (ELA) standards. We will outline the types of collaboration among teachers that yield effective standards-based instruction to meet the diverse academic and language development needs of students. Both instructional and noninstructional collaborative activities focused on the Common Core State Standards implementation are presented. Extensive research on both professional learning communities and teacher collaboration supports our notion that effective and successful implementation of the CCSS cannot happen without systemic collaboration.

WHY COLLABORATIVE PRACTICES HELP MEET THE COMMON CORE

In a recent publication on research-based literacy practices for English language learners (ELLs), Nancy Cloud, Fred Genesee, and Elsie Hamayan (2009) painted an accurate picture of emergent bilingual students as follows:

ELLs who are learning to read and write English have all of the challenges that mainstream English-speaking children face, and, in addition, they must acquire proficiency in English for both social and academic purposes; they must acquire background knowledge that is the foundation of the school curriculum; they must acquire enough knowledge of mainstream culture to integrate and function effectively in school and with their schoolmates; and they must keep up with the academic curriculum. (p. 14)

The complexity of the challenges ELLs and all diverse students encounter on a daily basis calls for a collaborative approach so teachers can pool their talents and resources and offer the best possible education to these learners. The implementation of the CCSS presents a unique opportunity for educators to collaborate on multiple levels to foster a shared mission and vision for diverse learners, to have honest conversations about instruction, to share instructional practices, to align curriculum, to create a student-centered approach to teaching and learning, and to perpetuate avenues for effective professional learning.

CORE COLLABORATIVE PRACTICES

Many teachers find engaging in ongoing professional dialogue with colleagues who share common concerns and experiences to be among the most rewarding experiences. Charlotte Danielson (2009) also noted that "it's through conversations that teachers clarify their beliefs and plans and examine, practice, and consider new possibilities" (p. 1). Most teachers agree, however, that while informal interactions keep teachers connected, they are not enough to support sustained, professional collaboration. For successful collaboration—especially with the CCSS in mind—formal structures and procedures must be developed, implemented, and maintained. Such formal collaborative practices may have a more or less direct instructional or noninstructional focus, as we discussed in greater detail in *Collaboration and Co-teaching: Strategies for English Learners* (Honigsfeld & Dove, 2010). Instructional activities include (1) joint planning, (2) curriculum mapping and alignment, (3) parallel teaching, (4) codeveloping instructional materials, (5) collaborative assessment of student work, and (6) coteaching. Noninstructional activities include (1) joint professional development, (2) teacher research, (3) preparing for and conducting joint parent-teacher conferences, and (4) planning, facilitating, or participating in other extracurricular activities. The following section details each of these collaborative activities as they pertain to aligning instruction to the CCSS.

Instructional Activities

1. Joint Planning

The purpose of a focused joint planning process—also referred to as cooperative or collaborative planning—is to allow specialists and classroom teachers to share their expertise as they (a) consider the Common Core expectations, (b) discuss students' needs and the specific challenges each learner has to overcome to meet the Common Core goals, and (c) plan lessons and units that they may deliver jointly or independent of each other. Sharing responsibility for the CCSS implementation through collaborative planning ensures that a sustained professional dialogue takes place. As a result, instruction offered by a team of teachers involved is aligned to the standards, rather than disjointed or fragmented. Joint planning helps ensure that the K–5 ELA curriculum is made accessible to all learners through scaffolding, tiering, or other differentiated instructional techniques. Joint planning opportunities must be part of the regular school schedule; common preparation time is often the most frequently cited obstacle to successful teacher collaboration.

A unique form of coplanning is when general education and ESL or bilingual teachers use the Sheltered Instruction Observation Protocol (SIOP Model) (Echevarria, Vogt, & Short, 2012) or the ExC-ELL protocol (Calderón, 2007) in conjunction with the CCSS. Classroom teachers may provide the ELA-specific content goals and objectives and the ESL/bilingual teacher contributes appropriately aligned language goals. Similarly, classroom teachers may present the required grade-appropriate ELA curriculum along with instructional resources commonly used to teach that curriculum, whereas the ESL/bilingual specialist provides supplementary materials and addresses the linguistic complexity in the core curriculum by adapting difficult texts, assignments, or assessment tools based on ELLs' needs as well as by planning on preteaching and reteaching select target language features.

Coplanning Basics. Regardless of grade level or instructional program model, key coplanning activities include the following:

- Identify the Common Core ELA standards and language proficiency standards for the lesson.
- Align language development objectives to ELA goals.
- Identify essential questions that scaffold meaning and clarify information.
- Select supplementary materials that help bridge new content to students' background knowledge.
- Develop multilevel, tiered activities that match students' language proficiency or readiness levels.

- Determine the types of instructional supports (multisensory, graphic, and interactive resources) needed to assist in making meaning from the required reading and assignments.
- Select target linguistics structures (word-, sentence-, and discourse-level language features).
- Plan standards-based learning activities that integrate the four language skills: listening, speaking, reading, and writing.
- Design formative assessment tasks and matching assessment tools that may offer data both about student progress and lesson effectiveness.
- Use individual student profiles to further differentiate instruction whenever possible.

Villa, Thousand, and Nevin (2008) suggested that coplanning could be most effective when there is a set agenda used as a framework for coplanning time to guide teacher conversations between specialists and classroom teachers. When planning time is scarce, teachers need to develop communication strategies that consistently keep all parties informed and allow for shared decision making. Resourcefulness regarding planning and implementing instruction is often supplemented with creative ways to communicate with each other about students, lesson ideas, teaching strategies, and instructional materials. A shared planbook or aligned curriculum maps can serve to frame the major concepts and skills that all students must learn for a particular unit of study and assist collaborating teachers to organize lessons. Teachers can also agree on a coplanning template (see Figure 8.1) or a coplanning agenda (see Box 8.1) to ensure effective use of their collaborative time. (A full page, reproducible version of the coplanning template is available at the end of this chapter.)

Figure 8.1   Common Core ELA Standard-Based Coplanning Template

Date:	Class:	Collaborative Teachers:
Common Core Standards Addressed		
Learning Objectives (Content/Language)		
Activities/Tasks (Rigor and Engagement)		
Resources and Materials		
Technology Integration		
Accommodations/Modifications		
Assessment Procedures		
Reflections/Special Notes		

Teachers engaged in regular coplanning may add additional lesson planning headings to this template. Similarly, the *Sample Common Core ELA Standards-Based Co-planning Agenda* in Box 8.1 may also be expanded and modified as needed.

Box 8.1 Sample Common Core ELA Standards-Based Co-Planning Agenda

1. Review previous unit/lesson and student assessment data.

2. Select target CCSS.

3. Determine unit or lesson goals/objectives.

4. Identify instructional procedures.

5. Differentiate instructional and assessment strategies.

6. Assign roles and responsibilities for individual follow-up planning.

---

2. Curriculum Mapping and Alignment

Curriculum mapping. Heidi Hayes Jacobs (1997), Udelhofen (2005), and others agree that curriculum mapping is an effective procedure for collecting data about the taught curriculum in a school or district using a yearly or monthly calendar as the framework. Even when standards-based collaboration is the ultimate goal, participating teachers may first independently map their own taught curriculum. Once such overviews of students' actual learning experiences are created, teachers engage in a dialogue to ensure alignment and explore possible misalignments of essential knowledge and skills taught in the general education, ESL, bilingual, or special education curriculum. As Jacobs (1999) noted,

> The fundamental purpose of mapping is communication. The composite of each teacher's map in a building or district provides efficient access to K–12 curriculum perspective both vertically and horizontally. Mapping is not presented as what *ought* to happen but what *is* happening during the course of a school year. Data offer an overview perspective rather than a daily classroom perspective. (p. 61)

With the CCSS, curriculum planning, mapping, and alignment among classroom teachers and support service professionals are receiving increasing attention. Most maps reveal five types of information: the content (essential knowledge taught); the standard which is addressed in the curricular unit; the processes and skills used to teach the content; the assessment tools; and key resources used in the unit.

Curriculum mapping may be carried out both by looking back (backward mapping) and looking ahead (forward mapping). Table 8.1 offers a useful summary to reflect on the advantages and disadvantages of different types of curriculum mapping from the ESL perspective.

Table 8.1 *Backward (Journal) Mapping Versus Forward (Projection) Mapping*

Initial Mapping Format	Advantages	Disadvantages
Backward Mapping *(Sometimes referred to as journal or diary mapping)*	• This type of mapping is less time-intensive; it requires a small amount of time on a regular basis to record the ESL and general-education content, language skills, and assessments taught each month. • When various levels of language proficiency are considered, this type of mapping allows for a more accurate account of what was actually taught to various groups of ELLs.	• It slows the completion of the initial mapping cycle, as teachers cannot proceed to the editing step until maps are completed. • The next steps probably would not occur until the beginning of the subsequent school year. • The curriculum mapping process can lose momentum. • Monthly check-ins must occur with each teacher to keep abreast of everyone's progress.
Forward Mapping *(Sometimes referred to as projection mapping)*	• The initial curriculum maps are completed within a short time frame, enabling teachers to move to the next steps of mapping much faster. • If a district allocates the appropriate amount of time, the initial cycle of mapping can be completed in one academic year.	• It is more time-intensive. • Some teachers may have difficulty projecting future teaching. • It is troublesome for teachers who wish to document their differentiated maps for the three language proficiency levels.

Source: Adapted from S. Udelhofen (2005). *Keys to curriculum mapping: Strategies and tools to make it work* (p. 19). Thousand Oaks, CA: Corwin; A. Honigsfeld & M. Dove (2010). *Collaboration and co-teaching: Strategies for English learners* (p. 68). Thousand Oaks, CA: Corwin.

Curriculum alignment. What effect has the standards reform movement had on the curriculum for ELLs and students with disabilities? Are districts able to incorporate the general education curriculum into the instruction of these youngsters?

In our investigation of districts with an ESL curriculum, we found that there are a number of curricular options.

1. A stand-alone ESL curriculum following a locally developed scope and sequence of language and literacy development

2. A stand-alone ESL curriculum following a statewide ESL curriculum framework

3. A stand-alone ESL curriculum based on a commercially available ESL program

4. A content-support ESL curriculum based on content standards

Developing an ESL curriculum with the CCSS in mind is expected to result in an ELA-standards-based curriculum aligned to grade-level literacy/English language arts expectation. If the ESL program does have a strong, purposeful connection to the grade-level ELA content through curriculum alignment, instruction in the mainstream classes becomes more meaningful for ELLs. Without such curriculum alignment, the ESL services may become fragmented, the lessons delivered in each class may become disjointed, and the skills introduced and practiced may become confusing for ELLs.

In further consideration of the CCSS to create more instructional rigor for all students, special education teachers need to collaborate with general education teachers in order to align students' Individual Education Plans (IEPs) with content curricula. The absence of knowledge of the general education curricula places both special education and ESL teachers in a position that often leads to the teaching of a narrow, skills-based curriculum for those pupils identified for these services. Furthermore, curriculum alignment through collaborative practices allows for a wider acceptance of shared academic goals and the use of differentiated instructional materials in all general education, second-language learning, and remedial programs.

3. Parallel Teaching

Academic intervention services (AIS), remedial reading, and ESL often continue to be implemented in the form of a stand-alone, pull-out program. At the elementary level, specialists often gather the children from one or more classrooms and take them to a designated room. What happens while those students are away from their regular classrooms? Their teachers are often puzzled by this challenge: what to teach and what not to teach during the pullout periods? One solution to this dilemma is for specialists and general education teachers to coordinate the objectives of their ELA lessons aligned to the CCSS. One recommendation is to use the grade-specific standards section of the CCSS, track the standards across two, three, or occasionally more grades and *back-map* to previous grade-level expectations when working with students who either need remediation or first-time skill-building as is the case with many ELLs.

4. Codeveloping Instructional Materials

When teachers collaborate with diverse students' needs in mind, their attention may be focused on not only creating CCSS-based lesson or unit plans together but also developing instructional materials, resources, activity sheets, inclass and homework assignments, and assessment tools. There are many already-available classroom items that can be easily adapted for diverse students. The following are examples of how students' lived experiences and out-of-school literacies are reflected in the ELA curriculum or the core content areas with a literacy focus:

- In kindergarten, when the topic of families is introduced, teachers consider each student's diverse family backgrounds—recognizing the importance of extended family members—and design oral language development activities around family histories.
- In first grade, when the three main types of communities (rural, urban, suburban) are explored, students' lived experiences are built into the curriculum. Their countries of origin or places they visited are featured in photographs, video clips, and other supplementary materials, including native language resources if applicable, while students are engaged in reading nonfiction selections about various communities.
- In second grade, when students learn about school areas and school personnel, they collaboratively develop a brief interview protocol and go on a tour of the school building. At each key location, they interview the school staff members about their jobs.
- In third grade, when students learn about important historic events, they also share current events happening in their communities.
- In fourth grade, as students are exposed to literature that revolves around heroes, they are invited to write a news article about a hero in their own lives.
- In fifth grade, when the geography of the world through the study of time zones and climate zones is introduced, students' unique experiences of living in or visiting various regions of the United States or the world are capitalized on.

The possibilities of joint ELA-standards-based and content-based material development are as diverse as lessons taught in the K–5 classroom!

5. Collaborative Assessment of Student Work

A powerful collaborative activity specialists and general education teachers may engage in is sampling and carefully examining representative work by diverse students. In one recently developed model, *Collaborative Analysis of Student Work: Improving Teaching and Learning,* Langer, Colton, and Gott (2003) suggested the use of rubrics within a framework of collaborative conversations and inquiry. Specifically, they proposed that participating teachers focus both on students' strengths and challenges and identify appropriate strategies to respond to patterns of learning difficulties. Using a protocol, members of teacher study groups analyze student work, offer plausible explanations for student performance levels, explore promising strategies to implement, and plan interventions. Once the teacher follows the collectively determined steps, new data are collected from the student, and the performance is assessed. This cycle is repeated, as teachers reflect on their students' learning and their own growth and needs.

In our work, we found it helpful to customize the protocol of examining student work by focusing on the challenges of specific students. For example, in order for teachers to jointly review the work of ELLs, we developed a protocol called *Sampling Work by English Language Learners* (SWELL) (Honigsfeld & Dove, 2010) as a guide for teachers to examine students' language, academic, cultural, and social-emotional development. See Box 8.2 for the entire protocol adapted for standards-based ELA instruction.

Box 8.2 Protocol for Sampling Work by English Language Learners (SWELL)

As you collaboratively examine student literacy work samples produced by English language learners, consider the following questions organized in four subcategories.

1. Linguistic Development

    a) What stage of second-language acquisition is evident?

    b) Which linguistic features has the student mastered and been able to use systematically?

(Continued)

(Continued)

    c) What are two or three prominent linguistic challenges the ELL's work demonstrates?

    d) Other comments:

2. Academic Needs

    a) What are two to three examples of successfully acquired ELA knowledge and/or skills?

    b) What are some noticeable gaps in the ELL's prior knowledge?

    c) What are some gaps in the ELL's new ELA skills and knowledge attainment?

    d) What ELA domain-specific skills does the ELL need to work on?

    e) Other comments:

3. Cultural Experiences and Challenges

    a) In what way are the ELL's cultural experiences reflected in his or her work?

    b) Is there any evidence that the ELL was struggling with cultural misunderstandings or misconceptions?

    c) Other comments:

4. Social-Emotional Aspects of Learning

    a) Is there evidence of motivated, self-directed learning in the ELL's work sample?

    b) Has the ELL been engaged in the task?

    c) Is there evidence of task persistence?

    d) Is there evidence of being engaged in cooperative learning (peer editing, etc.)?

    e) Other comments:

Source: Adapted from A. Honigsfeld & M. Dove (2010). *Collaboration and co-teaching: Strategies for English Learners* (p. 71). Thousand Oaks, CA: Corwin.

6. Coteaching as a Framework for Sustained Teacher Collaboration

Coteaching frameworks have been presented for special education inclusion models (Friend & Cook, 2007; Murawski, 2009; Vaughn, Schumm, & Arguelles, 1997; Villa, Thousand, & Nevin, 2008), as well as for English learners (Honigsfeld & Dove, 2010, 2012). In our work with ESL teachers and their general education colleagues, we have documented seven coteaching arrangements, which we refer to as *coteaching models*. In three of these models, both teachers work with one large group of students. In three additional models, two groups of students are split between the two cooperating teachers. In one final model, multiple groups of students are engaged in a learning activity that is facilitated and monitored by both teachers. Each of these configurations may have a place in any cotaught classroom, regardless of the grade level taught or the ELA standard targeted. We encourage our readers to consider both the advantages and disadvantages of each and pilot various models in their classes to see which ones allow them to respond best to both the students' needs, the specific content being taught, the type of learning activities designed, and the participating teachers' teaching styles and own preferences (see Honigsfeld & Dove, 2010, for detailed discussion of each model):

1. One Group: One Lead Teacher and One Teacher "Teaching on Purpose"

2. One Group: Two Teachers Teach Same Content

3. One Group: One Teaches, One Assesses

4. Two Groups: Two Teachers Teach Same Content

5. Two Groups: One Teacher Preteaches, One Teacher Teaches Alternative Information

6. Two Groups: One Teacher Reteaches, One Teacher Teaches Alternative Information

7. Multiple Groups: Two Teachers Monitor and Teach

What Is Unique About Coteaching?

During any of the above coteaching configurations, the partnering teachers share the responsibility for planning instruction, implementing the lessons, and assessing student performance and outcome. In a cotaught classroom, all students participate in CCSS-driven ELA lessons. When learning groups remain heterogeneous, students have the opportunity to work with others who have various academic capabilities and English language fluency. This is in contrast to remedial or pull-out programs, in which students are either grouped with youngsters who are struggling readers and writers or have no English language proficiency.

In our view, there are some basic ingredients of a successful coteaching program. Within a general education classroom, a specialist can demonstrate strategies during a cotaught lesson, and the classroom teacher can continue to use the same strategies with students when the specialist is no longer present. Very often, the exchange of ideas between both teachers allows for more risk-taking and the use of innovative strategies on the part of each teacher to benefit all students in the classroom.

Noninstructional Activities

1. Joint Professional Development

All teachers may benefit from participating in joint professional-development activities based on the CCSS either at their school, within their district, or outside their own professional environment. If they attend external, offsite training programs together, they have an open forum to share their experiences with standards-based ELA instruction, voice their concerns about the challenges the CCSS pose for diverse learners, and get feedback and responses both from colleagues from other school districts and from the course leader or workshop facilitator. Upon returning to their schools, teachers have the opportunity to share the information they gained both formally and informally with their colleagues. When they transfer the new information to their own practice and implement the new strategies in their own teaching, not only are they obtaining new skills, but they can also share these skills collaboratively with colleagues who did not attend the same training. When teachers train together, the benefit is even greater since they are able to support each other in their endeavors.

The collaborative professional development practices that yield the most effective partnership and team building between specialists and their general education colleagues have the following common elements:

1. Regular, work-based opportunities to reflect on and improve instruction

2. Shared topics of interest

3. Team membership and participation based on self-selection

4. Focus on teachers' instructional practices and students' learning

Below we outline three possible forms of collaborative professional development activities: (a) collegial circles, (b) peer observations, and (c) collaborative coaching or mentoring.

A. Collegial Circles. Collegial circles are small groups of teachers who meet on a regular basis to discuss common questions, share concerns, offer solutions to common problems, and discuss appropriate instructional techniques. However, to keep professional conversations on task, protocols or formats for discussion are often beneficial. In a classic educational resource, *Looking in Classrooms*, Good and Brophy (2000, p. 490) outlined a model for group discussion. To transfer this model to the current standards-based instructional context, we renamed the stages, adjusted the goals, and gave CCSS-specific examples for each stage, as seen in Table 8.2.

Table 8.2 *Phases of Group Discussions*

Phases	Types of Knowledge	Goals	Examples
Phase 1	External Knowledge: ↓ Review and Discover	• Explore existing, research-based information • Find out what experts say about the topic	• Find recently published articles on the CCSS and diverse learners
Phase 2	Personal Knowledge: ↓ Reflect and Relate	• Engage in active listening • Share personal experiences related to the topic or problem • Connect and compare external knowledge to group members' own experiences	• Discuss the challenges and opportunities the CCSS present for diverse learning needs • Invite everyone to share his or her personal experiences • Compare own challenges and successes to those documented in the literature
Phase 3	Future Actions: ↓ Revise and Devise	• Internalize new knowledge about the topic • Review and revise prior understanding of the problem • Develop a plan of action	• Evaluate recommended practices found in the literature and shared by group members • Develop a plan to experiment with and implement new CCSS-based instructional strategies

Source: Adapted from A. Honigsfeld and M. Dove (2010). *Collaboration and co-teaching: Strategies for English learners* (p. 82). Thousand Oaks, CA: Corwin.

B. Peer Observations. One powerful, school-based professional-learning opportunity for specialists and general education teachers is created by visiting each other's classes. When observing the teaching-learning process and monitoring student outcomes in a diverse classroom, teachers may set a specific purpose for the visit or choose one of the following:

> *Kid watching*: What are some of the observable challenges students face as the lesson unfolds? How do they respond to the literacy tasks and language focus activities presented by the teacher? How do they interact with their classmates? What opportunities do they have to meaningfully use and, thus, develop their English language skills? What percentage of the time are students engaged? What do students do differently in the observed class?

> *Teacher watching:* How clearly are the standards-based goals and objectives communicated? How does each teacher approach the varied needs of students? What types of adaptations are used? What percentage of the time is the teacher talking? In what ways are the assigned texts, tasks, homework assignments, and assessment practices modified (if at all)?

It is important to note that peer observations are not meant to be evaluative or judgmental, but rather serve as an opportunity for the teacher-observer to learn from the teacher being observed.

Allen and LeBlanc (2005) promote a simple yet effective collaborative peer coaching system they call the *2 + 2 Performance Appraisal Model*. The name suggests that teachers who engage in this form of peer support offer each other two compliments and two suggestions following a lesson observation. Table 8.3 offers possible target areas for the 2 + 2 models used with diverse learners.

C. Collaborative Coaching/Mentoring. When teachers participate in a mentor-coaching program either as a mentor-coach or as a mentee, opportunities to improve or learn new techniques for diverse learners while also aligning their instruction to the CCSS abound. Collaborative coaching and peer mentoring imply that teachers support each other's practice beyond conducting peer observations. Through a framework of coaching, teachers learn from each other, model effective instruction for one another, and benefit from sustained, job-embedded, and student-centered classroom assistance. Collaborative coaching requires an equal relationship between the two partners, such as the relationship between coteachers or those who collaborate formally in other ways to provide instruction. It is effective (a) when both participants possess knowledge about the topic or issue, such as high-stakes testing and test preparation for diverse learners or (b) when the coach understands one part

Table 8.3 Target Areas of Feedback in the 2+2 Model

General Feedback	Feedback Specific to Working With Diverse Learners	Comments
Clarity of lesson objectives	Alignment of lesson objectives to ELA CCSS standards	
Motivation	Connection to students' prior knowledge and experiences or building background knowledge	
Lesson sequence	Lesson accessibility, instructional supports	
Differentiated activities	Scaffolded and tiered activities	
Student engagement	At-risk students' participation	
Questioning techniques	Questions matched to students' language proficiency and readiness levels (and addressing all levels of Bloom's Taxonomy)	
Grouping techniques	Using flexible (heterogeneous and homogeneous) groupings (including bilingual peer bridging if possible)	
Assessment techniques	Differentiation of assessment for diverse learners	

Source: Adapted from A. Honigsfeld and M. Dove (2010). *Collaboration and co-teaching: Strategies for English learners* (p. 85). Thousand Oaks, CA: Corwin.

of a problem—content requirements for all students to pass a state exam, and the partner understands another part—ELLs' linguistic development (Dunne & Villani, 2007). Thus, collaborative coaching becomes a vehicle for professional growth both for the novice and experienced teacher.

2. Teacher Research

When teachers engage in classroom-based practitioner research, they may do so individually or collaboratively using a number of different formats. Working in research and development (R&D) teams, participating in collaborative inquiry groups, and engaging in collaborative action research or lesson studies are examples of this.

Research and development teams are formed by small groups of teachers who more formally decide on a particular instructional approach that they study collaboratively. In some districts, R & D projects and accompanying teacher portfolios that document teachers' success with the target strategy may be used in lieu of more traditional teacher evaluations (which are often based on observations by an administrator and may only yield limited data on the teacher's performance). After collaborating teachers review research related to the selected instructional approach, they jointly plan and implement lessons based on the approach, assess their own (and each other's) growth, and evaluate the student outcomes.

When teacher discussion groups or collegial circles elect to engage in more in-depth explorations, they may decide to form collaborative inquiry groups. They may investigate an overarching concept (such as the teaching-learning process or second-language acquisition patterns) or choose more specific topics that deal with ELLs' instructional needs (such as using effective note-taking strategies). A form of collaborative inquiry is conducting teacher research or action research. We use Johnson's (2008) definition of action research as "the process of studying a real school or classroom situation to understand and improve the quality of actions and instruction" (p. 28). When collaborative action research is woven into the school culture and supported strongly by both the administration and the faculty, it allows teachers to examine their standards-based practice systematically and participate in the highest level of professional learning (Cochran-Smith & Lytle, 1999).

Another form of teacher research is the lesson study concept originated in Japan as a professional-development movement for experienced inservice teachers who wanted to regularly engage in examining their teaching practices to improve their effectiveness (Lewis, 2002). In the classic format, participating teachers jointly plan a lesson in response to a preestablished study question or goal. One teacher teaches the lesson while others observe. Next, teachers discuss the lesson, revise it, and another team member teaches the lesson in a new class. This process of observation and discussion is repeated and ends with a written report (Fernandez & Chokshi, 2002). Yoshida (2004) emphasized that "lesson study helps to make teachers into lifelong learners. It is especially important to think of lesson study as a professional development activity, not as teacher training and lesson development. It creates opportunities for teachers to think deeply about instruction, learning, curriculum, and education" (para. 5).

3. Preparing for and Conducting Joint Parent-Teacher Conferences

When specialists and general education colleagues compare students' behavior, attitudes, and overall academic performance in their respective classes, they may observe that the same child acts quite differently in different settings.

When specialists and general education teachers write progress reports and quarterly, semiannual, or annual report cards based on collaboratively reviewed student work samples, portfolios, and test scores, multiple perspectives are included. Such collaborative effort is beneficial in assessing students' linguistic and academic progress since it leads to providing a clearer picture of areas of strengths and needs for both teachers and families.

4. Planning, Facilitating, or Participating in Other Extracurricular Activities

Jointly preparing and facilitating parent outreach and family involvement programs, as well as other community-based activities, also enhances collaboration. What are some common and uncommon collaborative practices?

1. Parent Teacher Association (PTA) meetings

2. Parent information or new family orientation night

3. Parent workshops (For example: Information about the advances/ shifts presented in the CCSS)

4. Family game night

5. Cultural events

6. Collaborative class, grade, or school newsletters

7. Family field day

8. Class and school plays, concerts, and talent shows

ANTICIPATED OUTCOMES

The successful implementation of the collaborative practices outlined here has been observed in numerous school districts around the United States (Dove & Honigsfeld, 2010; Honigsfeld & Dove, 2010, 2012). Most notably, collaborations that are anchored in the Common Core Standards allow teachers to use a shared framework and shared purpose, which leads to (re)examining not only their instructional practices and materials used in the general education and special program classes but the entire instructional service delivery system as well. The consistency and cohesion of the support services will have to be evaluated periodically to ensure diverse students receive rigorous, research-based services that lead to both academic language proficiency development and content-specific academic achievement. The establishment of a common set of goals and a shared language to talk about goals—as intended by the CCSS—contribute to effective collaborative practices.

CHALLENGES

Collaborating for the sake of diverse learners using the CCSS is no small feat! In order to establish the right context for such collaborations, school leaders—administrators, teacher- and parent-leaders together—must create an inclusive, welcoming school learning community with a shared vision of respect and acceptance of everyone's cultural heritage and background. Building a professional learning community (DuFour & Eaker, 1998)—that continually engages in collaborative inquiry on all students' needs as they are working toward meeting the CCSS—is a critical component of Common Core collaborations. Finally, addressing the logistics for these collaborative practices must include (a) using "flexible teaming" that allows for both horizontal (on grade level) and vertical (across grade level) teacher teams, as well as cross-disciplinary teamwork to support diverse students' curricular, instructional, and extracurricular needs, (b) time and place for collaborations, and (c) human and other resources that make collaborations possible in the short and long run.

COMMON CORE COLLABORATIONS— (UN)COMMON REFLECTION QUESTIONS

1. How do you define successful collaboration to meet the CCSS?

2. How do schools create the time and resources for Common Core collaborations to take place?

3. What type of school leadership is needed for collaborative practices to be implemented successfully?

4. How do schools accurately assess whether or not the CCSS are being addressed with diverse learners?

KEY RESOURCES

Professional Books

Friend, M. (2008). *Co-teach! A handbook for creating and sustaining classroom partnerships in inclusive schools.* Greensboro, NC: Marilyn Friend Inc.

Friend, M., & Cook, L. (2007). *Interactions: Collaboration skills for school professionals* (5th ed.). New York: Prentice Hall.

Jacobs, H. H. (2004). *Getting results with curriculum mapping.* Alexandria, VA: ASCD.

Murawski, W. W. (2009). *Collaborative teaching in elementary schools: Making the co-teaching marriage work!* Thousand Oaks, CA: Corwin.

Roberts, S., & Pruitt, E. (2009). *Schools as professional learning communities: Collaborative activities and strategies for professional development.* Thousand Oaks, CA: Corwin.

Online Resources

http://www.coteachingforells.weebly.com

http://www.powerof2.com

Multimedia Sources

Friend, M. (2005). *The power of 2.* DVD. Greensboro, NC: Marilyn Friend Inc.

St. Paul Public Schools (SPPS). (2007). *Coteaching.*DVD. St. Paul, MN: SPPS.

COMMON CORE ELA STANDARD-BASED COPLANNING TEMPLATE

Date:	Class:	Collaborative Teachers:
Common Core Standards Addressed		
Learning Objectives (Content/Language)		
Activities/Tasks (Rigor and Engagement)		
Resources and Materials		
Technology Integration		
Accommodations/Modifications		
Assessment Procedures		
Reflections/Special Notes		

References and Further Reading

Akhavan, N. (2009). *Teaching writing in a Title I school, K–3.* Portsmouth, NH: Heinemann.

Alber-Morgan, S. (2010). *Using RTI to teach literacy to diverse learners, K–8: Strategies for the inclusive classroom.* Thousand Oaks, CA: Corwin.

Allen, D. W., & LeBlanc, A. C. (2005). *Collaborative peer coaching that improves instruction: The 2 + 2 performance appraisal model.* Thousand Oaks, CA: Corwin.

Anderson, J. (2005). *Mechanically inclined: Building grammar, usage, and style into writer's workshop.* Portland, ME: Stenhouse.

Anderson, J. (2011). *10 things every writer needs to know.* Portland, ME: Stenhouse.

Ashcraft, M. H., & Radvansky, G. A. (2009). *Cognition* (5th ed.). Boston, MA: Pearson.

August, D., & Shanahan, T. (Eds.). (2006). *Developing literacy in second-language learners: Report of the National Literacy Panel on Language-Minority Children and Youth.* Mahwah, NJ: Erlbaum.

Avalos, M. A., Plasencia, A., Chavez, C., & Rascón, J. (2007). Modified guided reading: Gateway to English as a second language and literacy learning. *The Reading Teacher, 61,* 318–329. doi: 10.1598/RT.61.4.4

Barone, D. M., & Taylor, J. (2006). *Improving students' writing, K–8: From meaning-making to high stakes!* Thousand Oaks, CA: Corwin.

Beck, I. L., McKeown, M. G., & Kucan, L. (2002). *Bringing words to life: Robust vocabulary instruction.* New York, NY: Guilford.

Beck, I. L., McKeown, M. G., & Kucan, L. (2008). *Creating robust vocabulary: Frequently asked questions and extended examples.* New York, NY: Guilford.

Bennett, B., & Rolheiser, C. (2001). *Beyond Monet: The artful science of instructional integration.* Toronto, Ontario: Bookation.

Blachowicz, C., Fisher, P., Ogle, D., & Watts-Taffe, S. (2006). Vocabulary: Questions from the classroom. *Reading Research Quarterly, 41,* 524–539. doi: 10.1598/RRQ.41.4.5

Block, C. C., & Pressley, M. (2002). *Comprehension instruction: Research-based best practices.* New York, NY: Guilford.

Buehl, D. (2001). *Classroom strategies for interactive learning* (2nd ed.). Newark, DE: International Reading Association.

Burns, B. (1999). *How to teach balanced reading and writing.* Arlington Heights, IL: Skylight.

Butt, D., Fahey, R., Feez, S., Spinks, S., & Yallop, C. (2003). *Using functional grammar: An explorer's guide* (2nd ed.). Sydney, Australia: NCELTR/Macquarie University.

Calderón, M. E. (2007). *Teaching reading to English language learners, grades 6–12: A framework for improving achievement in the content areas.* Thousand Oaks, CA: Corwin.

Calkins, L., Ehrenworth, M., & Lehman, C. (2012). *Pathways to the Common Core: Accelerating achievement.* Portsmouth, NH: Heinemann.

Casagrande, J. (2006). *Grammar snobs are great big meanies: A guide to language for fun and spite.* New York, NY: Penguin Books.

Cloud, N., & Genesee, F. (2009). *Literacy instruction for English language learners.* Portsmouth, NH: Heinemann.

Cloud, N., Genesee, F., & Hamayan, E. (2009). *Literacy instruction for English language learners: A teacher's guide to research-based practices.* Portsmouth, NH: Heinemann.

Cochran-Smith, M., & Lytle, S. L. (1999). Relationships of knowledge and practice: Teacher learning in communities. In A. Iran-Nejad & C. D. Pearson (Eds.), *Review of Research in Education 24* (pp. 249–305). Washington, DC: American Educational Research Association.

Coleman, D. (2011). *Introduction to the Common Core State Standards for ELA & literacy.* Part 4 (Transcript). Retrieved from http://usny.nysed.gov/rttt/docs/bringingthecommoncoretolife/part4transcript.pdf

Coleman, R., & Goldenberg, C. (2010). What does research say about effective practices for English learners. Part II: Academic language proficiency. *Kappa Delta Pi Record, 46*(2), 60–65.

Collier, V. P., & Thomas, W. P. (1999). Making U.S. schools effective for English language learners, part 1. *TESOL Matters, 9*(4), 1–6.

Common Core State Standards for English Language Arts & Literacy in History/Social Studies, Science, and Technical Subjects (CCSS). (2010). Retrieved from http://corestandards.org/assets/CCSSI_ELA%20Standards.pdf

Crawford, J., & Krashen, S. (2007). *English language learners in American classrooms: 101 questions, 101 answers.* New York, NY: Scholastic.

Cummins, J. (1984). *Bilingualism and special education issues: Issues in assessment and pedagogy.* London, UK: Multilingual Matters.

Cummins, J. (2001). *Negotiating identities: Education for empowerment in a diverse society* (2nd ed.). Los Angeles: California Association for Bilingual Education.

Cummins, J., & Early, M. (Eds.). (2011). *Identity texts: The collaborative creation of power in multilingual schools.* Stoke-on-Trent, UK: Trentham Books.

Cummins, J., & Man, E. Y. (2007). Academic language: What is it and how do we acquire it? In J. Cummins & C. Davison (Eds.), *International handbook of second language acquisition* (pp. 797–810). Norwell, MA: Springer SBM.

Cunningham, P. M. (2008). *Phonics they use: Words for reading and writing.* Boston, MA: Allyn & Bacon.

Cunningham, P. M., & Allington, R. L. (2011). *Classrooms that work: They can all read and write.* Boston, MA: Pearson.

Cunningham, P. M., & Hall, D. P. (1994). *Making words: Multilevel hands-on developmentally appropriate spelling and phonics activities.* Torrance, CA: Good Apple.

Cunningham, P. M., Hall, D. P., & Defee, M. (1991). Non-ability-grouped, multilevel instruction: A year in a first-grade classroom. *The Reading Teacher, 44,* 566–571.

Cunningham, P. M., Hall, D. P., & Heggie, T. (2001). Making words: Multi-level, hands-on phonics and spelling activities. Columbus, OH: Good Apple.

Cunningham, P. M., Hall, D. P., & Sigmon, C. M. (1999). *The teacher's guide to the four blocks: A multimethod, multilevel framework for grades 1–3*. Greensboro, NC: Carson Dellosa.

Daniels, H. (2002). *Literature circles: Voice and choice in book clubs and reading groups* (2nd ed.). Portland, ME: Stenhouse.

Danielson, C. (2009). A framework for learning to teach. *Educational Leadership Online, 66*. Retrieved from http://www.Association for Supervision and Curriculum Development.org/publications/educational_leadership/summer09/vol66/num09/A_Framework_for_Learning_to_Teach.aspx

Diller, D. (2003). *Literacy work stations: Making centers work*. Portland, ME: Stenhouse.

Donohue, K., & Reddy, N. N. (2006). *180 days to successful writers: Lessons to prepare your students for standardized assessments and for life*. Thousand Oaks, CA: Corwin.

Dove, M. G., & Honigsfeld, A. (2010). ESL coteaching and collaboration: Opportunities to develop teacher leadership and enhance student learning. *TESOL Journal, 1*(1), 3–22.

DuBose, F. (2008). *Great Wall of China: A wall-to-wall history*. New York, NY: Kids Discover.

DuFour, R., & Eaker, R. (1998). *Professional learning communities at work: Best practices for enhancing student achievement*. Bloomington, IN: Solution Tree.

Dunn, R., & Dunn, K. (1992). *Teaching elementary students through their individual learning styles*. Boston, MA: Allyn & Bacon.

Dunne, K., & Villani, S. (2007). *Mentoring new teachers through collaborative coaching: Linking teacher and student learning*. San Francisco, CA: WestEd.

Echevarria, J., Vogt, M., & Short, D. J. (2012). *Making content comprehensible for English learners: The SIOP model* (4th ed.). Boston, MA: Pearson.

Education Northwest. (n.d.). *6+1 Trait® Writing Model*. Available at http://educationnorthwest.org/traits

Elmore, R. F. (2008). *School reform from the inside out: Policy, practice, and performance*. Cambridge, MA: Harvard Education Press.

Fang, Z. (2010). *Language and literacy in inquiry-based science classrooms, grades 3–8*. Thousand Oaks, CA: Corwin.

Fang, Z., & Wei, Y. (2010). Improving middle school students' science literacy through reading infusion. *Journal of Educational Research, 103*, 262–273.

Fearn, L., & Farnan, N. (2001). *Interactions: Teaching writing and the language arts*. Boston, MA: Houghton Mifflin.

Feldman, K., & Kinsella, K. (2005). *Narrowing the language gap: The case for explicit vocabulary instruction*. New York, NY: Scholastic.

Fernandez, C., & Chokshi, S. (2002). A practical guide to translating lesson study for a U.S. setting. *Phi Delta Kappan, 84*, 128–134.

Fiderer, A. (1998). *35 rubrics and checklists to assess reading and writing: Time-saving reproducible forms for meaningful literacy assessment*. New York, NY: Scholastic Professional Books.

Fiderer, A. (1999). *40 rubrics & checklists to assess reading and writing: Time-saving reproducible forms and great strategies for meaningful assessment*. New York, NY: Scholastic Professional Books.

Fillmore, L. W. (2009). *English language development: Acquiring the language needed for literacy and learning*. Retrieved from http://assets.pearsonschool.com/asset_mgr/current/201010/English%20Language%20Development.pdf

Fisher, D., & Frey, N. (2008). *Better learning through structured teaching: A framework for the gradual release of responsibility.* Alexandria, VA: ASCD.

Fisher, D., & Frey, N. (2011*). Teaching students to read like detectives: Comprehending, analyzing, and discussing text.* Bloomington, IN: Solution Tree.

Fisher, D., Frey, N., & Rothenberg, C. (2008). *Content-area conversations: How to plan discussion-based lessons for diverse language learners.* Alexandria, VA: ASCD.

Fitch, S., & Swartz, L. (2008). *The poetry experience: Choosing and using poetry in the classroom.* Portland, ME: Stenhouse.

Florida Center for Reading Research. (2005). *Florida assessments for instruction in reading (FAIR) search tool for links to instructional materials.* Retrieved from http://www.fcrr.org/FAIR_Search_Tool/FAIR_Search_Tool.aspx

Franklin, J. (2005). Finding the black ninja fish: Revision and writing groups in the first grade. *The Quarterly, 27*(1). Retrieved from http://www.nwp.org/cs/public/print/resource/2185

Frey, N., & Fisher, D. (2009). *Learning words inside & out: Vocabulary instruction that boosts achievement in all subject areas.* Portsmouth, NH: Heinemann.

Frey, N., Fisher, D., & Everlove, S. (2009). *Productive group work: How to engage students, build teamwork, and promote understanding.* Alexandria, VA: ASCD.

Friend, M. (2008). *Co-teach! A handbook for creating and sustaining classroom partnerships in inclusive schools.* Greensboro, NC: Marilyn Friend.

Friend, M., & Cook, L. (2007). *Interactions: Collaboration skills for school professionals* (5th ed.). New York, NY: Prentice Hall.

Fuchs, D., Fuchs, L., & Burish, P. (2000). Peer-assisted learning strategies: An evidence-based practice to promote reading achievement. *Learning Disabilities Research & Practice, 15*(2), 85–91.

Fullan, M. (2007). *The new meaning of educational change* (4th ed.). New York, NY: Teachers College Press.

Fullan, M. (2011). *Change leader: Learning to do what matters most.* San Francisco, CA: Jossey-Bass.

Gardner, H. (1999). *The disciplined mind: What all students should understand.* New York, NY: Simon & Schuster.

Gaskins, I. W., Guthrie, J. T., Satlow, E., Ostertag, J., Six, L., Byrne, J., & Connor, B. (1994). Integrating instruction in science, reading, and writing: Goals, teacher development, and assessment. *Journal of Research in Science Teaching, 31,* 1039–1056.

Genesee, F., Lindholm-Leary, K., Saunders, W., &. Christian, D. (2006). *Educating English language learners.* New York, NY: Cambridge University Press.

Gibbons, P. (2009). *English learners, academic literacy, and thinking: Learning in the challenge zone.* Portsmouth, NH: Heinemann.

Gibson, S. A. (2008). An effective framework for primary-grade guided writing instruction. *The Reading Teacher, 62,* 324–334.

Gillanders, C., Iruka, I., Ritchie, S., & Cobb, C. (2012). Restructuring and aligning early education opportunities for cultural, language, and ethnic minority children. In R. C. Pianta (Ed.), *Handbook of early childhood education* (pp. 111–135). New York, NY: Guilford Press.

Goldenberg, C. N. (1992). *Instructional conversations and their classroom application* (Educational Practice Report 2). Santa Cruz: The National Center for Research on Cultural Diversity and Second Language Learning, University of California, Santa Cruz.

Goldenberg, C. N., & Coleman, R. (2010). *Promoting academic achievement among English learners: A guide to the research.* Thousand Oaks, CA: Corwin.

Good, T., & Brophy, J. (2000). *Looking in classrooms* (8th ed.). New York, NY: Longman.

Gottlieb, M. (2006). *Assessing English language learners: Bridges from language proficiency to academic achievement.* Thousand Oaks, CA: Corwin.

Gottlieb, M. (2011, November). *From academic language to academic success.* Workshop presented at the Iowa Culture and Language Conference, Coralville, IA.

Gould, J. S., & Evan, J. (1999). *Four square writing method for grades 1–3.* Carthage, IL: Teaching & Learning.

Graves, D. H. (2003). *Writing: Teachers and children at work.* Portsmouth, NH: Heinemann.

Gray, R. (1997). Mnemonics in the ESL/EFL classroom. *The Language Teacher, 21*(4). Retrieved from http://jalt-publications.org/old_tlt/files/97/apr/mnemon.html

Griffin, C., Simmons, D., & Kameenui, E. (1991). Investigating the effectiveness of graphic organizer instruction on the comprehension and recall of science content by students with learning disabilities. *Reading, Writing, and Learning Disabilities, 7,* 355–376.

Hakuta, K., Butler, Y. G., & Witt, D. (2000). *How long does it take English learners to attain proficiency?* Retrieved from http://repositories.cdlib.org/cgi/view content.cgi?article=1001&context=lmri

Hale, C. (2001). *Sin and syntax: How to craft wickedly effective prose.* New York, NY: Broadway Books.

Hale, C. (2006). *Collaborative art & writing projects for young learners: 15 delightful projects that build early reading and writing skills, and connect to the topic you teach.* New York, NY: Scholastic.

Halliday, M. A. K. (1996). On grammar and grammatics. In R. Hasan, C. Cloran, & D. G. Butt (Eds.), *Functional descriptions: Theory into practice* (pp. 1–38). Philadelphia, PA: John Benjamins.

Harvey, S. (1998). *Nonfiction matters: Reading, writing, and research in grades 3–8.* Portland, ME: Stenhouse.

Harvey, S., & Daniels, H. (2009). *Comprehension and collaboration: Inquiry circles in action.* Portsmouth, NH: Heinemann.

Heard, G. (Ed.). (2000). *Songs of myself: An anthology of poems and arts.* New York, NY: Mondo.

Hill, J., & Flynn, K. (2006). *Classroom instruction that works with English language learners.* Alexandria, VA: ASCD.

Hill, J. D., & Flynn, K. (2008). Asking the right questions. *Journal of Staff Development, 49*(1), 46–52.

Hoffman, J. V. (1992). Critical reading/thinking across the curriculum: Using I-Charts to support learning. *Language Arts, 69,* 121–127.

Hoffner, H. I. (2010). *Literacy lessons, K–8: Connecting activities to standards and students to communities.* Thousand Oaks, CA: Corwin.

Honigsfeld, A., & Barnick-Eonidis, P. (2009). Do you speak mnemonic in the classroom? *Idiom, 39*(1), 8–9.

Honigsfeld, A., & Dove, M. G. (2010). *Collaboration and co-teaching: Strategies for English learners.* Thousand Oaks, CA: Corwin.

Honigsfeld, A., & Dove, M. (Eds.). (2012). *Coteaching and other collaborative practices in the EFL/ESL classroom: Rationale, research, reflections, and recommendations.* Charlotte, NC: Information Age Publishing.

Hoyt, L. (2008). *Interactive read alouds.* Retrieved from http://www.inter activereadalouds.com/overview.aspx

Irujo, S. (2007). *What does research tell us about teaching reading to English language learners?* Retrieved from http://www.readingrockets.org/article/19757/

Israel, S. E. (2008). *Early reading first and beyond: A guide to building early literacy skills.* Thousand Oaks, CA: Corwin.

Jacobs, H. H. (1997). *Mapping the big picture: Integrating curriculum and assessment K–12.* Alexandria, VA: ASCD.

Jacobs, H. H. (1999). *Breaking new ground in high school curriculum.* Reston, VA: NAASP.

Jacobs, H. H. (2004). *Getting results with curriculum mapping.* Alexandria, VA: ASCD.

Jensen, E. (2008). *Brain-based learning: The new paradigm of teaching.* Thousand Oaks, CA: Corwin.

Johnson, A. P. (2008). *A short guide to action research.* Boston, MA: Pearson.

Kagan, S. (1994). *Cooperative learning.* San Clemente, CA: Kagan Publishing.

Kagan, S., & Kagan, M. (1998). *Multiple intelligences: The complete MI book.* San Clemente, CA: Kagan.

Kletzien, S. B. (2003). *Informational text in K–3 classrooms: Helping children read and write.* Newark, DE: International Reading Association.

Korn, C. (1998). How young children make sense of their life stories. *Early Childhood Education Journal, 25,* 223–228.

Langer, G. M., Colton, A. B., & Gott, L. S. (2003). *Collaborative analysis of student work: Improving teaching and learning.* Alexandria, VA: ASCD.

Lederer, R., & Shore, J. (2005). *Comma sense: A fundamental guide to punctuation.* New York, NY: St. Martin's Press.

Lessow-Hurley, J. (2003). *Meeting the needs of second language learners: An educator's guide.* Alexandria, VA: ASCD.

Lewis, C. (2002). *Lesson study: A handbook of teacher-led instructional improvement.* Philadelphia, PA: Research for Better Schools.

Liberman, I. Y., Shankweiler, D., & Liberman, A. M. (1989). The alphabetic principle and learning to read. In D. Shankweiler & I. Y. Liberman (Eds.), *Phonology and reading disability: Solving the reading puzzle* (pp. 1–33). Ann Arbor, MI: University of Michigan Press.

Lorcher, T. (2011). *Context clue challenge.* Retrieved from http://www.brighthubeducation.com/high-school-english-lessons/6323-teaching-context-clues-activity

Lukeman, N. (2006). *A dash of style: The art and mastery of punctuation.* New York, NY: Norton.

Marinak, B. A., & Gambrell, L. B. (2009). Ways to teach about informational text. *Social Studies and the Young Learner, 22*(1), 19–22.

Marzano, R. J., & Pickering, D. J. (2005). *Building academic vocabulary: Teacher's manual.* Alexandria, VA: ASCD.

Mazur, A. J., & Doran, P. R. (2010). *Teaching diverse learners: Principles for best practice.* Thousand Oaks, CA: Corwin.

McCarrier, A., Pinnell, G. S., & Fountas, I. C. (2000). *Interactive writing: How language and literacy come together, K–2.* Portsmouth, NH: Heinemann.

McGregor, T. (2007). *Comprehension connections: Bridges to strategic reading.* Portsmouth, NH: Heinemann.

McKenzie, J. (2000). *Beyond technology, questioning, research and the information literate school.* Bellingham, WA: FNO Press.

McKeowan, M. G., Beck, I. L., & Worthy, M. J. (1993). Grappling with text ideas: Questioning the author. *the Reading Teacher, 46*(7), 560–566.

McNamara, D. S. (Ed.). (2007). *Reading comprehension strategies: Theory, interventions, and technologies.* Mahwah, NJ: Erlbaum.

McNamara, D. S. (2009). The importance of teaching reading strategies. *Perspectives on Language and Literacy, 35,* 34–40.

McNeil, M. (2011, April 28). Proportion of schools falling short on AYP rises, report says. *Education Week.* Retrieved from http://www.edweek.org/ew/articles/2011/04/28/30ayp.h30.html

Morrison, V., & Wlodarczyk, L. (2009, October). Revisiting read-aloud: Instructional strategies that encourage students' engagement with texts. *The Reading Teacher, 63,* 110–118.

Moss, B. (2004). Teaching expository text structures through information trade book retellings. *The Reading Teacher, 57,* 710–718.

Moss, B., & Loh, V. S. (2010). *35 strategies for guiding readers through informational texts.* New York, NY: Guilford Press.

Murawski, W. W. (2009). *Collaborative teaching in elementary schools: Making the co-teaching marriage work!* Thousand Oaks, CA: Corwin.

National Assessment of Educational Progress. (1999). *Report card for the nation and the states.* Washington, DC: National Center for Education Statistics. Retrieved from http://nces.ed.gov/nationsreportcard/pubs/main1998/1999500.asp

National Commission on Excellence in Education. (1983). *A nation at risk: The imperative for educational reform.* Washington, DC: U.S. Department of Education.

National Institute for Urban School Improvement. (2000). Spotlight on National Institute Activities (3rd ed.). Denver, CO: National Institute for Urban School Improvement.

National Institute of Child Health and Human Development. (2000). *Report of the National Reading Panel. Teaching children to read: An evidence-based assessment of the scientific research literature on reading and its implications for reading instruction* (NIH Publication No. 00–4769). Washington, DC: Government Printing Office.

Nell, K., Duke, N. K., & Bennett-Armistead, S. V. (2003). *Reading and writing informational text in the primary grades: Research-based practices.* New York, NY: Scholastic.

Nessel, D. D., & Dixon, C. N. (2008). *Using the language experience approach with English language learners: Strategies for engaging students and developing literacy.* Thousand Oaks, CA: Corwin.

Nevills, P., & Wolfe, P. (2009). *Building the reading brain: PreK–3* (2nd ed.). Thousand Oaks, CA: Corwin.

New York State Education Department (NYSED). (2012). Common Core in ELA/literacy: Shift 3: Staircase of complexity (online video). Retrieved from http://engageny.org/resource/common-core-in-ela-literacy-shift-3-staircase-of-complexity

Nichols, M. (2008). *Talking about text: Guiding students to increase comprehension through purposeful talk.* Huntington Beach, CA: Shell Education.

Noden, H. R. (1999). *Image grammar: Using grammatical structures to teach writing.* Portsmouth, NH: Heinemann.

Novak, J. D., & A. J. Cañas. (2008). *The theory underlying concept maps and how to construct them* (Technical Report IHMC CmapTools 2006-01 Rev 01-2008). Florida Institute for Human and Machine Cognition. Retrieved from http://cmap.ihmc.us/Publications/ResearchPapers/TheoryUnderlyingConceptMaps.pdf

Oczkus, L. D. (2007). *Guided writing: Practical lessons, powerful results.* Portsmouth, NH: Heinemann.

Olshansky, B. (2008). *The power of pictures: Creating pathways to literacy through art, grades K–6.* San Francisco, CA: Jossey-Bass.

Pearson, P. D., & Gallagher, G. (1983). The gradual release of responsibility model of instruction. *Contemporary Education Psychology, 8,* 112–123.

Pottle, J. L. (1998). *Writing frames: 40 activities for learning the writing process.* Portland, ME: J. Weston Walch.

Powers, S. W. (2011). Discourse/Instructional conversation: Connecting school and personal discourses. In R. Powell & E. Rightmeyer (Eds.), *Literacy for all students: An instructional framework for closing the gap* (pp. 190–226). New York, NY: Routledge.

Prensky, M. (2010). *Teaching digital natives: Partnering for real learning.* Thousand Oaks, CA: Corwin.

Primary Education Oasis. (2012). *Author Studies.* Retrieved from http://www .primary-education-oasis.com/author-studies.html

Raphael, T. E. (1982). Teaching children question-answering strategies. *The Reading Teacher, 36,* 186–191.

Raphael, T. E. (1986). Teaching question-answer relationships, revisited. *The Reading Teacher, 39,* 516–522.

Raphael, T. E., Highfield, K., & Au, K. H. (2006). *QAR now: A powerful and practical framework that develops comprehension and higher-level thinking in all students.* New York, NY: Scholastic Professional Books.

Reeves, D. B. (2000). Standards are not enough: Essential transformations for school success. *NASSP Bulletin, 84*(620), 5–19.

Roberts, S., & Pruitt, E. (2009). *Schools as professional learning communities: Collaborative activities and strategies for professional development.* Thousand Oaks, CA: Corwin.

Romance, N. R., & Vitale, M. R. (1992). A curriculum strategy that expands time for in-depth elementary science instruction by using science-based reading strategies: Effects of a year-long study in grade 4. *Journal of Research in Science Teaching, 29*(6), 545–554.

Roskos, K. A., Tabors, P. O., & Lenhart, L. A. (2005). *Oral language and early literacy in preschool: Talking, reading, and writing.* Newark, DE: International Reading Association.

Rowan, B., Correnti, R., Miller, R. J., & Camburn, E. M. (2009). *School improvement by design: Lessons from a study of comprehensive school reform programs* (ED507546). Philadelphia, PA: Consortium for Policy Research in Education.

Samway, K. D. (2006). *When English language learners write: Connecting research to practice, K–8.* Portsmouth, NH: Heinemann.

Scanlan, M., Frattura, E., Schneider, K. A., & Capper, C. A. (2012). Bilingual students with integrated comprehensive service: Collaborative strategies. In A. Honigsfeld & M. G. Dove (Eds.), *Coteaching and other collaborative practices in the EFL/ESL classroom: Rationale, research, reflections, and recommendations* (pp. 3–13). Charlotte, NC: Information Age Publishing.

Schumaker, J. B., Denton, P. H., & Deshler, D. D. (1984). *The paraphrasing strategy.* Lawrence: The University of Kansas.

Soto, I. (2012). *ELL shadowing as a catalyst for change.* Thousand Oaks, CA: Corwin.

Sousa, D. A. (2008). *Mind, brain, and education: Neuroscience implications for the classroom.* Bloomington, IN: Solution Tree.

Spandel, V. (2005). Foreword. In J. Anderson (Ed.), *Mechanically inclined: Building grammar, usage, and style into writer's workshop* (xi-xiii). Portland, ME: Stenhouse.

Stahl, S. A., & Nagy, W. E. (2006). *Teaching word meanings.* Mahwah, NJ: Erlbaum.

Strauss, V. (2010). *What Common Core State Standards are—and aren't.* Retrieved from http://voices.washingtonpost.com/answer-sheet/national-standards/ what-the-common-core-standards.html

Supovitz, J. A. (2006). *The case for district-based reform: Leading, building, and sustaining school improvement.* Cambridge, MA: Harvard Education Press.

Thomas, R. M. (2002). *Overcoming inertia in school reform: How to successfully implement change.* Thousand Oaks, CA: Corwin.

Tomlinson, C. A., & Imbeau, M. B. (2010). *Leading and managing a differentiated classroom.* Alexandria, VA: ASCD.

Truss, L. (2004). *Eats, shoots & leaves: The zero tolerance approach to punctuation.* New York, NY: Gotham Books.

Udelhofen, S. K. (2005). *Keys to curriculum mapping: Strategies and tools to make it work.* Thousand Oaks, CA: Corwin.

Vaughn, S., Schumm, J. S., & Arguelles, M. E. (1997). The ABCDEs of co-teaching. *Teaching Exceptional Children, 30*(2), 4–10.

Villa, R. A., Thousand, J. S., & Nevin, A. I. (2008). *A guide to co-teaching: Practical tips for facilitating student learning.* Thousand Oaks, CA: Corwin.

Vogt, M. E., & Echevarria, J. (2007). *99 ideas and activities for teaching English learners with the SIOP® model.* Boston, MA: Allyn & Bacon.

Walker, M., & Walter, T. (1996). *Amazing English! How-to handbook: Instructional strategies for the classroom teacher for cultural diversity, language acquisition, literacy, academic content, assessment.* Boston, MA: Addison-Wesley.

Walling, D. R. (2009). *Writing for understanding: Strategies to increase content learning.* Thousand Oaks, CA: Corwin.

Weaver, C. (1998). *Teaching grammar in context.* Portsmouth, NH: Heinemann.

WIDA. (2007). *English language proficiency standards prekindergarten through grade 5.* Retrieved from http://www.wida.us/standards/eld.aspx

WIDA. (2011). *Glossary of terms and expressions.* Retrieved from www.wida.us/get.aspx?id=412

Wilhelm, J. D. (2007). Imagining a new kind of self: Academic language, identity, and content area learning. *Voices from the Middle, 15*(1), 44–45.

Willis, J. (2006). *Research-based strategies to ignite student learning: Insights from a neurologist and classroom teacher.* Alexandria, VA: ASCD.

Winter Celebrations. (n.d.). Retrieved from http://kids.nationalgeographic.com/kids/stories/peopleplaces/winter-celebrations/

Wong Fillmore, L. (2011). *Supporting access to the language & content of complex texts for EL & LM Students.* Retrieved from http://www.cgcs.org/cms/lib/DC00001581/Centricity/Domain/25/ELA_retreat-Wong%20Fillmorepart2.pdf

Yoshida, M. (2004). *A summary of lesson study.* Retrieved from http://www.rbs.org/lesson_study/conference/2003/papers/defining/a_summary_of_lesson_study.shtm

Zike, D. (1992). *Big book of books.* San Antonio, TX: Dinah-Might Adventures.

Zwiers, J. (2008). *Building academic language essential practices for content classrooms.* San Francisco, CA: Jossey-Bass Teacher.

Zwiers, J., & Crawford, M. (2011). *Academic conversations: Classroom talk that fosters critical thinking and content understandings.* Portland, ME: Stenhouse.

Children's Literature Cited

Aboff, M. (2008). *If you were a prefix.* North Mankato, MN: Picture Window Books.

Aboff, M. (2008). *If you were a suffix.* North Mankato, MN: Picture Window Books.

Adamson, H. (2009). *Homes in many cultures.* North Mankato, MN: Capstone Press.

Arnold, T. (2000). *Parts.* New York, NY: Puffin Books.

Arnold, T. (2003). *More parts.* New York, NY: Puffin Books.

Arnold, T. (2007). *Even more parts.* New York, NY: Puffin Books.

Baker, J. (2004). *Home.* New York, NY: Greenwillow Books.

Bang, M. (1984). *The gray lady and the strawberry snatcher.* New York, NY: Simon & Schuster.

Berry, J. (2004). "Childhood tracks." In *Only one of me.* New York, NY: Macmillan.

Brooks, G. (1974). *The tiger who wore white gloves: Or what you are you are.* Minneapolis, MN: Sagebrush Education Resources.

Brown, M. (1954), *Cinderella.* New York, NY: Atheneum Books.

Buchanan, K. (2004). *The house is made of mud.* Lanham, MD: Cooper Square.

Burton, V. L. (1978). *The little house.* San Anselmo, CA: Sandpiper.

Butterworth, N., & Inkpen, M. (2008). *Jasper's beanstalk.* London, UK: Hodder Children's Books.

Cannon, J. (1993). *Stellaluna.* New York, NY: Harcourt Children's Books.

Ciardi, J. (1962). "About the teeth of sharks." In *You read to me, I'll read to you.* Philadelphia, PA: Lippincott.

Cleary, B. (1981). *Ramona Quimby, age 8.* New York, NY: HarperCollins.

Cleary, B. P. (2001). *Hairy, scary, ordinary: What is an adjective?* Minneapolis, MN: Carolrhoda Books.

Cleary, B. P. (2005). *Dearly, nearly, insincerely: What is an adverb?* Minneapolis, MN: First Avenue Editions.

Cleary, B. P. (2006). *I and you and don't forget who: What is a pronoun?* Minneapolis, MN: First Avenue Editions.

Cleary, B. P. (2011). *Skin like milk, hair of silk: What are similes and metaphors?* Minneapolis, MN: Millbrook.

Coburn, J. R., & McLennan, C. (2000). *Domitila: A Cinderella tale from the Mexican tradition.* Walnut Creek, CA: Shens Books & Supplies.

Dahl, R. (1990). "The dentist and the crocodile." Retrieved from http://www.npr.org/2005/12/16/5058489/poetry-speaks-to-children

Dahl, R., & Blake, Q. (2007). *Fantastic Mr. Fox.* New York, NY: Puffin Books.

Danziger, P. (2000). *A is for amber.* New York, NY: Scholastic.

Day, A. (1997). *Good dog, Carl.* New York, NY: Aladdin Paperbacks.

de Brunhoff, J. (1937). *Babar.* New York, NY: Random House Books for Young Readers.

dePaola, T. (1978). *Pancakes for breakfast.* San Anselmo, CA: Sandpiper.

dePaola, T. (1981). *The hunter and the animals: A wordless picture book.* New York, NY: Holiday House.

DiTerlizzi, T., & Black, H. (2003). *The Spiderwick chronicles.* New York, NY: Simon & Schuster.

DK Eyewitness Books. New York, NY: DK.

Fox, M. (1992). *Hattie and the fox.* New York, NY: Aladdin.

Gibbons, G. (1990). *How a house is built.* New York, NY: Holiday House.

Halfmann, J. (2006). *Alligator at Saw Grass Road.* Norfolk, CT: Soundprints.

Harris, N. (2010). *In these walls and floors (what's lurking in this house?).* North Mankato, MN: Heinemann-Raintree.

Heller, R. (1993). *Up, up and away: A book of adverbs.* New York, NY: Scholastic.

Heller, R. (1998). *Many luscious lollipops: A book about adjectives.* New York, NY: Puffin Books.

Heller, R. (1999). *Mine, all mine: A book about pronouns.* St. Louis, MO: Turtleback.

Heller, R. (2002). *A cache of jewels and other collective nouns.* New York, NY: Grosset & Dunlap.

Herman, G. (1997). *Storm chasers: Tracking twisters.* New York, NY: HarperCollins.

Hoban, T. (1984). *Is it rough? Is it smooth? Is it shiny?* New York, NY: Greenwillow Books.

Hoban, T. (1987). *Is it red? Is it yellow? Is it blue?* New York, NY: Greenwillow Books.

Hollander, J. (1991). *A Thanksgiving story.* Orlando, FL: Harcourt Brace Jovanovich.

Kinney, J. (2007). *Diary of a wimpy kid: Greg Heffley's journal.* New York, NY: Amulet Books.

Kline, S. (1997). *Horrible Harry.* New York, NY: Puffin.

Komatsu, Y. (2004). *Wonderful houses around the world.* Bolinas, CA: Shelter.

Kumin, M. (n.d.). "The quarrel." In E. Paschen (Ed.), *Poetry speaks to children.* Naperville, IL: Sourcebooks.

Leedy, L. (2009). *Crazy like a fox: A simile story.* New York, NY: Holiday House.

Lehman, B. (2004). *The red book.* Boston, MA: Houghton Mifflin.

Lillegard, D. (2000). *Wake up house.* New York, NY: Knopf Books for Young Readers.

Lionni, L. (1973). *The biggest house in the world.* New York, NY: Dragonfly Books.

Lobel, A. (1999). *Frog and toad.* New York, NY: HarperFestival.

Loewen, N. J. (2011). *Stubborn as a mule and other silly similes.* North Mankato, MN: Picture Window Books.

Louie, A-L. (1996). *Yeh-Shen: A Cinderella story from China.* New York, NY: Puffin Books.

Lowell, S. (1992). *The three little javelinas.* Flagstaff, AZ: Northland.

MacLachlan, P. (1985) *Sarah, plain and tall.* New York, NY: HarperCollins.

Marshall, J. (2000). *The three little pigs.* New York, NY: Grosset & Dunlap.

Martin, R. (1998). *The rough-face girl.* New York, NY: Puffin Books.

Mayer, M. (2011). *Octopus soup.* New York, NY: Amazon Children's Publishing.

Mayer, M., & Mayer, M. (2003). *A boy, a dog, a frog and a friend.* New York, NY: Dial.

McDonald, M., & Reynolds, P. H. (2010). *Judy Moody.* Somerville, MA: Candlewick Press.

McDonough, Y. Z. (2010). *Who was Rosa Parks?* New York, NY: Grosset & Dunlap.

McMillan, I. (1994). "Tempest Avenue." In *Dad, the Donkey's on Fire.* Manchester, UK: Carcanet.

Minarik, E. (2009). *Little bear.* New York, NY: HarperCollins.

Moore, M. (2009). *Homes around the world.* New York, NY: DK.

Morris, A. (1995). *Houses and homes.* New York, NY: HarperCollins.

Nash, O. (1994). *The adventures of Isabel.* Boston, MA: Little, Brown.

National Geographic Kids. (n.d.). *Vampire bats.* Available at http://kids .nationalgeographic.com/kids/animals/creaturefeature/vampire-bat

Newman, J. (2010). *The boys.* New York, NY: Simon & Schuster.

Noyes, A. (1952). *Daddy fell into the pond, and other poems for children.* London, UK: Sheed & Ward.

O'Dell, S. (1960). *Island of the blue dolphins.* Boston, MA: Houghton Mifflin.

Parish, P. (2001). *Amelia Bedelia.* New York, NY: HarperCollins.

Park, B. (1992). *Junie B. Jones and the stupid smelly bus.* New York, NY: Random House.

Paulsen, G. (2007). *Hatchet: 20th anniversary edition.* New York, NY: Simon & Schuster.

Perez, A. I. (2008). *My very own room/mi propio cuartito.* New York, NY: Lee & Low Books.

Pinkney, J. (2009). *The lion and the mouse.* New York, NY: Little, Brown Books for Young Readers.

Piper, W. (1961). *The little engine that could.* New York, NY: Platt & Munk.

Piven, H. (2010). *My best friend is as sharp as a pencil: And other funny classroom portraits.* New York, NY: Schwartz & Wade.

Piven, H. (2012). *My dog is as smelly as dirty socks: And other funny family portraits.* New York, NY: Dragonfly Books.

Priddy, R. (2010). *At my house: A lift-the-flap shadow book.* London, UK: Priddy Books.

Pulver, R. (2008). *Punctuation takes a vacation.* Pine Plains, NY: Live Oak Media.

Pulver, R. (2010). *Silent letters loud and clear.* New York, NY: Holiday House.

Pulver, R. (2011). *Happy endings: A story about suffixes.* New York, NY: Holiday House.

Raschka, C. (2011). *A ball for Daisy.* New York, NY: Schwartz & Wade.

Rey, H. A. (1973). *Curious George.* Boston, MA: HMH Books.

Rodriquez, B. (2010). *The chicken thief* (Stories without words). New York, NY: Enchanted Lion Books.

Rohmann, E. (1997). *Time flies.* New York, NY: Dragonfly Books.

Rosa-Mendoza, G. (2007). *My house/Mi casa.* Wheaton, IL: me+mi.

Rosen, M. J. (2011). *Home: A collaboration of thirty authors & illustrators.* New York, NY: HarperCollins.

Rosenthal, B. (2004). *My house is singing.* Boston, MA: HMH Books.

Rosing, N., & Carney, E. (2009). *Face to face with polar bears.* Washington DC: National Geographic Society.

Rowling, J. K. (1998). *Harry Potter and the sorcerer's stone.* New York, NY: Scholastic.

Rylant, C. (2002). *Tulip sees America.* New York, NY: Scholastic.

Scieszka, J., & Smith, L. (1996). *The true story of the three little pigs.* New York, NY: Puffin Books.

Shoulders, M. (2008). *The ABC book of American homes.* Watertown, MA: Charlesbridge.

Simon, N. (1997). *Wet world.* Somerville, MA: Candlewick Press.

Simon, S. (2009). *Wolves.* Washington, DC: Smithsonian.

Snicket, L. (2001). *A series of unfortunate events.* New York, NY: HarperCollins.

Spinelli, J. (1990). *Maniac Magee.* Boston, MA: Little, Brown.

Steel, F. A. (1976). *Tattercoats: An old English tale.* New York, NY: Bradbury Press.

Steptoe, J. (1988). *Mufaro's beautiful daughters: An African tale.* New York, NY: Scholastic.

Stevenson, R. L. (1885). "My shadow." Available at http://www.poetryfoundation.org/poem/171951

Taback, S. (2004). *This is the house that Jack built.* New York, NY: Puffin.

Terban, M. (2007). *In a pickle: And other funny idioms.* San Anselmo, CA: Sandpiper.

Trivizas, E., & Oxenbury, H. (1997). *The three little wolves and the big bad pig.* New York, NY: Aladdin Paperbacks.

Twain, M. (1885). *The adventures of Huckleberry Finn.* New York, NY: Charles L. Webster.

Wab, B. (1975). *Ira sleeps over.* San Anselmo, CA: Sandpiper.

Walters, J. M. (2010). "Forgive Billy the Kid?" *Scholastic News, 73*(5), 6.

Walton, R. (2011). *Around the house, the fox chased the mouse: Adventures in prepositions.* Layton, UT: Gibbs Smith.

Walton, R. (2011). *Bullfrog pops: Adventures in verbs and objects.* Layton, UT: Gibbs Smith.

Walton, R. (2011). *Herd of cows, flock of sheep: Adventures in collective nouns.* Layton, UT: Gibbs Smith.

Walton, R. (2011). *Just me and 6,000 rats: A tale of conjunctions.* Layton, UT: Gibbs Smith.

Walton, R. (2011). *Once there was a bull . . . (frog): Adventures in compound words.* Layton, UT: Gibbs Smith.

Wiesner, D. (2006). *Flotsam.* New York, NY: Clarion Books.

Williams, V. B. (1982). *A chair for my mother.* New York, NY: Greenwillow Books.

Wise Brown, M. (1949). *The important book.* New York, NY: HarperCollins.

Yolen, J. (1987). *Owl moon.* New York, NY: Philomel.

Yvonne, Y. (1998). "Wolf Pack." Available at http://www.angelfire.com/me/howlingwolfie/wolfpoems.html

Strategy Index